Scotland Yard's Casebook of Serious Crimes

DICK KIRBY

has also written:

Rough Justice: Memoirs of a Flying Squad Officer

The Real Sweeney

You're Nicked!

Villains

The Guv'nors: Ten of Scotland Yard's Finest Detectives

The Sweeney: The First Sixty Years of Scotland Yard's Crimebusting Flying Squad 1919–1978

Scotland Yard's Ghost Squad:
The Secret Weapon against Post-War Crime

The Brave Blue Line:
100 Years of Metropolitan Police Gallantry

Death on the Beat:
Police Officers Killed in the Line of Duty

The Scourge of Soho:
The Controversial Career of SAS Hero
Harry Challenor MM

Whitechapel's Sherlock Holmes:
The Casebook of Fred Wensley OBE, KPM, Victorian Crimebuster

The Wrong Man:
The Shooting of Steven Waldorf and the Hunt for David Martin

Laid Bare:
The Nude Murders and the Hunt for 'Jack the Stripper'

London's Gangs at War

Operation Countryman:
The Flawed Enquiry into London Police Corruption

Scotland Yard's Gangbuster:
Bert Wickstead's Most Celebrated Cases

The Mayfair Mafia:
The Lives and Crimes of the Messina Brothers

Scotland Yard's Flying Squad:
100 Years of Crime Fighting

Scotland Yard's Murder Squad

The Racetrack Gangs:
Four Decades of Doping, Intimidation and Violent Crime

IRA Terror on Britain's Streets 1939–1940: The Wartime Bombing Campaign and Hitler Connection.

Scotland Yard's Casebook of Serious Crimes

75 Years of No-Nonsense Policing

DICK KIRBY

First published in Great Britain in 2021 by
Pen & Sword True Crime
An imprint of
Pen & Sword Books Ltd
Yorkshire – Philadelphia

Copyright © Dick Kirby 2021

ISBN 978 1 39900 962 1

The right of Dick Kirby to be identified as Author of this work has been asserted by him in accordance with the Copyright, Designs and Patents Act 1988.

A CIP catalogue record for this book is
available from the British Library.

All rights reserved. No part of this book may be reproduced or transmitted in any form or by any means, electronic or mechanical including photocopying, recording or by any information storage and retrieval system, without permission from the Publisher in writing.

Printed and bound in the UK by CPI Group (UK) Ltd, Croydon, CR0 4YY.

Pen & Sword Books Limited incorporates the imprints of Atlas, Archaeology, Aviation, Discovery, Family History, Fiction, History, Maritime, Military, Military Classics, Politics, Select, Transport, True Crime, Air World, Frontline Publishing, Leo Cooper, Remember When, Seaforth Publishing, The Praetorian Press, Wharncliffe Local History, Wharncliffe Transport, Wharncliffe True Crime and White Owl.

For a complete list of Pen & Sword titles please contact

PEN & SWORD BOOKS LIMITED
47 Church Street, Barnsley, South Yorkshire, S70 2AS, England
E-mail: enquiries@pen-and-sword.co.uk
Website: www.pen-and-sword.co.uk

Or
PEN AND SWORD BOOKS
1950 Lawrence Rd, Havertown, PA 19083, USA
E-mail: Uspen-and-sword@casematepublishers.com
Website: www.penandswordbooks.com

To Ann:

I will give you the keys of my heart
And we will be married till death us do part.
Madam will you walk,
Madam will you talk,
Madam, will you walk and talk with me?

English Country Songs
Lucy Broadwood and J. A. Fuller Maitland, 1893

Praise for Dick Kirby's Books

'He treats criminals the only way they understand. His language is often shocking, his methods unorthodox.' **NATIONAL ASSOCIATION OF RETIRED POLICE OFFICERS' MAGAZINE**

'The continuing increase in violent crime will make many readers yearn for yesteryear and officers of Dick Kirby's calibre.' **POLICE MAGAZINE**

'His reflections on the political aspect of law enforcement will ring true for cops, everywhere.' **AMERICAN POLICE BEAT**

'Its no-nonsense portrayal of life in the police will give readers a memorable literary experience.' **SUFFOLK JOURNAL**

'A great read with fascinating stories and amusing anecdotes from a man who experienced it all.' **SUFFOLK NORFOLK LIFE MAGAZINE**

'A gritty series of episodes from his time in the Met – laced with black humour and humanity.' **EAST ANGLIAN DAILY TIMES**

'This is magic. The artfulness of these anti-heroes has you pining for the bad old days.' **DAILY SPORT**

'Crammed with vivid descriptions of long-forgotten police operations, races along like an Invicta tourer, at full throttle.' **DAILY EXPRESS**

'Rarely, if ever, have I been so captivated and moved by a book . . . the way in which Mr Kirby has gone about it is exceptional.' **POLICE MEMORABILIA COLLECTORS CLUB**

'Dick Kirby has chosen his fascinating subject well.' **LAW SOCIETY GAZETTE**

'Thrilling stories of gang-busting, murder and insurrection'. **BERTRAMS BOOKS**

'A scrupulously honest and detailed account of the unfortunate events leading to police shooting an innocent man . . . nobody is better qualified to write an account of this story than Dick Kirby.' **THE LONDON POLICE PENSIONER MAGAZINE**

'Dick Kirby knows his stuff!' **surrey-constabulary.com**

'Kirby looks to untangle facts from speculation and questions everything.' **GET WEST LONDON**

'Murder, torture and extortion all feature prominently as Mr Kirby investigates some of the most famous incidents of the post-war era.' **THE MAIL ONLINE**

'Only an insider with the engaging style of Dick Kirby could have produced this nakedly forthright page-turner.' **JOSEPH WAMBAUGH, AUTHOR OF THE CHOIRBOYS**

'Kirby's wit and extremely dry humour comes on straight away as early as the prologue which, of course, makes heavy reading subjects easier and creates a relationship between the author (narrator) and the reader.' **THE LOVE OF BOOKS**

'Dick Kirby's book gives precious insight into its exploits for over a century.' **PAUL MILLEN, AUTHOR OF CRIME SCENE INVESTIGATOR**

'Dick Kirby has written a book that all crime aficionados will want to read.' **THE WASHINGTON TIMES**

'Kirby does not hold back in detailing the grisly parts, bringing home to the reader the harsh reality that these ruthless killers had no boundaries.' **THE LONDON POLICE PENSIONER MAGAZINE**

Contents

About the Author		xi
Acknowledgements		xiii
Introduction		xv
Chapter 1	Greeno and the Safe-Blowers	1
Chapter 2	Barmy Army	11
Chapter 3	Devoted to his Wife and Seven Children	15
Chapter 4	Hit and Run?	19
Chapter 5	A Popular Jeweller's	23
Chapter 6	A Selection of Thieves, Dips and Conmen	31
Chapter 7	The Adventures of 'Australian Denny'	43
Chapter 8	'The King of the Blackmailers'	49
Chapter 9	Call in the Yard	61
Chapter 10	A Quartet of Gunmen	69
Chapter 11	A Wheeler-Dealer	77
Chapter 12	The Blackmailed Baronet	83
Chapter 13	The Battle of Heathrow – the Aftermath	87
Chapter 14	The Caseload of Peter Sinclair	93
Chapter 15	'The Velvet Kid'	99
Chapter 16	The Safe-Blowing at Martin's Bank	105
Chapter 17	'Peter the Plotter'	113
Chapter 18	Diamonds and Accusations	127

Chapter 19	'The Terrible Twins'	135
Chapter 20	A Pretty Collection of Villains	141
Chapter 21	Convicted by the Skin of his Finger	149
Chapter 22	A Zealous Cop	155
Chapter 23	An Old Master	163
Chapter 24	The Enigmatic German	171
Chapter 25	'Ray the Cat'	177
Chapter 26	The Safe-Blowing Cop	187
Chapter 27	Just When You Least Expect it!	195
Chapter 28	Scandal in Mayfair	207

Epilogue	215
Glossary of Custodial and Punishment Terms	217
Bibliography	221
Index	225

About the Author

Dick Kirby was born in 1943 in the East End of London and joined the Metropolitan Police in 1967. Half of his twenty-six years' service as a detective was spent with the Yard's Serious Crime Squad and the Flying Squad.

Before being discharged with an injury award and pension in 1993, Kirby was commended by Commissioners, Judges and Magistrates on forty occasions for displaying 'courage, determination and detective ability'.

Married, with four children and five grandchildren, Kirby lives in a Suffolk village with his wife. He appears on television and radio and can be relied upon to provide forthright views on spineless, supine senior police officers (and other politicians) with their insipid, uninformed, absurd and mendacious claims on how they intend to defeat serious crime and claim the streets.

He contributes regularly to newspapers and magazines, reviews books, films and music and is employed by a television company as a consultant and researcher. He also writes memoirs, biographies and true crime books which are widely quoted – this is his twenty-second.

Kirby can be visited on his website: www.dickkirby.com

Acknowledgements

My thanks go to Brigadier Henry Wilson for his support, together with many of the staff at Pen & Sword Books, Matt Jones and Tara Moran to mention but two; plus George Chamier for his welcome (and much-needed) editing and Jon Wilkinson for his impressive jacket designs. I write the books but it's Jon's designs that sell them.

I much appreciate the assistance given by Mick Carter of The ReCIDivists' Luncheon Club; Bob Fenton QGM, Honorary Secretary of the Ex-CID Officers' Association; Alan Moss of History by the Yard; the author Michael Nesbitt; and Susi Rogol, editor of the London Police Pensioner magazine. All of these were unstinting in their efforts to put everything into place.

My thanks go to John Benstead, Deirdre Bonner, Mervyn 'Taff' Gee, William 'Johnny' Johnson, Tony Pepper and John Troon for their kind input to the book.

The majority of the photographs are from the author's collection; whilst every effort has been made to trace copyright holders, the publishers and I apologise for any inadvertent omissions.

As always, my thanks go to my daughter Suzanne Cowper and her husband Steve for leading a blindfolded author safely through the minefield of cyber cock-ups and for the love and support from their children, Emma Cowper B Mus, Jessica Cowper B Mus and Harry Cowper, MTheatre. My gratitude goes to the rest of my family, Barbara Jerreat and her husband, Rich, plus their children Samuel and Annie Grace, my sons Mark and Robert and most of all to my dear wife Ann, who for many years has managed to steer my ramshackle ship through many a choppy sea.

Dick Kirby
Suffolk 2021

# Introduction

The Commissioner of the Metropolitan Police, Sir Joseph Simpson KBE, was well-liked by the rank and file, who affectionately referred to him as 'Joe'. He was the first commissioner to have walked the beat as a constable, in 1931; a compassionate man, he had made some much-needed changes in the police force – as it was then known.

The newly-appointed head of the Flying Squad, Ernie Millen, had similarly made changes in the running of the Squad, with the enthusiastic backing of the commissioner; the personnel had increased to almost 100 officers and the fleet to 32 vehicles. Millen, too, was 'a man's man'; he had served on the Squad twice before and like Sir Joseph he knew the job inside out. It was reflected in the return of work during 1961, Millen's first year in office; there had been 1,410 arrests, and stolen property to the value of £484,931 (or £9,165,195 at today's value) had been recovered. Millen was happy, and so was the commissioner.

Sir Joseph looked down at the buff-coloured docket that Millen had placed on his desk, adding with a grin, 'Thought you'd like to see this.'

The report dealt with a Flying Squad team led by an inspector who had surreptitiously followed a gang in their car, before shadowing them, even more cautiously, on foot into a shopping centre in Stockwell, South London.

The Squad officers' information was that the gang were planning to carry out an armed robbery; but where and when was a mystery.

It was a mystery soon solved, as the gang suddenly rushed into a bank. The Squad officers knew from experience that a bank robbery could be successfully carried out in an amazingly short space of time and from their position, over 100 yards away, they dashed towards the bank. As they approached its doors, the gang emerged and the leader, with his ill-gotten gains in one hand, raised the sawn-off shotgun he was holding in the other.

The detective inspector skidded to a halt, drew his .38 Webley & Scott revolver and shot the gang leader through the throat; he emitted a gurgling shriek and fell to the ground, swiftly followed to the pavement by his three associates, who flung their weaponry away and startled shoppers as they screamed, 'DON'T SHOOT!' at the tops of their voices.

The leader of the robbers recovered sufficiently to appear at the Old Bailey and croak, 'Guilty', as did his contemporaries (with rather clearer diction). They were all sentenced to fourteen years' imprisonment, and the Flying Squad officers collected some fulsome comments from the Judge.

These were the comments which Sir Joseph's eyes rested upon. None of the robbers had complained, therefore no internal enquiry needed to be instigated. It was just as well, because the commissioner had a healthy distaste for paperwork. Of course, commendations were another matter, requiring only a scrawled signature; and within the week, the Squad officers were pleased to see their names in *Police Orders*, along with compliments for their 'courage, promptness and determination displayed during their arrest of a dangerous gang of armed criminals'. Incidentally, the detective inspector in charge of the operation was promoted.

These were the days when police officers enjoyed firm backing from the judiciary, as well as from their senior officers.

In the sixty-odd years since these happenings, things, you may not be surprised to learn, have changed.

★ ★ ★

For a start, New Scotland Yard has moved twice since those halcyon days; and few, if any detectives inhabit it. Instead, it is infested with a civilian staff who do pretty much – or rather, as little – as they please. Any request for assistance that requires a modicum of work can be nullified by their quoting random acts of Parliament: the Data Protection Act (a favourite), Health and Safety regulations and anything else that comes to mind. No one at the Yard contradicts them; their managers support them to the hilt, for fear of losing their own bullshit jobs.

Next, the commissioners. Since Sir Joseph's day, few have displayed true leadership, two notable exceptions being Peter Imbert and John Stevens. Both were career detectives who rolled up their sleeves and got on with the job. Most of the others have been university products who never stopped gazing from the lofty spires of academia and who entered the police believing that whatever challenges might come their way would be 'really interesting'.

When Sir Robert Mark became commissioner in 1972 he decided to eradicate what he perceived as institutionalized corruption within the ranks of the Criminal Investigation Department. It is true that there was deep-rooted corruption among a small cadre of officers at the very top of the Department, and those officers were investigated and kicked out of the force, several of them into prison cells; and the vast majority of honest CID officers applauded that move.

But Mark believed that all CID officers were corrupt – and as he himself admitted, when he discovered he was wrong, it was too late. Instead of promoting the best of the rest of the detectives – and there were a good many of them, I can tell you – he filled the gaps left by the disgraced officers with senior officers from the uniform department. If they possessed any concept of detective work, it had dissipated many years before and, in the words of an old-time detective superintendent, 'they knew about as much about detective work as my arsehole knows about steam navigation.'

Mark introduced 'interchange' between uniform and CID; and for the Criminal Investigation Department it was a disaster. Valuable knowledge disappeared, helpful contacts were lost and officers rising through the ranks were encouraged to flit from one department to another, like butterflies, making wonderful reading for their CVs but leaving disaster in their wake. One uniform officer headed a team of young, inexperienced police constables tasked to infiltrate gangs of football hooligans. He knew nothing about this type of policing: how (and more especially, how not) to behave in difficult situations, what evidence could be given and how to record it; and neither did his young charges. There were hugely embarrassing acquittals at court, internal investigations and the threat of perjury charges hanging over the young officers' quaking heads; but not, of course for the chief inspector in charge, who by then had been promoted and moved on. 'Great fun!' he chortled. 'Wouldn't have missed it for the world!'

A little while ago, I telephoned one of the two Flying Squad offices, in buildings situated away from the Yard, and asked a detective constable the name of the officer in overall charge of the Squad. After a moment, he replied, 'Dunno', and then I heard him call out, 'Anyone know who's in charge of the Squad?' I assume there was a collective shaking of heads, because a few moments later, he replied, 'No one seems to know. Sorry.'

In the days recorded in the pages that follow, the names of senior CID officers were not only known to every member of the Department, they were known to many members of the public as well. Their names appeared on newspaper billboards when they travelled across the United Kingdom to investigate and solve murders. When Flying Squad ambushes were carried out – just like the one referred to above – they hit the headlines, because the senior officers of that department made sure the press knew about it.

Nowadays, it's different. Detectives do not appear at the Magistrates' Court with their protesting prisoners; instead, a pompous, suet-faced member of the Crown Prosecution Service (CPS) – many believe this stands for 'Couldn't Prosecute Satan' – will inform the television cameras, 'Having taken the decision that we believe there is a sufficiency of evidence to prosecute in this case and it being in the public interest to do so . . .' In the event of a successful prosecution, a representative of the CPS outside the Old Bailey will self-importantly suggest that they were responsible for the successful outcome; it's as though the police had no input into the investigation at all.

And in a case where a complaint is lodged against the police, it's the police chiefs who refer themselves to the Independent Office for Police Conduct; this is a body whose members have expertise in the worlds of accountancy, local government, the National Health Service, the humanities and psychology – but none, by law, has police experience. After making fawning, grovelling apologies to the person who has allegedly been mistreated by police, and/or their family, they set to work, often taking years after consulting with the CPS to come to the inescapable (although, for them, disappointing) conclusion that there was no evidence whatsoever of malpractice by the officers concerned.

For someone who was there, all those years ago, it's a sad state of affairs to see the apathetic, apologetic behaviour of the present day police chiefs, who have no sense of leadership and who, in a confrontational situation, think the best way of dealing with an aggressive, self-filming, chanting, bottle-throwing, police-hating mob is to plead with them, with moist, spaniel-like eyes, to 'build bridges' – but as we learnt from Neville Chamberlain in the run-up to the Second World War, appeasement never works.

Read the pages that follow; they're filled with luminaries like Ted Greeno ('I've given some villains some awful hidings'), Jack Capstick advising on the use of a truncheon ('I've hit quite a number of ruffians on top of the head and they've gone over, all right, but the best place to catch a man is right across the ear . . . it sounds brutal, I know') and Bob Fabian ('Treat your criminal rough, my boy; he's never heard of the Queensberry Rules. He'll respect you all the more for it').

Now before I go any further, there may be some readers amongst you who take the *Guardian*, are senior police officers, hug trees and fervently worship prisoners' human rights. If that's the case, I do strongly advise you not to continue any further, because what follows – certainly in your opinion – will make for fairly grim reading. Those of you who are made of sterner stuff, read on.

These old 'tecs (and others of the same ilk) will show you what *did* work . . .

CHAPTER 1

Greeno and the Safe-Blowers

In January 1921, an applicant for the Metropolitan Police was being medically examined in Whitehall. At 5 feet 9½ inches and 11 stone 6 lbs, it appeared he would have little trouble in proving his fitness, and when the 20-year-old former wireless operator from the Mercantile Marine was asked if he'd done any boxing he modestly admitted, 'A bit'.

'Keep it up', said the doctor, and the applicant – whose name was Ted Greeno – took him at his word. None of it, however, was carried out in the ring. He was far too busy catching thieves, but the pugilistic side of his nature was satisfied because few of them were prepared to be peacefully arrested. Posted to 'H' Division's Whitechapel district, he spent nine months in uniform before donning plain clothes; due to his encyclopaedic knowledge of racetrack thieves and gangsters, he was 'borrowed' by the Flying Squad for six years before officially being posted there, for a further eleven years.

Greeno's fighting was not confined to making arrests; if anybody challenged his authority, off would come his jacket, a makeshift ring would be formed and the challenger would be well and truly thrashed.

Much of his time was spent at racetracks, breaking up teams of gangsters and pickpockets. In addition, he cultivated his informants there; at a time when each piece of information was officially rewarded by 2s 6d from Scotland Yard's Informants' Fund, Greeno, having backed a winner, would unofficially lavish £25 or £50 on his informants; no wonder they provided him with top-notch information.

During the late 1930s, offences involving office-breaking with the use of explosives claimed the Flying Squad's attention; between March and November 1938, no fewer than thirty-six safes were opened with explosives. Greeno's informants identified a number of persons involved with that commodity, one of whom pretended that his name was William Smith; in reality he was George Henry Chatham and he possessed three previous convictions. Let's leave Greeno in abeyance, just for the moment, and concentrate on Chatham; there's a sound reason for this, I assure you, because I need to introduce the reader to the antecedents of a young man who progressed to being one of Britain's most audacious and persistent criminals, with and without the use of explosives.

His first conviction came in 1931, when Chatham was nineteen; he took a car without the owner's consent and was fined £15 – quite a large sum for that time, especially for a first offence. But he failed to profit by it; just a few weeks later, Chatham and an associate took a car from Kensington and it was found abandoned outside Chatham's address at 16 Garvan Road, Fulham. A search of the car revealed identifiable items belonging to both men, both were arrested and on 29 October 1931 Chatham was sentenced to six weeks' hard labour.

It was a short, sharp shock which should have worked, but it didn't.

His third conviction merits rather further discourse because it points the reader into the direction that Chatham's life would take.

Hardly had he been released, when together with 25-year-old John Robins, Charles Mitchell aged thirty-three and Joseph Chandler aged twenty-two, Chatham broke into a garage in Lessam Mews, Kensington during the early hours of 21 December 1931 and stole a car. From there, with Chatham driving, the four men went to a butcher's shop in Lavender Hill and, with the aid of a jemmy, forced entry. They were surprised by two patrolling police constables, John Wallis and Lester Barrett, who jumped on to the running boards of the stolen car, whereupon Chatham drove off, swerving wildly and mounting the footpath. Both officers were attacked with jemmies, sustaining head injuries, and PC Barrett was also kicked in the stomach, thrown off the car and hospitalized. With the assistance of Percy Tester, a coffee stall proprietor, and William Todd, a taxi driver, Chatham and Robins were arrested at the scene.

Three hours later, Chandler was arrested in bed at his address in Anselm Road, Fulham and told Detective Sergeant Smith, 'Yes, I was with them but I didn't strike or kick anybody. It wasn't me.'

At 7.30 that morning, the same officer arrested Mitchell in Halford Street, Fulham who said, 'Not me.' However, taken to North Fulham police station and seeing Chandler in the station doorway, Mitchell said, 'That's done it. I thought you were trying to get me to admit something but now you have the others, I need not say a word.'

That admission was repeated by the officer at South Western Police Court a few hours later and drew a furious denial from Mitchell, who said, 'You're telling lies. It's a deliberate lie!'

That – considering the severity of the charges – was not the wisest statement to make, especially when all four defendants were applying for bail, an application that was strongly opposed by the police.

'This is a very serious matter', said the Magistrate. 'We will see about bail next week', and he added ominously, 'if there are any grounds for it.'

There wasn't; Christmas came and went, and in the New Year all four were committed in custody to the Old Bailey.

Charged with shop- and garage-breaking, possessing housebreaking implements by night, stealing a car and inflicting grievous bodily harm on the two police constables, the quartet appeared before the Recorder of London, Sir Ernest Wild KC, who was told that Chatham 'had been strongly suspected of smash and grab raids and stealing motor cars and was a most violent and persistent criminal and expert motor driver.'

It is interesting to note that while Chatham was the junior of the defendants by several years he was the acknowledged prime mover and leader of the gang.

The Recorder's comments were no less severe:

> There is no religion, morality or respect left in a certain class in the community, and the gravest crimes of violence are being perpetuated by young men, under the age of twenty. The prisoners are extremely fortunate not to be charged with murder.

He then commended the actions of the two constables to the commissioner and gave monetary awards to the two helpers, Messrs Todd and Tester. While Mitchell was sent to hard labour, Robins, Chandler and Chatham were each sentenced to three years' penal servitude.

So before he had reached his twentieth birthday, Chatham was a hardened and dangerous criminal, having served sentences of hard labour and penal servitude. He emerged from Wandsworth Prison determined to continue his life of crime.

★ ★ ★

On 9 November 1938, Chatham went to Uxbridge Road Station, Shepherd's Bush to collect a suitcase which contained a packet of gelignite and thirty detonators. Unfortunately, the clerk in the parcels office had been replaced by a Flying Squad officer, who tipped the wink to Greeno when Chatham fetched the case.

There then ensued an extremely violent disagreement between the two men. Chatham flung the case into the road, where it was almost run over by a passing bus, Greeno's truncheon was produced (not for the first and certainly not for the last time), and Chatham was 'sticked', which brought his arrest to a successful conclusion.

At the Old Bailey, Chatham plaintively told the jury that he was collecting the case for somebody else and that he had done so under the impression that it contained cigars. Not even Mr Christmas Humphreys' sheer ineptitude as a prosecutor could save him, and Chatham was convicted of possessing the items in such circumstances as to give rise to a reasonable suspicion that he did not have them for a lawful purpose.

'I would describe him', said Greeno – who by then held the rank of divisional detective inspector – 'as a most persistent, dangerous and desperate criminal. He has been associated with active criminals, some of whom have appeared before this court in connection with explosives charges and house-breaking.'

The Common Serjeant, Mr Cecil Whiteley KC, was not the most sympathetic of judges – indeed, he was a firm believer in supporting the police – and sentencing Chatham to five years' penal servitude, he said:

> What strikes me about this man is that he is only twenty-six now. When he was given his first prison sentence he was only nineteen. He was never bound over. That is what I call manufacturing criminals. Thank God it is not going on now.

To his dying day, Chatham would say that he was in possession of just one detonator (not thirty), had been sentenced to six years (not five) and had been 'fitted up'. In fact, his arrest was what's known in the trade as 'a set-up'. It also has a Latin tag – *quid pro quo*. Wanting to use it for his own piece of work, Chatham had double-crossed the gang who had possessed the gelignite, and they had been getting their own back by informing on him.

And there, for the time being, we can leave George Henry Chatham – he would later be known to the underworld as 'Taters' Chatham – but never fear, he will be returning to these pages later on, in stunning style.

★ ★ ★

Greeno's next confrontation with criminals who possessed explosives occurred just nine days after Chatham's arrest.

When John Fairley, a 33-year-old labourer, ventured south from his habitat at Dykemuir Street, Springburn, Glasgow, to meet up in London with James Robertson and James Albert Paynter, it did not escape the attention of one of Greeno's snouts. In fact, Greeno was provided with details of precisely what the larcenous trio were planning and, what was more, where it was going to be carried out. I hasten to add that not all information possesses the same exactitude; but then again, Greeno's snouts were of the highest calibre.

It led to a Flying Squad team, under the direction of Detective Chief Inspector Bill Parker, staking out Cranbrook Road, Ilford on the evening of 18 November 1938. At 9.15 pm the officer saw Paynter standing in a passageway; within a few minutes, Robertson and Fairley joined him. The three men climbed over a wall and were seen to enter the premises of a department store, Wests & Moultons Ltd, through a fanlight. Parker ascended a fire escape and entered the top floor.

Meanwhile, Greeno and Detective Sergeant Cyril Green had also entered the store, and in the showroom they could hear the sound of metal being sawn through. At 9.40 they saw the three men come up the stairway and, after entering two other rooms, go into the office, where they could hear the sounds of metal tapping metal. The three men emerged into the showroom, where they took off their coats, and although it was very dark, they must have seen Green, because Robertson said, 'The watchman – do him!'

That was their first mistake; the second was when Fairley and Paynter advanced towards Green to carry out Robinson's instruction.

'We're police officers!' shouted Greeno and, drawing his truncheon, went into action, 'sticking' Fairley, then Paynter. The three of them rolled about on the floor, with Greeno lashing out quite indiscriminately before subduing them. Green, too, had disabled Robertson. He took his prisoner into the office to make a telephone call and arrange transportation for the prisoners, when Fairley and Paynter, who were still on the floor, began to kick out at the officers. There was another fight and later, at Stratford Petty Sessions, Greeno, seeking to insert a note of regret in his voice, stated, 'I again had to use my truncheon.' What he didn't tell the Justices was that he had also told the prisoners, 'One move and I'll belt you again!'

When the showroom lights were switched on, Greeno admitted that even he was appalled at the sight. With the injuries inflicted and the amount of blood that had been shed, he described the floor as resembling the interior of a jam sandwich.

Fairley told him, 'All right. I've had enough. I've got some dangerous explosives in my pocket – detonators – and they're liable to go off if they get knocked.'

His associates were in a confessing mood as well. Fairley told DCI Parker, 'Be careful of my jacket, you'll find some detonators in the pocket', and Parker did – six of them in a matchbox.

Robertson said, 'There's some gelignite in my coat pocket', and when Parker searched him he discovered that the prisoner was right; eight and a half sticks of Polar Ammon. It was slightly amazing that in giving out such a bashing Greeno's and Green's truncheons had not detonated the three criminals – and themselves.

And that wasn't all. Also in their possession were a coil of fuse, a jemmy, three pairs of gloves and a torch covered in brown paper so that the light was concentrated through a pin-hole. There was also a bar of soap; this was to be used for sealing up the lock of the safe into which the gelignite was going to be inserted. In fact, they had already made a start; the sounds of the metal tapping heard by the officers was the safe's lock cover being bent and fixed away from the hole.

The trio were herded into Ilford police station, where the duty officer's face drained of colour when he saw the state of the prisoners; and the following morning at court, Greeno assured the Justices that no, an interpreter would not be required, since the defendants were not turbaned Indians but only bandaged villains.

The officers were commended by the Justices, the prisoners were committed to the Old Bailey, where Robertson was sentenced to three years' penal servitude, Fairley to five years' penal servitude and 24-year-old Paynter was – rather surprisingly – bound over in the sum of £5 for three years and placed on probation.

The commissioner highly commended Greeno and Green, and when they were presented with £10 cheques from the Bow Street Reward Fund, the Magistrate, Sir Rollo Graham-Campbell, said:

> I think there can be no doubt that both officers are deserving of the highest commendation for their courageous action. I am sure they acted in a way in which we expect all Metropolitan police officers to act and I congratulate them and wish them all success in their further career in the Force.

These were sentiments which would have been shared by many of us; but it does beg the question, had those arrests been carried out eighty years later, is it possible that the Crown Prosecution Service and the Independent Office for Police Conduct would have taken the same view?

★ ★ ★

Greeno could now concentrate on a gang who had claimed his attention for some time. Eddie Chapman was an Army deserter, thief, conman and womanizing blackmailer, who had turned his attention to acquiring the contents of safes. It had started in a fairly modest way, ripping the back off an old safe belonging to the Fyffe's Bananas warehouse with a chisel. But it soon became clear that newer, stronger, more sophisticatedly constructed safes, holding bigger prizes than those contained in the banana firm's dilapidated safe, would need something better than a chisel to permit entry.

Explosives, of course, were the answer – but not an unequivocal one. In strengthening their products, the safe manufacturers ensured that when a safe was blown, for a split second the lock mechanism would bulge outwards, thereby making it impossible to open. Of course, this could be circumvented by the safe-breakers using a greater amount of explosive, but apart from this creating a much louder bang, increasing the chances of it being heard, it also intensified the risk of blowing the safe to smithereens, thereby destroying any currency contained therein.

However, Chapman was able to avoid such a mishap. After inserting a small amount of gelignite in the safe's lock and sealing it in place with chewing gum (thereby giving rise to the suspicion that, due to the use of that commodity, an American gang was responsible) he took the office's heavy typewriter and tied it to the safe's handle with string. In that split-second when the explosion occurred, the weight of the typewriter pulled down the handle, causing the door to swing open effortlessly.

The following morning, when the banditry was discovered, the office typist would have been nonplussed to find that her machine was in a different position to where she had left it the previous night. If any of those now ancient ladies are reading these words, they'll understand why.

Chapman enlisted the aid of George Darry, whose real name was Anthony Latt and who was the possessor of two previous convictions, and also of Hugh Anson. The latter had not been previously convicted, but his real name was Anton Stromberg; his job was to drive the other two. Chapman did not run the risk of stealing cars to aid their escapades; he enlisted the help of Leonard

Eric Groves, who did not accompany them on their safe-blowings but hired cars for them to use and also hid the explosives for them.

From July 1938 onwards, the three men blew safes not only in London but also all over the country. On 22 November 1938, the gang stole £438 from a blown safe at the Odeon Cinema, Bournemouth, and four days after that they blew a safe at the Co-op store in Leicester and obtained £256. From there they went to Yorkshire, then back down again to Lincolnshire, before turning again to the north. Checking into an Edinburgh hotel, they blew the safe at St Cuthbert's Co-op but were caught in possession of explosives. Amazingly, they were bailed from Edinburgh High Court and fled south, once more to Bournemouth. But it was a cinema in York that was their next target, on 28 January 1939, when they stole £200 before checking into a Bournemouth hotel on 2 February. Three days later, the safe of the Parkstone & Bournemouth Co-op was hit, and the men got away with £476 3s 0d. Then the mistakes began to be made.

Chapman, always ostentatious, decided to settle the hotel bill by producing a roll of notes so thick that the receptionist would later recall he was unable to get his hand around it. He also tipped the chambermaid £1 – an enormous amount for 1939, the equivalent of £60 at today's values. It was a piece of generosity that would help to cause the gang's downfall; she permitted detectives to examine the contents of her vacuum cleaner, and there, amongst the dust, was a red rubber band of the variety used to encircle notes in the Co-op's safe.

Darry sent a letter to his girlfriend saying that he and the others intended to go to Jersey; unfortunately, the letter was intercepted and the local police were alerted.

When seven members of the Jersey police dashed into the Hotel de la Plage at Havre-le-Pas they swiftly arrested Darry and Anson, but the guests enjoying lunch were astonished when Chapman dived through the dining room window and escaped.

Darry and Anson were returned to England, where their baggage and clothing was examined. The suitcases revealed copper casings that had come from a detonator, as well as two black crystals which were proved to be large-grain blasting gunpowder of the type used in mining operations. The mens' pockets and trouser turn-ups contained mahogany dust which exactly matched the Co-op safe.

Leonard Groves received a visit from Greeno at his address at Sutherland Place, North Kensington. Initially denying any knowledge of Chapman, Darry or Anson – or any of their aliases – he grew rather apprehensive when a search of his property revealed

134 detonators in a tobacco tin wrapped in a piece of lined notepaper. This was hidden behind the gas meter; a further search resulted in the finding of sixteen more detonators in a cupboard, together with two 2oz cartridges of Polar Ammon gelignite and twelve pieces of safety fuse.

Groves – who had two previous convictions – sullenly told Greeno, 'I know nothing about the stuff. Chapman and the other boys have visited me. I can't help what they do.' Later, he would change his mind.

A letter in Darry's possession was on the same type of notepaper used to wrap the cigarette box found in Groves' basement. It led police to the address of Darry's sister where, in a chimney, were found more gelignite, powder fuse and four detonators.

On 7 March 1939, Anson and Darry were committed from Bournemouth Police Court to the Old Bailey, where they met up with Groves, who had similarly been committed from West London Police Court.

Both Darry and Anson claimed to have alibis, although Anson had previously made a statement to Bournemouth police stating that he had simply driven Darry and Chapman to various locations and thought that the money they had given him afterwards came from their winnings at dog tracks. He then rather spoilt that by making a further statement in which he said that Chapman and Darry had told him that there had only been £275 in the Co-op safe, of which his share had been £40.

It simply wasn't good enough, and on 23 March, both men were found guilty of possessing explosives and conspiracy, and Greeno was able to inform the Common Serjeant that since the gang's arrest, all safe-blowing throughout the country had ceased.

Darry was sentenced to seven years' penal servitude, and Groves, charged only with possessing explosives and who pleaded guilty, was sentenced to three years' penal servitude.

Anson's sentence was postponed until the next sessions, and on 25 April, Greeno told the Judge that Anson was now asking for five other similar offences to be taken into consideration. He was given the surprisingly compassionate sentence of twelve months' imprisonment; perhaps this leniency was because the Old Bailey had no jurisdiction over the other offence which Anson had admitted, that of the safe-blowing at St Cuthbert's Co-op in Edinburgh; it would have to be there, from where Anson had skipped bail, that he would be tried. It was possible that the vengeful Edinburgh High Court would not be quite as merciful as the Old Bailey's Common Serjeant had been.

But what of Eddie Chapman – alias Arnold Edward Chapman, Edward Arnold Chapman, Edward Edwards, Edward Simpson, Arnold Thompson and Edward Thompson – on the run in Jersey? The day following his escape, he broke into the West Pavilion nightclub, cracked open a safe and helped himself to the contents. Arrested, he appeared at the Royal Court of Jersey, pleaded guilty and was sentenced to two years' hard labour. Within four months he had escaped but was re-arrested the following day on Plémont beach, where he put up a struggle which only ended when one of the officers punched him in the stomach. He was as fortunate as Greeno's prisoners in Ilford had been, some eight months previously. Inside Chapman's pockets were eight sticks of gelignite and fifteen detonators which he'd stolen from L'Etacq quarry; had the punch been delivered three inches either way, it would have meant the end of Chapman, his pursuers and most of the sunbathers on north-west Jersey's nicest beach.

For that, plus a series of other offences committed during his 24 hours of freedom, Chapman appeared at the island's Criminal Assizes, where he was sentenced to twelve months' imprisonment, to run consecutively to his two-year sentence.

Fate intervened when, with the outbreak of the Second World War, the Germans overran the Channel Islands and Chapman volunteered to work for them as a spy. He was accepted and after training was parachuted into England. Initially giving his name as 'George Clarke', he volunteered to work as a double-agent for British Intelligence and they, too, accepted him.

Having been awarded a small fortune (plus an Iron Cross) by Germany, Chapman also negotiated a deal with the British authorities by which all the crimes he was wanted for were expunged from the records.

When he returned to England, with the war at an end, Chapman was saved the inconvenience of about ten years' penal servitude; just as importantly, he was spared an almost certain bruising arrest at the hands of Ted Greeno.

CHAPTER 2

Barmy Army

The other day, I came across an instance of indiscipline in the British Army which spilled over into civilian life. This was the case of Percy Lane, who was born in 1891. At the age of seventeen he was convicted of theft and was sentenced to three weeks' imprisonment. Barely had he been released when he was bound over for stealing a bicycle. The following year, he joined the Army but was dismissed with ignominy, and in 1911 he acquired another conviction at Tunbridge Wells. At the outbreak of war he joined the Army once more and rose to become a battery sergeant major. But then he was reduced to the rank of sergeant and, after he had absented himself, he was finally reduced to the rank of gunner. I mention this because although his Army discharge was implausibly marked 'Honest, sober and good character', an inspector at the Old Bailey (with certainly more accuracy) described Lane as being 'a man with an ungovernable temper'.

This is what happened to inspire that intemperate description.

On 14 November 1921, in the guise of 'Detective Inspector Drew of Scotland Yard', Lane entered London's Kismet Restaurant, told the proprietress that he was investigating the passing of forged currency and asked to see her cash register; unconvinced of his bona fides, the lady refused to comply. Next stop was the Brownie Restaurant in Victoria Street, where he made the same request to the cashier, Mrs Kavanagh, saying, 'We have got a man who has been passing counterfeit treasury notes, and I want you to show me all the notes you have taken today.' She did so, Lane examined them, handed them back and said he would return the following day.

However, Mrs Kavanagh was as unimpressed with Lane's authenticity as the proprietress of the Kismet Restaurant had been, she communicated with the police, and the following day, Detectives Charles Martin and Percy McDoull from Rochester Row police station secreted themselves in the restaurant's passageway to await the arrival of 'Inspector Drew'.

When he did arrive and asked to see the notes in the till, Martin stepped out and challenged him, whereupon Lane admitted that he was not a police officer. But when Martin told Lane he was arresting him, Lane pulled a revolver from his hip pocket and pointed it at the officer. Martin gripped the revolver, and two shots were fired in quick succession; to stop any further shots being fired, Martin took hold of the revolver's cylinder, and for the following ten minutes there was a tremendous struggle. McDoull joined in, and during the melee he was flung around and his head smashed the glass in the restaurant's door. Eventually, however, Lane was disarmed and subdued.

When he was charged, Lane replied:

> I was desperate owing to my wife's delicate state of health and I had read in the paper how a man had obtained treasury notes by saying he was a detective and I thought it was easy ... Break the news gently to my wife. This has happened because I was out of work and I had deceived my wife by saying I was in work.

At the Old Bailey, Lane pleaded not guilty to shooting at the officers with intent to do them grievous bodily harm; giving evidence, he told the court that he had 'scrounged' the revolver from the battlefield while he was serving in France. He said that he loaded the revolver in 1919 after 'firing in the New Year' but was unable to say why it was in his possession on 15 November 1921; he did not intend to injure anyone.

This, of course, was complete and consummate bollocks. One does not put a fully loaded service revolver in one's hip pocket, where it makes a heavy (2½lbs) and uncomfortable bulge, for no reason. Lane's intention was to use it to threaten Mrs Kavanagh should she demur in handing over the currency; he had not done so the previous day because the revolver was not then in his possession. The fact that he had pulled it out when he was stopped by the detectives was an indication of – as Inspector Aldridge later put it – his 'ungovernable temper'.

But not according to Lane:

> When Detective Martin came for me in an aggressive manner, I was afraid I would get shot in the struggle. I put my hand to pull out the revolver which Martin gripped and it went off. That seemed to pull me to my senses and I immediately fired it again to put the wind up them.

It did not explain to the jury's satisfaction why the struggle continued for ten minutes, why Lane failed to voluntarily relinquish his hold on the gun or, in fact, the need to smash the unfortunate Detective McDoull's head through the restaurant door.

Found guilty, Lane made a pathetic appeal, claiming that he was not the 'out-and-out criminal' which his record seemed to indicate, but Mr Justice Avory obviously thought he was and, telling him that crimes committed by persons with loaded firearms 'must be put down', he sentenced him to twenty months' hard labour.

Six weeks later, both officers were awarded £5 by Mr Chester Jones from the Bow Street Reward Fund, and in the 1923 New Year's Honours they were awarded the King's Police Medal.

But it does leave a question in one's mind as to what would have happened if Mrs Kavanagh had not gone to the police and if she had then decided not to hand over the money? I've got a pretty good idea, but then there are some who'd say I'm prejudiced . . .

CHAPTER 3

Devoted to his Wife and Seven Children

I first saw the name of Detective Inspector Charles Young on a report which he penned to the head of the Flying Squad, dated January 1931, bemoaning the fact that the sluggish Crossley Tenders, which had been in service with the Squad for the previous eleven years, were no match for the faster, more powerful cars used by 'The Motor Car Bandits' and citing recent instances when this had been the case. What he didn't say, and what I found out later, was what happened – in his particular case, three months earlier – when faster Flying Squad cars were used . . .

The story begins on 4 September 1930, when a light blue Morris saloon was stolen from Albion Road, Lewisham. Then, on 27 September, George Ressier, the sub-postmaster at the Atlantic Road Post Office, Brixton, locked up for the night, leaving stamps and cash valued at £300 in the safe. At 3 o'clock the following morning, Detective Sergeant Brooks was called to the premises; he found that the door had been opened by sawing through a staple which held a padlock, the interior was 'in great disorder' and the safe was missing.

The person responsible for both those offences was John Jackson – he also liked to be referred to as 'Slater', and a pretty horrible character he was, too. Born in 1893, he was sent to Borstal detention for three years in 1913 and then, in 1922, he appeared at the Old Bailey for robbery with violence, for which he received six years' penal servitude and fifteen lashes of the cat-o'-nine tails. Married, with seven children, he lived apart from his wife.

Then, on the morning of 6 October, Police Constable Barwick was patrolling West Wickham and discovered the safe behind a hedge in Layham's Road. The back had been ripped off and the handle broken; the only contents left were two empty bank bags and papers with 'Brixton Post Office' stamped on them.

But the stolen car's details had been circulated, and later that evening, Detective Inspector Young, together with Detective Sergeants Charles Reid and James Wakeling, was on patrol in a

Flying Squad car – a fast one – when at midnight, they spotted the distinctive stolen Morris being driven near Oxford Circus. They gave chase, and Jackson suddenly turned off into Wardour Street. A build-up of traffic initially stopped the Squad car from following, but the stolen car was soon seen again, this time in Shaftesbury Avenue. The chase recommenced, straight across Cambridge Circus, into Charing Cross Road and right across the busy junction with New Oxford Street and into Tottenham Court Road. Jackson took the next right turn into Great Russell Street, tore past the British Museum and through Russell Square, before coming to a halt in Tavistock Square, with the Squad car right behind him.

The three officers leapt from their car, and whilst Reid and Wakeling jumped on to the Morris's nearside running board, Young did the same on the offside. Jackson now set off again and swerved into the middle of the road, hoping to throw the detectives off, but Young got the driver's door open and grabbed hold of the steering wheel. While Jackson tried to stop the other detectives from getting into the car, Young swung the car around and it crashed into a barrow by the kerb and bounced back into the middle of the road, where Young succeeded in switching off the engine.

Wakeling and Weir had now managed to get into the car, and Jackson shouted, 'Get out or I'll shoot!' and punched Wakeling in the face. Jackson was trying to pull something from his back pocket, but Wakeling trapped his arm and from Jackson's hip pocket took out an automatic pistol. Weir pinioned Jackson's arms, and despite Jackson's frenzied struggles, the officers overpowered him and took him into Tottenham Court Road police station.

There it was discovered that the automatic pistol was loaded with nine rounds – and there was more: Jackson was searched and in his possession was a £5 silver bag, together with the Atlantic Road date stamp.

Sergeant Wakeling was placed on the sick list for some time; during the furious melee with Jackson he had torn the ligaments in his chest and his back muscles. However, it's to be hoped that he had made a full recovery by New Year's Eve 1930, when the three officers were highly commended by the commissioner for exhibiting 'great courage' when making the arrest.

Back, now, to 18 November 1930, when Jackson appeared at the Old Bailey before the Recorder of London, Sir Ernest Wild KC. He denied everything, having told Young, 'I know nothing about the burglary' and telling the court that he had hired the

Morris and that the pistol, which he had been told was defective, had been handed to him to ascertain what was wrong with it.

It wasn't quite good enough, and he was found guilty of possessing a loaded firearm with intent to endanger life, receiving a stolen car and a date stamp. The Recorder sentenced Jackson to a total of ten years' penal servitude, after Inspector Young said that he was 'a very dangerous and resourceful thief and a leading light of a gang of car bandits and shop-breakers'.

This description of his attributes, asserted Jackson, was not correct. He did not dispute Young's additional statement that – according to Jackson – he made an allowance to his deserted wife and children of £4 per week. However, since that was approximately the weekly wage received by a police constable, the Recorder may have formed the opinion that Jackson was either, as Young had stated, 'a resourceful thief' or that Jackson and the truth were incompatible, and he had taken it into consideration when passing sentence.

CHAPTER 4

Hit and Run?

When 21-year-old Sidney George Morath (he also liked to be known as Sidney Davies) of Grinstead Road, Deptford walked out into the street from the London Sessions on 6 October 1931 he must have expelled a sigh of relief, because he and a fellow scoundrel had just been acquitted of attempting to steal a motor car. Quite possibly he thought, 'If I could get away with that just now, I'll be able to get away with it again in the future.' If that was the case, it was a rather irresponsible prediction . . .

Just over one year later, a garage in Peterborough Road, Fulham was broken into and a Morris saloon car was stolen; that was followed by a shop-breaking a matter of yards away at Hurlingham Road, where the thieves helped themselves to a quantity of cigarettes and tobacco.

It was 1.30 in the morning of 22 December 1932 when three officers from 'X' Division – Detective Sergeants John Black and Albert Champion with Detective Constable Harry Rawlings – were on patrol in a police car in the Uxbridge Road, when they saw the Morris being driven towards them. Since there were four men in the car – Morath was driving and was accompanied by Harold Hillier, James Grant and James Pointing – this not unnaturally excited the officers' interest, and DS Black turned the car around and gave chase. The police car overtook the Morris at Ealing Broadway, and DS Champion shouted at Morath to stop, blew his whistle and flashed his lamp; but Morath ignored him and kept driving. The chase continued until the Morris suddenly stopped and a piece of metal was flung at the police car's windscreen; Black swerved, the metal bar missed, and when a second weapon was thrown, that too was avoided. As the chase resumed and the cars roared through the night, packets of cigarettes were thrown from the Morris and then its back seat was torn out and flung at the pursuing car in an effort to impede its progress. At Hanwell, Black crashed the police car into the rear of the Morris, and as the cars approached Southall, he rammed the Morris once more; but those collisions failed to stop it.

It was when the two cars entered Southall High Street and Black struck the offside wheel of the Morris with his nearside front wheel that the chase came to an end; the Morris mounted the pavement and turned over completely, trapping the four occupants underneath it.

Cigarettes and tobacco were strewn all over the pavement, the men were arrested and packets of cigarettes were found in the pockets of Morath and Grant; Hillier had a pair of white cotton gloves on him. There was also the matter of a jemmy found in their possession; and DS Champion, who must have been a very astute officer, was able to say that it was the jemmy which had produced the striations on the shutter of the Peterborough Road garage from where the Morris had been stolen.

At a remand appearance at Ealing Police Court, Hillier and Grant pleaded guilty to being in possession of a stolen car and cigarettes, Pointing pleaded not guilty to everything and Morath pleaded guilty to possessing house-breaking implements but denied the other offences.

Morath told the court that on the night of the incident he had seen two men with a car outside the tobacconist's shop and became suspicious when they ran off. He looked inside the car and saw the tobacco and cigarettes. He then said:

> Having no money, I got into the car and drove it away. I did not know what to do with it, so I took it round to Hillier's house. I told him what I had done and asked him if he knew anybody who would have it. He and Grant got into the car and later we met Pointing . . . I was challenged by a police car. I tried to get away. They eventually overtook us. Finally at Southall, they hit the car and overturned us, pinning the four of us underneath.

The four men were committed for trial to the Middlesex Sessions and on 10 January 1933 they were convicted and received lengthy prison sentences. The three police officers were commended by the jury and also by the chairman, Sir Montagu Sharpe; they were highly commended by the commissioner; and on 4 May 1933, at Bow Street Court, the Chief Magistrate, Sir Rollo Graham-Campbell, praised them for 'their acts of conspicuous bravery' and awarded them cheques from the Reward Fund, £10 for Black (soon to be a detective inspector with the Flying Squad) and £5 each for Champion and Rawlings.

And this was no one-off achievement by the officers; in the same edition of *Police Orders* in which the officers had been highly commended there was a further separate commendation for

Hit and Run?

Champion and Black, this time for 'vigilance, zeal and ability in effecting the arrest of twelve persons for loitering, larceny and other offences in four cases'. Additionally, Champion was also commended in two of the cases and Black in one case by the Justices at the Ealing Petty Sessions.

It's said that there have been times during hair-raising car chases such as the one described above, when the pursuing officers are reminded of their own mortality and, upon apprehending the originators of their discomfort, have smashed the living shit out of them. If that were true, I have no doubt that anyone reading these words would consider that type of behaviour utterly reprehensible, as indeed I do.

But there was one rather unsettling aspect of the case, because when the prisoners made their first appearance at Ealing Police Court, Pointing was not amongst them. He had been hospitalized, and DS Black had explained to the court that when the car was lifted off the prisoners, Pointing took this as a heaven-sent opportunity to escape but had been 'knocked down'. Black did not expand upon this statement, nor did the Bench demand any further details. Perhaps they inferred that he had been struck by a passing vehicle, although I find it difficult to believe that there was an excess of traffic in Southall at two o'clock in the morning in December 1932.

Naturally, it's a matter that has caused me some concern.

Chapter 5

A Popular Jeweller's

It's difficult to say if Frank Colbard suffered from an identity crisis or whether he had a defective memory, but it appeared he had difficulty recalling his baptismal name, since he also claimed to be Edward Perkins and John C. Webber. He and his associate, Thomas Johnson, both stated their profession to be 'clerk' and said that they had no fixed abode. This may or may not have been true, but one thing was for certain: these 20-year-olds were a pair of thoroughgoing villains.

At the opposite end of the social scale was Sir Ernest Wild KC (who has been mentioned previously and will be again). He was sixty-four years of age at their one and only meeting, on 20 July 1933. Sir Ernest had qualified as a barrister in 1912, was knighted in 1918 and since 1922 had held the position of the most senior judge at the Old Bailey, the Recorder of London. Both parties held strong views on law and order: Messrs Colbard and Johnson wished to circumvent it, Sir Ernest decided to ruthlessly enforce it.

Their meeting came about as a result of Colbard and Johnson's activities one month previously, on the evening of 20 June 1933. Just as a Mr May and his staff were about to close Dibden & Co., a jeweller's shop in London's Sloane Street, at 6.15pm, they were attacked by the two men in possession of a sawn-off shotgun, two pieces of lead piping and a dagger; Mr May was struck across the head, and whilst his bowler hat saved him from more serious injuries, he was also hit across the hand as he tried to defend himself from further attack. Three other employees were held at bay by Colbard, who levelled the gun at them, while Johnson ransacked the showcase, taking eleven pearl necklaces, studs and buttons, valued at £280 – or approximately £20,000 at today's values.

The loot went into Johnson's 'happy bag' (since it had also housed the weaponry) and an attaché case, and the two men ran from the shop.

They were spotted by two patrolling police constables, 243 'B' William Bunce and 207 'B' Frederick Hawkes, who commandeered a passing motorist's car and took up the chase. The robbers got into a taxi, but hearing the shouts and whistles of the pursuing officers, the cab driver refused to move. Colbard threatened Hawkes with the cocked shotgun, but the officer slammed the cab's door on him, causing the barrels to crash through the window. Drawing his truncheon, Hawkes 'sticked' Colbard, but Johnson attacked both officers with the dagger, Hawkes suffering cuts to his arm and jaw. Both men escaped from the cab, but with the aid of Mr May and two passers-by, a Major Elwell and Captain Phillips, they were disarmed and arrested.

Having pleaded guilty to robbery with violence at the Old Bailey, Detective Sergeant Harold Smith told the Recorder that 'this is the first occasion when the American gangster method of sawing off a shotgun has been used in this country.' Some thirty years later, this accompaniment to robbery would have become all too common, but in 1933 it was considered sensational news and it flashed round the globe, even gaining a mention in Canada's *Calgary Herald* on 31 August.

But now it was time for retribution; Johnson was sentenced to five years' penal servitude and eighteen strokes of the birch, while Colbard received four years' penal servitude and twelve strokes of the cat-o'-nine tails. The Recorder praised the efforts of the passers-by and directed that a reward of £5 should be paid to each of them. He also expressed admiration for the two constables, who were later both highly commended by the commissioner, presented with cheques for £8 from the Bow Street Reward Fund and awarded the King's Police Medal in the 1934 New Year's Honours List.

Dibden's appeared to be a popular venue for thieves; also for the handing out of gallantry awards. This is what happened two decades later . . .

★ ★ ★

If Frederick Mark Stone was not the model for Charles Atlas' original seven-stone weakling, destined in the advertisements to have sand kicked in his face by the beach bully, he came pretty close. As a boy, his legs were encased in callipers but he dreamt of becoming a champion swimmer. It says much for Stone that exercise rid him of the callipers, he taught himself to swim and he became a proficient cyclist, boxer, wrestler and rugby player.

He joined the Royal Navy, serving during the First World War and leaving after seven years' service, and in 1921 at the age of twenty-three he joined the Metropolitan Police. Stone was a compassionate man who befriended many of the homeless people he encountered along the banks of the River Thames as he patrolled the beats on 'A' Division.

It was one of those unfortunates who, desirous of ending his life, jumped into the Thames from Westminster Bridge at midnight on 28 June 1927. Seeing the man floating in the water, Stone stripped off his tunic and leaving that, his helmet and boots on the bridge, climbed on to the parapet and dived 22ft into the river.

He reached the man, and swimming across the tide with him, made for the steps of the LCC building, 100 yards away. However, the fellow simply didn't want to be rescued and began struggling wildly, whereupon Stone punched him – he was not *that* compassionate! By now the tide had swept them past the steps; fortunately, Stone saw a chain hanging from the wall, grabbed hold of it and hung on until they were rescued by a River Police launch.

He had been injured during the rescue and now he was showered with awards: a commissioner's high commendation, a bronze medal and certificate from the Royal Humane Society, an inscribed silver watch from the Carnegie Hero Trust Fund, £10 from the Bow Street Reward Fund and finally, the King's Police Medal for gallantry.

What was not generally known was that Stone, who was married with two sons, took the man home, nursed him back to health and found him a job.

Shortly afterwards, Stone transferred to 'C' Division, where as Police Constable 281'C' he became an assistant warrant officer at Marlborough Street Police Court. Not that the new posting curtailed his philanthropic activities; in his off-duty hours he utilized his athletic ability to run sports clubs and keep youths off the streets. With the arrival of the Second World War, Stone helped families whose homes had been bombed and destroyed.

His next, astonishing act of bravery came in 1941; a building had been completely demolished by an explosion and people were trapped inside. Gas and water had escaped from the fractured mains, and the water level was rising rapidly in the basement. Police officers attended the scene, including Stone, who was off duty. One casualty was successfully removed before the officers tunnelled down to the cellar, now flooded to a depth of 4ft. Due to the escaping gas, the officers were only able to work in short shifts, but they rescued three women. For 2½ hours the men worked on, despite the fact that a 30ft high wall was in danger of collapsing. Told to evacuate the area, they refused, because two people were still unaccounted for, but after an unsuccessful search, they were obliged to leave; just as they did so, the unstable wall crashed down on the area where they had been working.

For this, Stone was one of two officers awarded the British Empire Medal for gallantry.

Ten years later, 53-year-old Stone was walking along Chelsea's Sloane Street in plain clothes on 17 April 1951, when he encountered his greatest challenge, one engineered by three formidable opponents.

* * *

Albert Edward Bathie was just twenty-two years of age when he appeared at Marylebone Police Court in 1931, charged with stealing a car and its contents valued at £235. The former Borstal boy obviously believed telling the Bench that after being jilted he had drowned his sorrow in drink would act as suitable mitigation, but he was wrong and he went down for four months.

He had just finished an eighteen-month sentence when he obtained a dodgy visiting order to see a chum in the same prison and was spotted; that was swiftly followed by a sentence of three years' penal servitude for a series of smash and grab raids.

In September 1938, Bathie and another man were caught after two smash and grab raids in Wolverhampton netted them diamond rings valued at £1,939 – they had also stolen a car worth £150 in which, 'driving like a madman', they endeavoured to escape. An enterprising Police Constable Watkins 'knocked out the driver, cold.' After Wolverhampton Quarter Sessions heard that 'Baby-face' Bathie was a 'stick-at-nothing' jewel raider who often disguised himself as a woman to commit these offences, he went to penal servitude again, this time for five years.

By 1945 he had acquired what the Recorder at West Bromwich Sessions described as 'a dreadful record', and for taking a car without the owner's consent (and injuring a police officer who tried to stop him), he was sentenced to twelve months' imprisonment.

So that was the same Albert Edward Bathie who stole a Vauxhall saloon from a car park at the junction with Cromwell Road and Thurloe Street on the morning of 17 April 1951; he was in company with 32-year-old James John Ford, described by the police as being 'an extremely violent and dangerous criminal', and Frederick Adams aged thirty-nine, also the possessor of an appalling record.

At 11.45 that morning, the staff at Messrs Dibden, the jeweller's at 189 Sloane Street, were alarmed when Adams, armed with an iron bar, shattered the shop window and tried to grab a handful of jewellery; a £450 bracelet was later found in the gutter. Meanwhile, Bathie leaned well back in the driver's seat of the stolen car, and Ford held aloft a heavy bronze instrument which he used to threaten any passers-by who might be brave enough to intervene.

Fred Stone was one such passer-by. Dashing forward, he dived at Adams' legs, who promptly hit him several times with the iron bar. Stone managed to grab the bar, and the manager of a nearby business, Mr D. J. H. Golby (later to receive a Binney Certificate), rushed forward and jumped on Ford's back; but he was thrown off, and now Ford joined in the attack, viciously clubbing Stone on the head with the bronze item.

'I tried to grab his legs from under him and got more blows on the back of the head', Stone said later, adding, 'I tried to dodge and take them on my shoulder.'

A small crowd had gathered, but apart from Mr Golby no one intervened in the struggle. Stone was now starting to slip into unconsciousness, but help from an unexpected quarter was at hand.

* * *

Mrs Phyllis Holman Richards was just about to alight from a No. 22 bus when she heard the crash of glass from Dibden's jeweller's and saw Ford wielding what she described as being 'somewhat like a truncheon and rather like a hammer'.

Despite having one arm strapped to her side, due to a broken rib, the 53-year-old welfare worker immediately tackled Ford, grabbing hold of the arm grasping the weapon; he threw her off but, undeterred, she grabbed him by the waistcoat, shouting for help and trying to prevent any further harm coming to Stone.

Ford pushed her to one side and, despite the number of onlookers, nobody tried to stop him. He jumped into the stolen car which, driven by Bathie, roared off along Sloane Street towards Knightsbridge, past two constables who noted both the registration number and a description of the driver. The car was discovered abandoned in Lowndes Place the following day, and two days later, Bathie was arrested and accurately picked out on an identification parade.

Meanwhile, Adams had been overpowered by Mr Golby and the manager of the jewellery shop, and when the police arrived, he whined, 'I'll come quietly. I've had enough.'

Fred Stone had had enough, as well. He was taken to St George's Hospital, where a trepanning operation was carried out to relieve pressure on his brain. Eight days later, he was transferred to Atkinson Morley Hospital in Wimbledon, where a silver plate was inserted in his skull to replace the lost bone. He was sent to the Metropolitan Police Nursing Home at Denmark Hill but he was still extremely ill; when he was first allowed out of bed, six weeks after the attack, it was for a maximum of half an hour.

In July 1951, at the Old Bailey, for shop-breaking and inflicting grievous bodily harm, Adams was sentenced to eight years' preventative detention, and Bathie, for shop-breaking and taking and driving away, received six years' imprisonment.

Stone was severely disabled, having suffered brain damage, and was medically discharged from the police in December 1951 after 30½ years' service with a 100 per cent disability pension. He was plagued with headaches and sleeplessness thereafter; the running of his beloved youth clubs became a thing of the past.

Highly commended by the commissioner, Stone was awarded £15 from the Reward Fund at Bow Street, the Chief Magistrate, Sir Lawrence Dunne, telling him, 'No more striking example of heroism has ever come before this court.'

The Magistrate at Stone's place of work, Marlborough Street Court, was no stranger to courage himself; Eugene Paul Bennett VC, MC stated:

> We are saying goodbye to an old friend and a brave man. He just saw his duty clearly and did it without the slightest hesitation. Had some of the onlookers seen their duty as clearly, a third man involved would not have got away.

Former PC Stone was awarded the George Medal by King George VI on 12 February 1952. Mrs Richards was awarded the Binney Medal for the bravest civilian act in assisting law and order during the previous year on St George's Day 1952 by the Lord Lieutenant of London, Field Marshal Viscount Alanbrooke, who said:

> When we see ladies coming to the fore and throwing themselves into the rough and tumble with men armed with iron bars and axes, we remember that they are the fairer sex and therefore, more credit is due to them. The winner of the medal this year deserves special congratulation for the great part she played – a most astoundingly gallant act.

Later in her life as a welfare worker, Mrs Richards was also appointed OBE.

Meanwhile, Stone was given the job of security officer at Westminster Hospital. Was this a sinecure? Without wishing to be offensive, I rather think it was.

But what of the gallant James John Ford who, thanks to the lack of resolution on the part of the onlookers, as Mr Bennett accurately pointed out, had made good his escape?

Following the attack, Stone saw him in the street, twice more, once in Soho, once in Kennington.

You see, Stone knew him – and Ford knew Stone.

Ford's father was a close friend of Stone's and had assisted him with rescue operations during the Blitz – Ford Jr. had attended one of Stone's youth clubs, although in his case the attempts to keep him 'on the straight and narrow' had spectacularly failed.

Churchill's physician Lord Moran once said, 'Courage is a capital sum, reduced by expenditure', and that was true in Stone's case. The effect of the attack on him had been so profound that the man who ordinarily would have tackled this thug without hesitation could only phone the police on the first occasion of seeing him; on the second, he could not even do that. He simply went home and went to bed.

But eighteen months after the attack, Ford was arrested in Brighton and stood his trial at the Old Bailey in January 1953. He denied attacking Stone but was found guilty of shop-breaking and inflicting grievous bodily harm. Sentencing him to eight years' imprisonment, Mr Justice Byrne told him:

> You are a dangerous criminal. You and Adams are responsible for Mr Stone's retirement from the police force and his state of health at the present time.

His colleagues on 'C' Division did not forget Fred Stone, and in January 1958 a report was submitted with the request that a service subscription be made on his behalf; in his minute to the commissioner, Assistant Commissioner Robertson stated:

> This case is a most unusual one. Ex-PC Stone by his bravery and devotion to duty has caused his wife much anguish, and she has been robbed of many years of happiness which she would otherwise have shared with her husband. Physically, Stone is a wreck and his expectation of life is very short; indeed, he may die at any time due to the terrible injuries he received while doing his duty. In the circumstances you may agree with me that a service subscription is justified and if it is made in time, we may be able to present it to him personally as a rather belated testimonial, instead of to his widow as a memorial.

A cheque in the sum of £1,689 – £33,172 at today's values – was presented to Stone on 3 March 1958 by the Commissioner,

Sir John Nott-Bower (himself the recipient of a King's Police Medal for gallantry), when Stone's remarkable career was revealed on the BBC programme, *This is Your Life*.

Yet Stone outlived all the predictions of his early death. He retired to Broadstairs, Kent, where he involved himself with church activities and was secretary of the local branch of LEPRA, the international society formed to beat leprosy in all parts of the world. There he lived quietly and died at his home at Dene Cottage, aged eighty-one.

The Metropolitan Police has thrown up many brave men and women who have rightly been awarded medals for gallantry; but has there ever been an officer like Fred Stone, who was honoured with the King's Police Medal, the British Empire Medal and the George Medal – three of the highest civilian awards for bravery?

I don't think so – but let me know if you disagree.

CHAPTER 6

A Selection of Thieves, Dips and Conmen

Confidence tricks have been around since time immemorial; nowadays they're referred to as 'scams', normally perpetrated over the phone or the internet and pretty successfully, too. I suppose the victims can be compartmentalized into roughly two groups: those who are greedy, who believe they're getting something for nothing – or if not nothing, at very little risk to themselves – and those who are genuinely, innocently duped. There's a smattering of both in the stories that follow, as well as an assortment of villains, all of them plausible and all strangers to the truth.

Let's start with Reginald Wallace, who apart from being a conman was quite a nasty bit of work as well.

Wallace was born in 1900, enlisted in the British Army when he was under age and served in France during the First World War. This was to his credit, but the acclamation surrounding his selfless action took a bit of a dent when in 1917 he was convicted of wearing decorations to which he was not entitled and sentenced to six months' hard labour. This was followed by twenty-two months' hard labour at District Court Martial at Warwick for desertion, attempting to escape and destroying public property; that was the end of his Army career, and he was discharged with ignominy.

He was caught in May 1924 after attempting to break into the residence of Dr Butler Smythe at 78 Brook Street, Mayfair at 3.30 one morning; he and an older criminal were found to be in possession of certain house-breaking implements by night, notably two hacksaw blades, a candle, a screwdriver, a torch and two pairs of gloves.

By the time he was twenty-eight, Wallace had served two terms of penal servitude, and from his latest 'journey' of four years he had been released in December 1928. Three days later, he launched a mini-crime wave. Assuming a military appearance, Wallace would visit well-known West End clubs to steal attaché cases belonging to the members, extracting from them cheque books in which he would then forge the holder's signatures and obtain cash at the English Speaking Union, the Conservative Club and the National Liberal Club.

Newly promoted Detective Sergeants Bob Fabian and Albert Greenacre were assigned the case and soon realized that it was Wallace they were looking for; acting on a tip-off, in April 1929 they kept observation at Mayfair's Connaught Hotel. But there were two surprises in store for them: first, when Wallace arrived, he did not match the description given by his CRO file. He was disguised, affecting the voice and bearing of an Army officer with greying hair and a bristling moustache, together with a slight limp. But there was one thing he could not camouflage: a tattoo on his left wrist. Telling the officers his name was Marshall, he refused to permit them to examine his wrist; and with that, satisfied that he was Wallace and not 'Marshall', they seized him and bundled him into a taxi.

But the second surprise awaited the officers upon their arrival at Vine Street police station; Wallace suddenly reached into his hip pocket and tried to extract a fully loaded six-chambered revolver. A terrific struggle ensued with Fabian and Greenacre, who finally subdued and disarmed him. Wallace then told them, 'You're lucky to have got me like this; otherwise you both would have been in hell.'

Also in his pockets were cheques, stolen and forged. His address was searched, and pens, coloured inks and more cheques were found, together with a notebook containing names and addresses of West End club members.

On 14 May Wallace, smartly attired in a double-breasted blue overcoat and brown spats, appeared at the County of London Sessions and pleaded guilty to thirteen counts of larceny, obtaining money by false pretences and possessing a revolver and ammunition with intent to endanger life; he also asked for twenty-four other cases of false pretences to be taken into consideration. His plea of guilty may have been provoked by the prosecutor at Marlborough Street police court telling the magistrate that the charge of possessing the revolver with intent to endanger life alone merited a sentence of twenty years' penal servitude. He was sentenced to eleven years' imprisonment – four years' penal servitude plus seven years' preventative detention for being a habitual criminal.

'Thanks', he said, superciliously. 'I expected at least fifteen!' and then had the grace to wait until he was taken to his cell before bursting into tears.

* * *

Jack Capstick had been appointed detective constable less than three years after joining the Metropolitan Police in 1925, and that, I can assure you, was very fast moving indeed – although it was hardly surprising. As a police constable and an aid to CID at Bow Street, he had amassed a remarkable number of arrests and made a considerable number of contacts amongst the market porters at Covent Garden and in the underworld. He had been commended time and again, and his work rate had been noted by 'E' Division's Divisional Detective Inspector Walter Hambrook, who as a detective inspector had headed the first motorized Flying Squad raid. Now, in 1929, he had been promoted to chief inspector to head the Flying Squad and with a keen eye for ability 'borrowed' Capstick to utilize his talents.

It was a prudent move; Capstick knew many of the shoplifters, pickpockets (or 'dips') and conmen who infested the West End. Two likely customers were Portuguese nationals, Abel Cerinadas and Agostiono Anastacio, and together with a third man they were kept under observation by Capstick outside the Coliseum Theatre. He saw the men jostle a contractor's manager, Mr Bateman Brown Tarring, and Cerinadas take the wallet from Tarring's pocket and pass it to Anastacio. Capstick grabbed the team; the third man escaped, but the other two appeared before Mr (later Sir) Rollo Graham-Campbell at Bow Street police court. Capstick was able to say that Cerinadas was a member of a gang of international pickpockets and had been convicted in London and Lisbon; in fact, he had been convicted nine months previously and deported for attempting to pick the pockets of theatregoers at the Hippodrome. Sentencing Cerinadas to four and Anastacio to three months' hard labour, the magistrate also recommended them for deportation, adding that they were 'dangerous thieves'.

The same magistrate dealt with George Clarke, described as 'an international thief and frequenter of fashionable hotels and clubs'. It would have been difficult to find a more fashionable hotel than the Savoy, and it was there that Capstick tailed him, having initially seen the 67-year-old thief acting suspiciously across the road in the luggage department of the Strand Palace Hotel. Clarke was followed across the Strand and into the Savoy's grill-room, lounge and writing room; and as he reached out his hand towards a woman's fur, Clarke became aware, all too late, of Capstick's presence. After hearing that Clarke had served two terms of penal servitude, including one for stealing £500 from a bank, as well as being convicted in Munich and Berlin, Sir Rollo weighed him off with three months' hard labour.

'This is a time when pickpockets, no doubt, are reaping a rich harvest', said Sir Rollo's fellow magistrate, Mr Dummett, when confronted with 42-year-old Arthur Purvis, who was arrested loitering with intent to steal from women's handbags outside Buckingham Palace. It was true, said Capstick, that Purvis had no previous convictions, but he made up for this deficit by informing Mr Dummett that Purvis was an associate of confidence tricksters and that since arriving from Australia four years previously he had 'been living on his wits'. This was an expression much used by detectives (including the author) to indicate that the person in the dock was as straight as a pretzel but hadn't yet been caught. One month's imprisonment.

Mind you, when Capstick mentioned confidence tricksters to the Beak he knew what he was talking about.

He knew men like Gary Cecil Colman, a theatrical producer who, less than a week after being released from a twelve-month sentence for fraud, had stated that he was about to found a £500,000 theatrical company in Norwich which would provide employment for 300 artistes. He was negotiating with some of those artistes to raise capital for this non-existent company and had actually persuaded a young actress to part with some money; indeed, he intended to marry her on the very day Capstick nabbed him.

'It's very fortunate you were able to stop this so quickly', Mr Fry, the Magistrate, told Capstick, adding, 'He's a very dangerous person.'

This view was reinforced when he was informed that 26-year-old Colman had served a three-year term of Borstal training and had three convictions recorded against him in Canada. He was sentenced to three months' hard labour.

Ernest Henry Watts (who also liked to be known as Henry Warren) was in the company of Phillip Smith when they approached various foreigners and colonials in the vicinity of the Waldorf and Strand Palace Hotels, with Watts representing himself as an Australian who had been in the country for only four days and offering to sell what would turn out to be worthless watches. He was giving this sales pitch to a Rhodesian when he was nabbed by Capstick, who had had him under surveillance for half an hour. Smith melted away into the crowds but had his collar felt when he arrived at Bow Street Court the following day to see how his associate was faring. Watts had been convicted of a similar offence in Perth, Australia, and Smith was 'an associate of confidence tricksters'; that was sufficient for them to be sent to hard labour, three months for Watts, six weeks for Smith.

So Capstick was no slouch when it came to dealing with conmen. Therefore, when he had dealings with the infamous Wolfe family, there should have been no trouble in packing them off to quod. Well, there was and there wasn't.

* * *

The expression 'ringing the changes' is not used so often nowadays as it was years ago, but although the trick has different guises, it usually takes the form of the fraudster paying for a small item with a large denomination note; then, when change is given by the shopkeeper, the conman states that he had the correct money after all, asks for his original banknote back and, with sleight of hand and some very quick patter, pockets most if not all of the change as well.

This was what happened in Wolverhampton, when 17-year-old Jack Kaufman Wolfe obtained 10s 0d by ringing the changes at Thomas A. Welling's tobacconist shop in Green Street on 18 May 1921. Then he tried the same trick again at another of Mr Welling's shops in Lichfield Street on the same day and was caught. But when, after a brief remand, he appeared at court a week later, he was merely bound over to keep the peace for twelve months.

This was because the police had told the Bench that he was of previous good character and that he came from a respectable family.

The officer in question must either have been less than diligent in carrying out his background checks or (and far more likely) have taken a stonking great bung, because young Jack was one of five similarly larcenous sons of patriarch Charles Wolfe, one of the biggest villains unhung. Born in 1875, Charles had first come to the attention of the authorities in 1904 when he appeared at the County of London Sessions. He was accused of obtaining £450 by means of a confidence trick, and since that sum represented over £55,000 at today's value, this was no drop in the ocean. It was reflected in his sentence of twenty-three months' hard labour for a first offence. Since then, Charles had travelled the world on ocean-going liners, swindling people left, right and centre and collecting convictions in the USA (New York, Pittsburgh, New Orleans and Jacksonville) as well as in London, Peterborough, Paris, Brussels and Dublin.

The Dublin offence was committed when Charles and another of his sons, Benjamin, befriended a priest, one Father Joseph Hegarty. The reverend gentleman had arrived in Dublin to book a passage to Australia, and father and son professed to be natives of that country. On 31 December 1923, after Charles asked the priest how much money he had in his possession and was told £140, he suggested that Hegarty hand over £100 of it for Charles to invest for him. He did so, but when he later returned to the Hibernian Hotel where they had all been staying, there was no trace of father and son; the Wolfes were arrested by Detective Sergeant Gibney of the Garda Siochána the same evening.

Charles, without success, tried to hide his conman's box of tricks: 'tops and bottoms' (a bundle of paper cut to the size of banknotes, then topped and tailed with genuine notes) and worthless bills of exchange (written orders to a person requiring them to make a specified payment to the signatory or a named person), as well as cheques, a passport and a passbook. Then he told the officer, 'I'll get the money. You can do a lot for me if you like. It'll mean £100 for you tomorrow, if you get me out of this.'

When this ruse failed to work, Charles said, 'Oh, you can let the boy out', and a very sullen Benjamin said, 'I'll say nothing', adding, 'I know nothing about it.'

At the Dublin Police Court the priest was repaid his £100 (and told to keep a closer eye on his money in future), Charles was bound over, his son was released and both were told to 'leave the Free State, or you'll be arrested', although precisely on what charge was not made clear

Benjamin failed to profit from Dublin's clemency because, like his older brother Jack, he tried to ring the changes by attempting to obtain 10s 0d at an off-licence in the Wandsworth Road, Clapham. Unfortunately for him, Mrs Florence Smith, the off-licensee, had seen that particular trick tried before, and he duly appeared at South-Western Police Court on the morning of 11 June 1924. Since no money had been obtained, and what with his plea of guilty, Benjamin might have hoped for leniency – until Detective Sergeant Francis informed the court that only the previous month, he had been bound over for a similar offence, and the Magistrate, Mr Marshall, sentenced him to three months' hard labour.

Time, now, to be reunited with Detective Sergeant Albert Greenacre, fresh from his triumph in subduing the deeply unpleasant Mr Wallace and separating him from his six-chambered revolver, and now working with Jack Capstick.

★ ★ ★

Charles Wolfe and his son, Jack Kaufman Wolfe, were kept under observation for some time by the two officers. They were seen – in the words of the prosecuting counsel – to 'force themselves' on a victim at his hotel in the Strand. The victim in question was a Mr Pauly, who was a member of the retinue of a Maharajah taking part in an Indian conference in London.

Father and son claimed that they had just come from New Zealand, where they had been sheep farming, and produced Bills of Exchange which were quite worthless. They invited Mr Pauly to lunch, but by now Detectives Greenacre and Capstick were in very close proximity to the conmen and, prior to the luncheon meeting, heard Jack say, 'You leave him to me', while his father advised, 'Stick to him.' During the lunch, the men made enquiries as to their victim's bank, and when paying the bill they produced bundles of banknotes; as the prosecutor later told Bow Street Police Court, they 'looked as though they had more money than they knew what to do with.'

Wolfe senior told Pauly that he was going to Scotland and asked him to 'look after his son' while he was away; but now the officers were busying themselves obtaining the necessary warrants for conspiracy, since no power of arrest was possible without them.

Shortly afterwards, Jack alone was arrested and made a spirited attempt to dispose of a wallet which contained tissue paper cut to the size of banknotes plus imitation $1,000 notes. He refused to admit his identity, but after he was remanded in custody at Bow Street on 27 November 1930, his father was spotted in the public gallery and he, too, was arrested.

The 55-year-old crook, who was in possession of a false passport, gave his name as Mr Denny; although he later admitted his true identity he refused to give his address and he, too, was remanded in custody.

But when they appeared again at court on 4 December, it appeared that the Maharajah would shortly be travelling to Paris and wished Mr Pauly to accompany him. Since the conspiracy charge could only be dealt with at a higher court, and probably not for several weeks, it was decided to deal with the defendants on a charge of being suspected persons, loitering with intent to commit a felony by means of a confidence trick. Found guilty, Charles Wolfe's chequered past was revealed, as was Jack's, who had served three years in Borstal and had since been convicted of stealing by means of a trick. Describing them as 'arrant rogues', the Magistrate, Sir Chartres Biron, sentenced both father and son to three months' hard labour, additionally stating that the police officers concerned had 'acted with great skill and were deserving of very great credit.'

But one year later, Charles and Jack, this time with Benjamin Wolfe, were arrested once more by Capstick for exactly the same offence, after he had seen them accost a foreigner named McDonald in High Holborn. Jack had said to the other two, 'He's no fool; take your time.' To this, Benjamin said, 'Leave him to me, Dad', while Charles advised caution: 'It may take a couple of days; he will not be easy.'

However, the family's solicitor, Mr Ricketts, told the court that this overheard conversation was quite consistent with an innocent transaction, that Mr McDonald was in court and, if necessary, the defence were quite prepared to call him as a witness. This last may have been nothing more than bullshit, but it was sufficient for Sir Rollo Graham-Campbell to dismiss the charges.

One of the necessary attributes of a conman is arrogance; this was displayed by Charles Wolfe when he summoned the commissioner at Bow Street to show cause why he should not deliver to him the eleven £10 notes which had been in his possession and seized by police at the time of his arrest in High Holborn, on a charge of which he was, of course, quite plainly innocent.

Capstick stepped smartly into the witness box to successfully oppose the application, saying that some of those notes were part-proceeds of a £9,500 swindle and obtained by means of a confidence trick by a man currently in South Africa; and that when he returned to this country, it was quite possible that proceedings would be taken against him.

★ ★ ★

Following an appearance at Greenwich Coroner's Court in October 1927, where three of the Wolfe brothers – Benjamin, Joseph and Jack – all admitted perjury, on 30 November 1932, Charles Wolfe appeared at the *Assizes de la Seine* in Paris in the guise of 'Sir Charles Wolfe', an Australian. He was accused of swindling a Danish visitor to Paris of £4,000, but there was a problem. 'Sir Charles' had grown a beard, and his hair was now so long that none of the witnesses could identify him. The French judicial system refused to be defeated: 'Get his hair cut and have him shaved!' demanded the Judge, and after this draconian order was carried out, the witnesses were indeed able to identify 57-year-old 'Sir Charles', who was sentenced to eight years' imprisonment.

Freshly released from quod in France, Charles Wolfe (now minus his knighthood) was soon back in Blighty and up to his old tricks. On 5 February 1938, he appeared at Bow Street Police Court charged with obtaining £110 from a certain Mr Simon Sacks by means of a confidence trick; but the case collapsed when the victim told the court that he did not believe there was any intention to defraud him, and Charles walked free – but not for long.

What he did next is unknown, but whatever sentence he received it must have been a short one, because he was released on 6 June 1938 and it was not too long before he and his son Henry, now aged twenty-nine and referring to themselves as Charles Graham (uncle) and Jimmy Graham (nephew), got to work again.

The 'nephew' fell into conversation in Southampton Row with Alfred Clyde Boswell, a storekeeper from Taranaki, New Zealand; Boswell and his wife were on holiday in London. It started innocuously enough with Henry (saying that he had just arrived from Canada) asking the way to a certain hotel. A number of other meetings followed, then on 1 September 1938, Boswell was introduced to Charles Wolfe, masquerading as Henry's uncle, and they arranged to have lunch in Cheapside.

But Boswell was not the complete mug that the larcenous duo took him to be, and prior to the luncheon, he went to Gray's Inn Road police station, where he received certain pertinent advice.

After lunch, Boswell was informed that it was possible to win money on a horse even if it didn't win its race, and in this way, father and son attempted to obtain £150 from him. They pleaded not guilty at Clerkenwell police court, but not even the best efforts of the devoted family solicitor, Mr Ricketts (who accused the police of fabricating evidence since 'they were desperate to obtain a conviction'), could save them. Detective Sergeant Gowan set out the antecedents of Charles in stunning style and then told the court:

> There is no doubt that he has been responsible for the training of the family in crime; his five sons have all been convicted of confidence tricks and he has given them every encouragement. He is a menace to foreign and colonial visitors, and the sums of money which have been obtained by this family through confidence tricks have amounted to many thousands of pounds. The younger prisoner is believed to be a single man and has been convicted on two occasions.

Mr Ricketts was not going to stand for that, saying that the reference to other members of the family who were not in court to defend themselves was introduced to prejudice Henry in the eyes of the court.

'Perhaps it is in his favour, as showing that he seems to have been brought up to this', remarked the Magistrate, Walter Hedley KC, mildly, before sentencing both to hard labour, six months for Charles, four months for Henry.

Charles and Henry pass out of the picture now, and it's time to review the fortunes of Benjamin, who was up to his old tricks again in 1947, this time in company with an older man, James Ryan. They met Harry Cartwright, a racehorse owner, at Nottingham Races on 27 October, and Ryan told him that he had backed a winner. When Ryan left their company, Benjamin told Cartwright, 'He's one of the shrewdest judges of racing in this country and works some big stable commissions.'

When Ryan returned he was stuffing what appeared to be a substantial wad of notes in his pocket, saying, 'This is only a little bit I put on', and adding carelessly, 'Actually, I put on £4,000 for the stable.'

He later told both men that he was about to execute a very large ante-post commission for the Manchester November Handicap and wanted both of them 'to be in on it'.

They may have thought that they'd found a mug in Mr Cartwright, but they were wrong, because he went straight to the police, and when the trio met again at the Queen's Hotel, Birmingham, officers were watching. Ryan repeated his offer, saying the horse's name was Billet and stating, 'I've got to put £30,000 on this horse for Harry Wragg, the trainer and patrons of the stable.'

Charged with attempting to obtain £1,500 by means of false pretences, they appeared at Birmingham Stipendiary Court, where Harry Wragg gave evidence. He agreed that Billet had been trained by him for the Manchester November Handicap and he had thought the horse had an excellent chance, but it had finished at the tail end of the field; more importantly, no commission was placed by the stable on the horse and he did not know either of the defendants.

Both were committed for trial at Birmingham Sessions on what appeared to be an open and shut case, but on 15 January 1948, after the jury had deliberated for 75 minutes, both men were surprisingly found not guilty.

Well, that was good enough for Benjamin's brother, Jack Kaufman Wolfe, because two weeks later, in company with 60-year-old Joseph Henry Cockayne, they were at Colwick Park racecourse, Nottingham. There they saw Leonard Wood, a young miner (later described by the prosecution at Nottingham

A Selection of Thieves, Dips and Conmen

Guildhall as having 'more money than sense'), who had won £120 by successfully betting on two races.

Jack got into conversation with him and then, referring to Cockayne, said, 'That man has had a good bet.' Wood subsequently parted with £10, £20, then £40 to Cockayne to place a bet for him. When Cockayne then disappeared, Wood complained to Detective Inspector Corbett, who arrested the two men. Cockayne said, 'There was no trick. I put the money on the horse and it lost', while Jack contented himself with, 'Not guilty. I know nothing about it.'

In Cockayne's possession was £95 8s 8d and two similar-looking bundles made up of paper topped and tailed with £5 notes, which he tried to dispose of; Jack had £38 14s 0d in his possession.

When they appeared at the Guildhall on 18 February, a new complainant appeared. This was Raymond Claude Lewis, who had also attended the race meeting; he recognized the two men who had swindled him out of £20 at Cheltenham race course in December 1947.

'I intend bringing evidence to prove that the time Lewis alleges he was at Cheltenham races, Wolfe was having lunch with two of his friends in a London restaurant!' roared Mr Wise for the defence, but he didn't bring it, which was probably just as well – because on 3 March 1948, both men were found guilty. Whilst Cockayne had been fined on a number of occasions for gaming offences, Inspector Corbett told the Bench that between 1921 and 1942, Jack had been convicted on ten occasions, having been sent to Borstal, imprisonment and penal servitude.

Now that they had been found guilty, Jack swiftly abandoned his restaurant alibi, and both asked for Mr Wood's offence to be taken into consideration when they were sentenced, six months' imprisonment for Jack and two months for Cockayne, with both ordered to pay compensation and costs.

There, we shall leave the depredations of the Wolfe family and their associates – some they won, some they lost, but as Humphrey Bogart was prone to remark, 'That's the way the piss-pot cracks.'

Chapter 7

The Adventures of 'Australian Denny'

He was born in New South Wales, hence the nickname 'Australian Denny', and while the year of his birth might have been 1866, then again, it might not have been. His baptismal name could have been David Alfred Delaney, but that's debatable; he also called himself David Harris, but he was invariably charged in the name of Dennis Harris, and when that occurred, he changed his date of birth by several years. So Dennis Harris he'll be referred to as from now on. Slim, 5 feet 7¾ inches tall, with a fresh complexion, brown hair and eyes, it was said that he had been a steeplechase jockey and that he had fought in the Boer War. That might have been true; one never knows. What is known is that he served terms of penal servitude for robbery, house-breaking and shop-breaking in Johannesburg, and that when he came to the United Kingdom, before the First World War, he was acquitted with two other men in March 1914 at the Old Bailey on charges of house-breaking and stealing a quantity of jewellery from 25 Agate Road, Hammersmith. He was convicted of unlawful wounding and stealing jewellery from a dwelling house in London's West End, for which he was imprisoned, but he was released just in time to be caught on 2 June 1917 when the Excell Restaurant at 65 St Mary Axe in the City of London was broken into. The back of the restaurant's safe had been ripped off and £22 18s 9½d stolen, as well as ten shillings from the Red Cross Hospital box. The area was surrounded by City of London police, and Harris and an associate were chased across the rooftops, during which pursuit a police sergeant slipped and fell, injuring himself severely.

Harris was found in a small yard at the rear of 72 Houndsditch; asked what he was doing there, he replied, 'Nothing'. Asked how he got there, he said, 'I fell off the roof' and added that he had forgotten where he lived. In circumstances such as that, his pockets full of the safe's contents, in possession of house-breaking implements and giving smart-arse replies – when the arresting officer's companion had sustained serious injuries whilst trying to apprehend him – Harris might have qualified for a smart bit of summary justice in that secluded area; although if this happened, he made no mention of it.

Just over two weeks later at the Old Bailey, the Recorder of London described Harris as 'an expert in house-breaking' and packed him off to penal servitude for three years.

Four years later, between 12 and 13 March 1921, a warehouse belonging to Messrs Collard, Parsons & Co. at Cork Street, London was broken into and cloth valued at £3,718 was stolen. The following day, police in Leeds visited a house in Tramway Street and discovered sixty of the seventy-four stolen bales of cloth, as well as Harris and another man, both of whom disclaimed all knowledge of the goods. Brought down to London for trial, this time Harris went down for four years' penal servitude.

But it seemed that 'Australian Denny' was unstoppable. He now met up with three associates, John James, John Russell and Edward Wood (who also liked to be known as 'Flood'), but this did not go unnoticed. Detective (later Detective Inspector) John Smith of the Flying Squad, disguised as a match-seller, kept them under observation for a week. On 24 November 1924 he saw the men in the Orange Tree public house in the Euston Road and heard enough of their conversation to realize that that evening, they intended to break into a warehouse owned by Messrs Ewart & Son Ltd, also in the Euston Road.

George Cornish had joined the police in 1895, had worked in Whitechapel in the East End and Kennington in South London and was later dubbed 'The Murder Wizard' after solving a number of those cases in London and the provinces. Now a divisional detective inspector at Marylebone, he was informed of this impending raid on his patch and he, together with Divisional Detective Inspector Walter Hambrook (one of the founding fathers of the Flying Squad), Detective Inspector Eggboro and several other Squad officers, kept watch on the warehouse.

At 9.45 that evening, Smith saw James and Russell in the Euston Road; they were joined by Harris and Wood, and all four men went to the side entrance of the premises. At midnight, Wood emerged from the warehouse and stood opposite the premises, looking up towards the first floor, which was where the safe, containing hundreds of pounds, was situated. He then produced a handkerchief which he drew sharply across his face, obviously a signal that the street was clear and that his companions could proceed.

Wood then crossed the road to a passageway which, unfortunately for him, was occcupied by two officers, who grabbed him and divested him of his bowler hat and mackintosh;

then one of the officers – Detective John Rutherford, who that day had received his King's Police Medal for gallantry at Buckingham Palace – put the hat and coat on and took up Wood's original position. The other officer took Wood to Albany Street police station, where due to the inclement weather, and being without the protection of his hat and mackintosh, he arrived soaking wet.

An hour later, Harris left by the warehouse's side door and was arrested; he had a pair of gloves in his possession and an electric battery, which he unsuccessfully tried to discard on his way to Albany Street.

Russell and James got out on the roof, where they were found hiding under a bench in a workshop. Russell said, 'If we had followed the others we should have beaten you. We got suspicious half an hour ago, and split up.'

Explosives and a fuse were found in the safe's lock, and in the same room were six pieces of iron tubing, three claw cutters, three jemmies, a brace and five drill bits, a hatchet and chain, a punch, chisel and screwdriver, a piece of black alpaca and two iron wedges.

These items made an impressive display at Marlborough Police Court, where the Magistrate, Mr Hay Halkett, told Detective Smith that he 'deserved great credit' and then, tongue in cheek, suggested to DDI Cornish, 'It is not safe to give any of them bail?' to which Cornish sharply replied, 'No!'

As the prisoners left the court, Wood called out that he was innocent, and he reaffirmed this at the Old Bailey before Judge Atherley Jones KC, when both he and Harris irrationally claimed mistaken identity but were found guilty; James and Russell had already pleaded guilty. Harris and James, the oldest, aged sixty-four and sixty respectively, were each sentenced to three years' penal servitude, Wood to fifteen months' hard labour and Russell to six months' imprisonment in the second division. Cornish was commended and promoted.

After his release, Harris avoided breakings; instead, he concentrated his efforts on smash and grabs but acquired the reputation of being a 'slicer' (or 'slasher'), someone who failed to share the loot fairly with other members of his gang. Consequently, he was grassed up time after time to the Flying Squad, but although he was frequently arrested he was never again convicted. In many ways he was the forerunner of the notorious Billy Hill; his jobs were meticulously planned, and vehicles – sometimes a horse and cart – were used to block pursuit before a changeover vehicle was utilized. He regularly changed the members of his team, swapped receivers for stolen gems on a regular basis and would often agree a price for the goods and a venue where the transaction would take place before carrying out the smash and grab; he knew exactly what he was looking for. Following a smash and grab in the Burlington Arcade which had all of Harris' hallmarks, a Flying Squad car shot straight round to his address. There was Harris with two of his associates, and they were brought into Vine Street police station. None of them was picked out by the witnesses and there was no trace of the valuable rings, so they were released. A few days later, an informant asked the officer in charge if he had noticed that Harris had been wearing a bandage. He had; the rings were underneath it.

It was thought that his ill-gotten gains were in safe deposits all over London under different names, and when he died suddenly in 1934, London jewellers breathed a collective sigh of relief.

★ ★ ★

Fred 'Nutty' Sharpe was an officer who followed Harris's career with interest. A former coal miner and captain of his local rugby team, Sharp joined the Metropolitan Police in 1911 and was thrown into the deep end of policing, in Whitechapel. Violent crime was rife, particularly garrotting, and Sharpe was in his element; working in plain clothes, he would lie down in the gutter, offering himself as a drunken sailor to be robbed, and then arrest those who tried to take advantage of his apparent helplessness. Physical toughness was a requirement in that era; Sharpe was told it was commonplace for the local tearaways to hit a copper on the head with a chopper, 'for a lark!' He was an expert on the thieves and pickpockets of the area; when he was co-opted into the Flying Squad in 1922, his expertise and range of operations grew wider. Sharpe may have been keeping an eye on the pickpockets at Wetherby, or any of the racecourses in the area, but in any event, Wakefield is 190 miles from Sharpe's home territory. It was there at 10 o'clock in the evening of 18 November 1922 that he arrested John Hamilton, who tried to pick the pocket of a fellow traveller on a tramcar. Sharpe was able to tell the Bench at Wakefield Police Court that Hamilton's correct name was Arthur Gill, and although he was a baker by trade he was in fact an expert pickpocket, who for the past fifteen years had done little else than follow crowds at football matches and racetracks. Sentenced to three months' hard labour, Gill notched-up his twenty-seventh conviction.

After Sharpe arrested a pickpocket at Earl's Court tube station, five of the arrestee's associates crowded into the lift occupied by the officer and his prisoner and, having knocked

Sharpe unconscious, escaped, together with the prisoner. The incident was reported in the 6 April 1924 edition of the *Sunday Post*. 'The cowardly attack by a gang of pickpockets on Detective Sergeant Sharpe will, it is hoped, meet with a speedy punishment', thundered the newspaper, and although it took Sharpe a year to catch all six of the miscreants, the newspaper was right – they did receive 'a speedy punishment'.

Sharpe could be relied upon to provide the press with good copy; nailed up inside a packing case with eyeholes, he had himself delivered to a warehouse that had been experiencing thefts, and he hit the headlines again when he arrested nine pickpockets on a bus. At the Old Bailey, when thirteen months' imprisonment in the second division was passed on James Thompson for bigamy, Sharpe told the court, 'Thompson admitted to me that he has a weakness for women, and during the war he was made such a fuss of by women that he lost his sense of proportion.'

As a detective on 'J' Division, Sharpe arrested a man for offering to sell two bottles of 'whisky' at four shillings each to a dupe; they contained a mixture of vinegar and water. Told that the police could dispose of the evidence as they saw fit, the Magistrate, Mr Wilberforce, said, 'I hear that the police had an entertainment, last night?' to which Sharpe replied, "H' and not 'J' Division, sir!'

The amusement in court at these remarks was not shared by the defendant, David Sidney McWilliams, who had a number of previous convictions and was now sent off to serve three months' hard labour.

★ ★ ★

Dan Gooch was a former gamekeeper from Weston, Norfolk, who joined the police in 1909; he served twice at the Yard before the formation of the Flying Squad, in which he spent much of his career thereafter. He was commended on a remarkable 109 occasions by the commissioner, and one of his cases showed his remarkable sense of fairness.

Edward Durrant was released on licence from a sentence of three years' penal servitude in May 1928. One month later, goods valued at £60 were stolen from a shop in Welwyn Garden City by three men in a car; Durrant was the driver. Stopped by police, Durrant offered to drive them to the police station, but once they were on board, he accelerated and the car crashed, although its occupants were overpowered. Remanded by the magistrates, Durrant asked to go to the lavatory and escaped through a window. He was seen no more until 14 July, when he was arrested in Old Bond Street for attempting to steal a car. After being remanded at Marlborough Street Police Court, Durrant and another prisoner were put into a police van to convey them to Brixton prison. When the van stopped at Rochester Row police station, Durrant seized the opportunity to lift up the floorboards and squeeze out; the second man was arrested almost immediately, but Durrant once more got clean away.

The following day, Inspector Gooch led a Flying Squad team to the house occupied by Durrant's wife. Her husband was seen trying to get out of a bedroom window in his pyjamas, the door was forced, and after a violent struggle he was arrested.

He appeared at the London Sessions; while he was waiting in the cell passageway to be brought up, he climbed up one of the ventilator shafts and got out of a window on top of the court, but was recaptured after injuring his ankle jumping from one wall to another.

Now, finally, he appeared at the London Sessions once more. 'He is a most courageous man and it's a pity he turned to crime', said Gooch. 'He is absolutely without fear.'

Durrant's barrister asked, 'You would not reproach him for his love of liberty?'

'Oh, no' replied Gooch. 'I admire some of his characteristics.'

Sentenced to eighteen months' hard labour, Durrant said, 'I consider you have given me a chance – thank you very much.'

★ ★ ★

The common denominator between Hambrook, Cornish, Sharpe and Gooch was not that they knew criminals, knew how to arrest them in a no-nonsense fashion and knew how to present clear-cut evidence in court; that was common amongst detectives of that era. What linked these four was that, successively, all became head of the Flying Squad.

Chapter 8

'The King of the Blackmailers'

Blackmailers used to stand a good chance of getting away with their crimes, far better than armed robbers or burglars. In the latter two cases, the victims wanted their possessions restored and the perpetrators caught, charged and sent to prison. But in the case of blackmail, especially when sexual activity was involved, the victim's testimony was required to obtain a conviction, even if the police knew that the offence was being committed. But such testimony was not always forthcoming, especially when sex between two males was involved. The difficulty was aggravated when the victim was of high social standing; reputations could be destroyed, families divided and any hope of advancement in parliament, the law, the clergy or the armed services gone forever.

Nowadays, matters have changed, inasmuch as it's downright desirable to be openly gay, both from a social point of view and to achieve promotion in the workplace; brave indeed is the person who has the temerity to challenge anyone on the matter of their sexuality. But in the days when sexual activity between males was not only a crime but an outrage to the social circles they moved in, a blackmailer stood a pretty good chance not only of getting away with it but also of becoming extraordinarily rich.

Such a man was Harry Raymond, who was crowned 'The King of the Blackmailers'. Born Arthur Gould in 1905, he changed his name when he entered the acting profession. In fact, Raymond – or 'Harry the Vain' as he was known – was a pretty good actor, appearing from 1928 at London's Wyndham's Theatre in such stage successes as *Firebrand* and *Rising Generation*. When the author Edgar Wallace took a lease on the theatre, Raymond appeared in the production of Wallace's *The Ringer*. Thereafter, he became stage manager to a theatrical touring company, but then he decided that his looks and his acting ability could be put to a more lucrative use. In 1931, he purchased a café in London's Carnaby Street, and it became the meeting point for degenerates of the same persuasion as Raymond, one of whom was 21-year-old Frank Bernard Neale, whom Raymond met in January 1932. In June of that year, Neale met a married man with a child who would subsequently become known as 'Mr X'. Having formed an unwise connection with young Mr Neale, Mr X had written him several affectionate and rather compromising letters. But it was at the end of July, when Mr X told Neale that he did not wish to continue the relationship, that Raymond, purporting to be Neale's brother, suddenly appeared, produced the letters and demanded money for their return; otherwise they would be handed to Mr X's wife.

In this way Raymond obtained sums amounting to £75, but when Mr X paid over the last instalment he decided to take out an insurance policy. He prepared a document for Raymond to sign in which he (Raymond) admitted blackmailing Mr X to the extent of £75 in respect of certain letters that he had written to Frank Neale. This document further stated:

> I hereby solemnly promise that I will never in any way communicate with Mr X again. I swear that we hold no further letters or photos which can in any way compromise Mr X. If we do, Mr X is to use this as evidence of blackmail in a police court or a court of law.

Raymond did indeed sign the document across a 6d stamp, although he used the signature 'Leslie Neale'. Being in possession of this extraordinary piece of paper, Mr X no doubt thought he was safe from any further approaches – but he was wrong.

On 15 December 1932, Raymond saw Mr X in Duke Street and told him that his brother was in trouble with the police and needed money. Mr X flatly refused to provide any.

The next morning, Mr X received a letter from Raymond asking for an appointment, which he kept. Raymond produced another letter which Mr X had sent to Neale and asked for £50. Mr X had had quite enough by now and told Raymond that if he pestered him again, he would go to Vine Street police station; in return, Raymond stated that unless he coughed up, he and Neale would go and see Mr X's wife.

Having consulted a solicitor, Mr X did indeed go to the police; and during their next assignation in Duke Street, greedy Raymond was so obsessed with extorting more money from his victim that he took no notice of a courting couple who were strolling nearby.

'I must have a final settlement', said Mr X. 'How much do you want?'

'I must have £35', replied Raymond. 'You can have this letter. It's signed by both of us. It's worth it to you.'

Suddenly, Raymond felt that things were not quite as they should be. Turning, he looked into the face of Detective Sergeant MacDonald, the male half of the 'courting couple', who grabbed Raymond by the arm and told him that he was well and truly nicked.

Charged with demanding £110 with menaces, Raymond appeared at Marlborough Street Police Court, where the prosecutor, Mr Vincent Evans, told Mr Dummett, the Magistrate, that there was another man wanted in connection with this matter.

'Will the other man be arrested before the case comes on again?' asked the Magistrate, to which Mr Evans replied, 'I hope so.'

Evans' optimism was rewarded when Neale was arrested the very next day at a hotel in Chelsea. He told Divisional Detective Inspector Bill Thompson, 'Yes, I read about the case in the papers. I knew he had letters from Mr X. I had no idea he had got so much money out of it. £20 is exactly all I had.'

By the time the two had been committed to the Old Bailey to stand their trial on 1 February 1933, Mr X had inexplicably become Mr W; but irrespective of whether their victim was 'X' or 'W', the charmless duo were found guilty of blackmailing him.

Sergeant MacDonald told the court that Raymond's café had been the meeting place of a gang of blackmailers who were convicted the previous year; however, the officer added that Neale sponged off his friends when he could not obtain employment as a professional dancing partner.

'Do you mean he is a man whom elderly women take to dances?' gasped the Recorder of London, Sir Ernest Wild KC; and obviously feeling that this occupation was almost as bad as being a participant in a sordid blackmail case, he packed Neale off to penal servitude for three years. The shock of the revelation may have contributed to Sir Ernest's death, eighteen months later.

Additionally, the Judge was in no doubt that Raymond was the principal in 'engineering a wicked scheme of blackmail' and sentenced him to five years' penal servitude.

* * *

Thereafter, Neale passes out of the picture. Raymond, of course does not, and neither does Inspector Thompson. In fact, it's time to introduce two more pieces of dreg into Raymond's world of blackmail.

Joseph Kinsella had already been fined for assault in Ireland and he was one of two men convicted of assault with intent to rob the manager of a Holloway cinema; armed with an imitation pistol, Kinsella had hit the manager with a banister rail so hard that it broke in two. In January 1933 at the Old Bailey, he was sentenced to three years' penal servitude and eighteen strokes of the birch.

Later, in November 1933, David Sellars Baird appeared at the same court; in a completely different case, he was convicted of assault with intent to rob and shooting at a pursuer and he, too, was sentenced to three years' penal servitude. He and Kinsella met up with Raymond in Maidstone Prison, where they exchanged ideas on the way their future careers might progress – and that was not all.

Also serving their sentences at that time were a gang of really professional blackmailers, who over a period of 3½ years had screwed the sum of £10,754 (now, a staggering £662,307) out of a man referred to in court as 'The Captain' and who in reality was the very wealthy Captain Richard Dixon. Following a Scotland Yard investigation six men appeared at the Old Bailey in June 1927, and the ringleader, convicted of blackmail, was sentenced to penal servitude for life. The other gang members were sentenced to penal servitude for periods of fifteen, twelve, ten, ten and eight years. Women in court shrieked and fainted when the sentences were passed, although the wife of the prisoner sentenced to fifteen years was not amongst them, since she was currently serving an eighteen-month sentence with hard labour, also for blackmail.

These characters met up with Raymond when he joined them in prison, and Dixon's name was mentioned.

Released in October 1936, Raymond lost no time in acquiring new premises, known variously as The Philary or Harry's Restaurant, in Lisle Street, Leicester Square, and which also became the haunt of prostitutes of both genders; in September 1937, Raymond was fined £1 on each of five summonses for harbouring prostitutes on the premises. Not that that caused him any concern.

He took off after the unfortunate Captain Dixon, now aged seventy-two and already bled white by the blackmailers; after his initial fright, Dixon arranged a meeting at his London club, but Raymond, doubtless fearing a set-up (and he was probably right), did not attend. However, he had plenty of other schemes afoot, because in his one year of freedom Raymond amassed a small fortune and was said to be worth anything between £15,000 and £60,000.

In 1936 a popular men's tailoring store known as the Fifty Shilling Tailors provided very decent suits at that price to the man in the street; Raymond's suits cost eight times as much (£1,420 at today's prices) – and he possessed thirty of them. An inveterate gambler, he placed bets at racecourses using £50 and £100 notes; when Mid-Day Sun was the favourite for the St Leger at Doncaster in 1937, Raymond put £1,200 on the horse to win; Mid-Day Sun started off well, but came in third. Raymond smiled, shrugged and walked away. The loss was of little consequence to him, since he was organizing blackmailing events from Cornwall to the Shetlands.

He planted his agents – young men who were beautiful as well as being beautifully tailored – in smart hotels and restaurants, waiting to be picked up by wealthy clients so that Raymond could compromise them.

Meanwhile, Joseph Kinsella had met a certain 'Mr A' in October 1936, and following a dissolute encounter at a cinema, both he and David Baird went to Mr A's village, where they demanded £5,000 from him as a fee for their silence. In fact, they received £3,100, which they divided between them; with his share, Baird opened a small business for a woman friend in Brighton, spent £150 on furniture for his flat and another £155 on a car.

This business was simply too good to be true; in April 1937 Kinsella approached Mr A in London and this time demanded £10,000 as the price of his silence. Mr A offered him £3,000 but said that nothing could be done until after King Edward VIII's coronation.

A meeting was set up between Kinsella and Mr A in a Piccadilly Hotel; but by now the police had been informed and the meeting was overheard by Detective Inspector Slyfield and another officer.

'What is your final?' asked Mr A, and Kinsella replied, 'Eight.'

'Hundreds?' asked Mr A, only to be told, 'Thousands.'

Asked what would happen if he refused to pay, Mr A was told that Kinsella would inform Mr A's brothers and his son – and that was quite sufficient for Inspector Slyfield to emerge from concealment and arrest him.

'I had no intention of stealing the money', Kinsella quickly stated. 'It was a loan promised me.'

This was the defence relied upon by him and by Baird, who was arrested later, but both men were convicted at the Old Bailey in September 1937, with the Recorder of London telling them:

> It would be difficult to invent a story containing worse elements than are to be found in the crime you have committed. I have not the slightest doubt that you knew of the prosecutor's

weakness. You designed and succeeded in getting him to commit an immoral act with the intention of getting all the money you could from him afterwards.

Kinsella was then sentenced to ten years' penal servitude and Baird to five.

Raymond was not arrested; he had been involved with Kinsella, but on the advice of the Director of Public Prosecutions no proceedings were taken against him for two very good reasons. First, the evidence against him was not as strong as it might have been, and second, he was right up to his neck in trouble where the evidence was far stronger.

The police were fully aware of what Raymond was up to; they gathered statements from ten of his victims. One was the accomplished painter Edward Seago, who in time became a great favourite of the Queen Mother, to whom he would present two paintings a year.

But in 1936 Seago had more pressing problems than the merits of oils and watercolours for his post-impressionist works; he had become enmeshed with one of Raymond's beautiful young men and had given him £35, then £45 and paid his rent, as well as introducing him to his mother. Raymond paid Seago a call at his country home and made his usual demands, but without success.

Neither Seago nor eight other victims were particularly keen on appearing in court, and the police wanted someone who could be relied upon to provide them with a copper-bottomed, watertight case. The tenth victim was 'Mr A', who had met 16-year-old Alfred Bird in 1932; over the years he had had sexual assignations with him at Mr A's flat and various hotels. Bird discovered Mr A's financial position – a considerable one – plus details of his family.

On 3 May 1937 Raymond, using the name Vincent Axford, met Mr A and told him that he had private detectives following both him and Bird, but that rather than disclose their findings, the detectives would settle the matter for £450. That was just the beginning; the following day, Mr A paid £350, on 13 May he paid £500 and between 12 and 20 May, another £2,500 – altogether, in under three weeks, a whopping £3,800. A letter which purported to come from the firm of private detectives in question stated:

> We, the undersigned, admit that we have received the sum of £800 and the sum of £3,000 from Mr A. If we should approach or worry him again in any way, he is quite in order to place

this matter in the hands of Scotland Yard and charge us with blackmail.

This, too, was signed over a 6d stamp.

Mr A must have thought his troubles were over and so they were – until 15 October 1937. It was then that Raymond made his next demand – for £5,000 – and it was the straw that broke this particular camel's back. At 3 o'clock on the afternoon of 21 October, in the Empire Restaurant, Victoria, two men were seated at a table adjacent to the one occupied by Raymond, Bird and Mr A. They appeared to be studying racing form in the pages of their newspapers, but in fact Divisional Detective Inspector Bill Thompson and Detective Inspector Arthur Thorp were jotting down in the 'Stop Press' column every word uttered by both men.

'I suppose you want some money?' said Mr A, to which Raymond replied, 'Five thousand pounds', adding, 'You know I can ruin you unless you pay.'

Mr A said he wanted the matter settled at once, whereupon Raymond became rather agitated. 'I don't like your attitude', he remarked. 'It's rather hot here. We had better go', and as they left the room, they did – to Vine Street police station.

At the Old Bailey a very fierce defence was mounted, but on 2 December they were found guilty. Bird burst into tears when the Common Serjeant sentenced him to twenty months' imprisonment, but Raymond, who was still on licence from his previous sentence until the following January, was more composed. Sentenced to ten years' penal servitude, he murmured, 'Thank you, my lord.'

★ ★ ★

Raymond was released in 1946, but now matters became slightly reversed. He was also a receiver of stolen jewellery, and when he was approached by two of the founders of the Ghost Squad, Detective Sergeants John Gosling and Matthew Brinnand, he felt a deep sense of unease. It is possible that he was soothed by Gosling's avuncular manner, but not by Brinnand; he had known Brinnand from his days on 'C' Division and he was terrified of him. Brinnand had a thorough dislike of criminals in general, but reserved his particular loathing for ponces. At this stage the Ghost Squad was only six months old. They needed results fast, and the only way to achieve this was to recruit informants; nor were they particularly fussy about how they did so.

So Raymond was told that he had better stick up some work, pronto, the rationale being that whilst the Ghost Squad was concentrating on other criminals, their gaze would be averted from Raymond's activities.

He did so on 6 July 1946, when he alerted the officers to the activities (and the whereabouts) of an active gang of housebreakers, who had helped themselves to jewellery valued at £3,147 from a house at Thorney Court, Kensington, the previous day. The gang was pulled in and five of them were sentenced to two years' imprisonment, the sixth receiving eighteen months.

'We will never ask you to divulge your sources of information', the Assistant Commissioner (Crime) had told the Ghost Squad personnel; in Raymond's case it was just as well. For the purposes of the informant's report he was known as 'Harry Vevy'.

So while the Ghost Squad concentrated on lorry thieves, hi-jackers and warehouse-breakers, Raymond got on with his own brand of work and in 1947 formed The Pygmalion Kama Society. This was an association which devoted itself and its members – and there were 320 of them in the first three months of its fortunately short-lived existence – to the rituals of sex, lust and passion. These members paid subscriptions of between £3 and £5, but that, of course was just the beginning.

One such member was Mr Alan Vyvyan Insole – naturally, an extremely wealthy man – and just before Christmas 1947, Raymond arrived at Insole's house in Sussex and introduced himself as 'Master B' of the Society. With him was Joe Joiner, who had led a bit of a charmed life. For the first six of his convictions – larceny, receiving and being on enclosed premises – he had had never been sent to prison. Matters were slightly rectified when he was later sent to Borstal; he was also an Army deserter.

Raymond returned on New Year's Eve 1947 and told Insole that Joiner was 'in very great trouble', so much so that it could endanger the existence of the society. It was possible that £1,000 could save it; Insole coughed up, as he did two days later, when he parted with another £350.

It was clear that Insole had been completely taken in; he asked Raymond if he could supply him with what he described as 'a Negro servant', and on 5 January, Raymond did just that in the form of Solomon Fahm, a highly dangerous individual with convictions for larceny, shop-breaking, inflicting grievous bodily harm, assault and wounding. Insole was so taken with this personage that he gave Raymond £50 to buy him decent clothes to replace his shabby ones. In fact, he did more; he handed over to Raymond books which he had printed dealing with sex religion and sex education.

Can you see the way things are going? So can I.

The next person to arrive was William Peter Heap, who had served Borstal training and prison sentences for larceny and house-breaking. He told Insole and his wife that he was a member of a gang who had kidnapped Raymond (in his guise as 'Master B') and had 'knocked all his teeth out' to make him confess; but now that he had, the gang was aware that Insole had 'committed a certain crime' and they wanted £200 to keep silent about it. Pointing to the expensive-looking ring on Mrs Insole's finger, he told her, 'That's worth £800; don't try pleading poverty with me.'

After Heap had left, the Insoles wasted no time in getting on board the next London-bound train and heading in the direction of Scotland Yard.

Fahm had told Insole that he knew the head of the society, a certain 'Master G'. Did Insole want to meet him? You bet your life he did. But when Fahm arrived on 31 January with Master G, aka Francis Una, also black, Detective Sergeant Chadbourne from Scotland Yard's newly-formed company fraud department and other officers were in hiding to record the conversation that followed.

Joiner, the two men told the Insoles, was in possession of Mr Insole's sex religion book and they could retrieve it, with Una telling Mrs Insole, 'You must cooperate.'

'What is the meaning of cooperation?' enquired Mrs Insole.

'We shall require £50 to begin with', replied Una.

'Do you really think these books could do us any damage?' asked Mrs Insole, only to be told, 'Your reputation, Madame.'

Both men were arrested, as was Joiner, nine days later.

'Who am I supposed to have conspired with?' he asked, and the following day, Heap was arrested when he arrived at the house.

'I don't see how you can make a demand when I didn't get any money', be protested. 'I suppose I have to thank Joe Joiner for this. I shouldn't have gone there.' But as he reached the gate of the house he turned and shouted to the occupants, 'We'll be back to see you again!'

That was an unfortunate remark because it pretty well ensured a remand in custody for everybody in the dock.

At the committal proceedings at Tunbridge Wells County Magistrate's Court, both Una and Fahm were offered legal aid; they refused. This meant that they defended themselves (as indeed they did later at Lewes Assizes) and were given far greater latitude than if they were defended by lawyers, something they were fully aware of.

Fahm took great delight in cross-examining Mrs Insole (with Una sometimes offering to assist in interpreting for him, which of course, was not needed), and the purpose of the questioning was simply to humiliate her, as follows:

'On the Sunday at 2am, did your husband come down to my room and call me up to his bedroom where you were in bed?'

'It is the most utter and absolute lies!'

'Do you remember the Sunday night when Mr Insole asked me to go in bed with you?'

'Absolute lies!'

'Do you remember telling me that Mr Insole could not do anything?'

'Good gracious, no!' and then turning to the Magistrate, she asked, 'Do we have to listen to this?'

Well, it seemed that they did, and Fahm played an early unsuccessful race card when Sergeant Chadbourne was obliged to deny saying, 'If I had my way, none of you niggers would remain in this country.'

Nevertheless, they were all committed for trial, and on 16 March 1948, Joiner was found guilty of conspiring with Raymond to obtain £1,350 by false pretences and was sentenced to two years' imprisonment.

The others were all found guilty of blackmail, and Mr Justice Oliver told them, 'It is difficult to speak without anger.' To 22-year-old Heaps, he said, 'If you were older, I would send you to penal servitude for seven years; instead, you will go for five.'

Fahm received a similar sentence, and Una got four years' penal servitude.

But of Raymond, there was no sign. A warrant was issued for his arrest; it was thought he might be in Northern Ireland. Nine months later, he was arrested but he was dealt with at the London Sessions, not at Lewes Assizes. Charged with five cases of blackmail, he pleaded not guilty, and that was accepted by the prosecution. Instead, he pleaded guilty to seven charges of obtaining a total of £227 by false pretences and asked for fifteen similar offences, amounting to £2,871, to be taken into consideration. He was sentenced to five years' penal servitude.

Now in his forties, Raymond slipped from public attention, but the case left unanswered questions. Why the dropping of the charges that could have seen him imprisoned for life? Were there matters in those charges in respect of very wealthy and influential personages that could have proved embarrassing to individuals up to and including members of the government – or perhaps even higher?

Had Raymond struck some kind of a deal, much like the one he had engineered with the Ghost Squad? Gosling would later say, 'We threatened him with a big stick if he did not mend his ways', but it seemed very likely that Raymond had taken out his own insurance policy.

CHAPTER 9

Call in the Yard

Police Constable Arthur Collins, a member of the Warwickshire Constabulary, had just come off duty and was getting into bed with his wife Marjorie close to midnight on Sunday, 23 June 1946, when he heard the sound of breaking glass. It had come from the Buyers & Sellers Agency, Warwick Market Place, almost opposite the Collins' flat in Theatre Street. By the time he had got up and dressed in his uniform, the breaking had been successfully carried out and a portable gramophone, radio sets, cameras and other items valued at £72 7s 6d had been taken. This was the second breaking by those responsible; the first was at the Civil Defence Stores, also in the Market Place, where forty-two pairs of gumboots had been stolen, valued at £46 6s 0d.

Thirty-year-old PC Collins didn't hesitate when he confronted the three men responsible; and neither did they. Collins' truncheon was snatched from his hand and he was savagely and repeatedly struck with it. Hearing the commotion, Mrs Collins put a coat over her nightdress and rushed downstairs. Outside the Liberal Club, she saw a large man repeatedly hitting her husband with the truncheon, and screaming, 'Help! Murder! Police!' she flung herself at her husband's attacker, only to have him hit her on the shoulder with the truncheon, knocking her aside.

George Wollington, a club steward, heard Mrs Collins' screams and ran into the roadway, where he saw the unconscious body of PC Collins. The attackers had fled by now, and Mrs Collins had run, barefoot, the 200 yards to Warwick Police Station, where in a very distressed condition, her hands and nightwear covered in her husband's blood, she gasped out what had happened to Police Sergeant Wild, who ran back with her to the Market Place.

PC Collins was conveyed by ambulance to the Queen Elizabeth Hospital, Birmingham, where he would remain for weeks. His bloodstained truncheon, uniform coat, helmet and lamp would become exhibits, but Collins would not recover sufficiently to testify against those responsible for his plight.

However, there was something that might turn the tide and help find the culprits. When the truncheon-wielding thug used it to strike Mrs Collins, she already had a firm grip on his jacket lapel, so much so that when she was knocked aside, the lapel was torn right off. It had come from a dark double-breasted jacket with alternate blue and chalk stripes in the pattern; and it would lead to the downfall of PC Collins' attacker.

For five days PC Collins lay unconscious in hospital; it was only on Friday, 28 June that his condition showed a slight improvement and he began to slowly recover consciousness, but he could provide no useful information to the detective sitting at the foot of his bed. So serious was his condition that the offence was classified as attempted murder; and no one would have been unduly surprised if Collins had expired. In the meantime, the Warwick police were working flat out to discover who was responsible; tailors and managers of clothing stores were shown the piece of torn-off cloth. Did it come from their stock? Had they seen it before? Dustbins were searched, and anywhere else that rubbish might be disposed of, looking for the rest of the jacket, discarded or burnt; but all without success.

PC Collins had been a member of the constabulary for ten years; he was a well-known and popular member of the community, and emotions were running high amongst the townspeople. Police vehicles with loudspeakers attached slowly trawled the streets of Leamington and the surrounding districts appealing for anyone who had information as to the identity of the perpetrators to come forward; but nobody did. And all the while, Collins' life hung in the balance.

After ten days the investigation was no further forward, and the Chief Constable of Warwickshire finally decided to call in the Yard.

* * *

It might seem odd that the head of the Flying Squad should be chosen to head up this investigation, but the fact was, at that time, that the Squad was still part of C1 Department at the Yard – there would be another two years before it became a separate entity, to be known as C8 Department – and therefore the detective chief inspector in charge was as liable as any other chief inspector to be part of the C1 rota, to be sent out to investigate serious crime.

Consequently, it was Bob Fabian who was sent to Warwick to help; with him he took Detective Sergeant Arthur Veasey, who would spend almost twenty-two of his thirty-two years' service with the Flying Squad.

The Warwickshire investigation had been thorough, but it was parochial. Fabian was a big believer in utilizing maximum publicity in an investigation and he had the piece of cloth photographed, then copies of the photograph sent to newspapers all over the country – and it worked. The cloth was identified as material used in a demob suit. At the end of the war, members of the armed forces who were demobilized were issued with a raincoat, a hat, a tie, two shirts, underwear, a pair of shoes – and a suit.

Bear in mind that by the time this offence was committed, 2,250,000 demob suits had been issued to returning service personnel. It was a daunting investigation, made all the more complex because many soldiers, dissatisfied with the quality or cut of the cloth, had sold their suits to spivs hanging about outside the depots; they, in turn, sold them on to dealers. Fabian could only hope and pray that it hadn't happened in this case.

First stop was the Ministry of Supply, Birmingham, where the cloth was identified as pattern No. DES 1012; it had been manufactured in Somerset. Of the 5,000 yards of woven cloth, most had gone to Birmingham, although 900 yards had gone on a separate order to Glasgow.

Back to Birmingham; the two factories who had received the bulk of the cloth were visited, and the detectives discovered that it was still in their warehouses, waiting to be made into suits. On, then, to Glasgow, where a tailor identified the torn lapel's stitching as his; he had made it from pattern No. DES 1012 into a suit, specially cut for a very large ex-serviceman, 6 feet 2½ inches tall, with a 45-inch chest. The suit had been sent to 8 Holly Place, Wright Street, Birmingham by recorded delivery for Patrick Dominic Sutcliffe, who had been discharged from the army on 18 January 1945.

On 2 July Sutcliffe was traced to Wilmcote, near Stratford-upon-Avon, where he was arrested by Detective Superintendent Spooner of the local constabulary, as was the norm when Scotland Yard officers had been called into a provincial investigation.

Spooner's accusation was met with a denial. 'I know nothing at all about it', said Sutcliffe. 'I was in Birmingham.'

The denials continued after he was taken into Stratford-upon-Avon police station. 'If I had done that', he said, referring to the assault, 'I should have walked into a police station and given myself up.'

But when he was taken to Warwick police station he had a change of heart. In the absence of the superintendent, he was left in charge of Sergeant Arthur Veasey; despite the nickname 'Squeaker', because of his high-pitched voice, there was nothing remotely soft about Veasey. A tough veteran of the First World War, he was an even tougher member of the Flying Squad. He had been one of three officers under the control of Detective Inspector Jack 'Charlie Artful' Capstick who, during the Christmas period of 1943, had arrested a violent gang of warehouse-breakers. Capstick pulverized two of the gang with his truncheon, and when two more tried to escape, as Capstick later recounted, 'It was a pleasure to see the workmanlike way in which Squeaker dealt with them.' Only three of the warehouse-breakers arrived at Clerkenwell police station; the other three were in hospital, receiving much-needed treatment for their injuries.

So this was the officer who had Sutcliffe – someone who had almost killed a fellow police officer – under his care, during Superintendent Spooner's absence. It appears that there was discourse between them, because Sutcliffe told Veasey, 'I feel a bit worried about the whole matter; what would you advise me to do?'

Veasey must have provided helpful advice, because when the superintendent returned, Sutcliffe said that he would 'tell them the whole story'. In admitting that he and two other men decided to break into the Buyers and Sellers Agency, he added that they were disturbed:

> The policeman came running up and I at once hit him with his staff. With that, I lost my head . . . I hit him a number of times. Whilst I was hitting him, a woman came up and said something. I must have lost my head, but I didn't hit the woman, I may have pushed her but I didn't hit her – oh, no. I pushed her off and ran away up a jetty and threw the policeman's staff away. I jumped into the car and drove off home.

Whose car? And who were the other men? What happened to Sutcliffe's jacket? A little more questioning resulted in answers and further arrests.

When Thomas Joseph Parkinson was arrested at his home at 261 Charles Road, Small Heath, Birmingham, he immediately replied, 'OK. I'm glad it has come. I was dead scared.'

When his wife asked the reason for this outburst, he replied, 'Don't worry. I went with some pals to Warwick, broke into a place. The others knew where it was. I had never been before, but I didn't have anything to do with the beating up of the policeman.'

Next, William George Evans from a demolition site at Warwick Market Place was arrested; he too admitted the warehouse-breaking.

Anthony Richard Allen admitted that Sutcliffe had borrowed his car on the night of the attack; Allen had then gone to the home of Gurdas Ram at 58 Golden Hillock Road, Birmingham and described to the officers what happened when Sutcliffe arrived at about 12.30am. 'He was in a hell of a mess. His jacket was torn, his left lapel was torn completely away and he looked as though he'd been in a rough house. Sutcliffe told me he was disturbed at the warehouse when they were ready to get the stuff away and he hit the copper with his truncheon. Sutcliffe's clothing was later burned in the fire.'

Charged with attempting to murder PC Collins, as well as the two breaking offences, Sutcliffe replied, 'I never intended to knock the policeman about like that; I lost my head.'

Ram and Allen were charged with harbouring Sutcliffe and receiving stolen property. Allen replied, 'Paddy is a pal. I lent him a suit but it was not me who burnt the torn one', while Ram said, 'I only tried to shield Paddy; he is a good friend.'

Of course, Allen and Ram knew precisely that Sutcliffe was out to break into premises; Allen had lent him his car, and why else would he have gone to Ram's address at after midnight? Why else would Sutcliffe have also gone there, if it wasn't to hand over the stolen property?

More corroborative evidence was now forthcoming: two women who knew both Sutcliffe and Evans saw them in the evening, before the attack, drinking in the Green Dragon public house at Warwick; and at Warwick Magistrates' Court, a witness from Taunton identified the piece of cloth as being made by his company for demob suits, as did another from Glasgow, who identified the stitching on the lapel as his own work.

But there was a dramatic moment at court when four of the prisoners appeared in the dock handcuffed and Sutcliffe appeared in shackles. It caused the solicitor appearing for Ram to roar, 'I have never in my life seen prisoners handcuffed in a public court and I raise great objection to it at this stage!'

In fact, he did have a point. It was something stage-managed by the police to show the gravity of the charge against Sutcliffe, and while there was very good reason for him to be shackled, it really was a bit over the top for the other defendants, who had not shown any violence. Then again, the solicitor could have exercised more tact; there was an angry crowd, both in the court and outside it, who had vociferously booed the arrival of the prisoners and would demonstrate their disapproval again at their departure. Superintendent Spooner, obviously not used to dealing with outraged solicitors, made some fairly drippy comments, the Bench decided they had no jurisdiction in the matter, and the prisoners remained handcuffed.

At the committal proceedings, the court was told that only the previous day, 24 July, had Collins been permitted to go home from hospital. There he would be treated for some considerable time, after which he would convalesce for a lengthy period. It would be quite impossible to call him for court proceedings. Over forty witnesses were called and thirty-six exhibits were produced, and after a two-day hearing the defendants were committed to Northampton Assizes for trial. By now the crowd was so furious – one woman in particular complaining that she had queued for an hour and a half and *still* hadn't been allowed in – that the prisoners had to be smuggled out of court.

★ ★ ★

The proceedings at Northampton Assizes were a bit of a mishmash; the warehouse-breaking charge at the Civil Defence Stores was dropped, so were the receiving charges against Allen and Ram, who were found guilty of harbouring Sutcliffe on 26 October 1946 and were each sentenced to three months' imprisonment.

The attempted murder charge against Sutcliffe evaporated; much was made of the fact that he had two trifling convictions for larceny and that he was 'very sorry' for the attack on the officer. Instead, he was allowed to plead guilty to wounding PC Collins with intent to resist arrest, but he was told by the Commissioner, Mr F.E. Pritchard:

> Had it not been for the gallant attempt on the part of this policeman's wife, you might well have stood in this dock on a charge of murder . . . The police of this country have a very difficult task to perform – a task which is made more difficult by the actions of people like you and the people who stand in the dock with you. When it has been proved – as it has been proved in this court – that they are obstructed in their duties by violence, such as you administered to this unfortunate man, the law rises in its wrath to come to their aid. For breaking and entering the B&S Agency, you will go to prison for twelve months with hard labour and for the attack on the policeman, you will go to penal servitude for four years, the sentences to run concurrently.

Evans was told, 'The time has come in this country when shop- and house-breakers must be stopped; you will go to prison with hard labour for twelve months'; and referring to Parkinson's Army record, the Commissioner said, 'I take into account the fact that you stood by your country in her hour of need; you must serve six months' hard labour.'

The Chief Constable of Warwickshire was delighted; he and his wife gave a garden party, and Fabian and Veasey were guests of honour – later, both officers were quite rightly commended by the Metropolitan Police commissioner, which marked Fabian's fortieth and final commendation.

It was not until 11 February 1947 that PC Collins returned to duty, but he was a broken man. As the police surgeon, Dr Worthington had told the Assize Court:

> Further improvement is probable but I do not anticipate a full recovery. Since being injured, he has become more loquacious and treats his disability with abnormal levity. He has frequent headaches, has lost his sense of smell and his sense of taste is impaired.

Collins was transferred to Rugby, his wife's home town. Had he been medically discharged with eleven years service (as he fully deserved to be), his ill-health pension would have been negligible. So it was an act of kindness for his force to find him a job in Rugby's police office – but it was a sinecure, nothing else. He would be kept on full pay until retirement, while being conveniently tucked out of the way – because PC Collins would never walk the beat again.

Chapter 10

A Quartet of Gunmen

There are gunmen and gunmen; they come in all shapes and sizes – all temperaments, as well. Let's take a look at four of them, as different as different can be, and we can start off with 'a regular, right-down bad 'un', which was how Mr Noah Claypole unwisely referred to Oliver Twist's mum in Dickens' eponymous novel.

He was born Alan Ivor Philips, but that didn't seem quite grand enough, so Alan Philips was transformed into Philip Devereux, and one September night in 1932, he was spotted by Detective Inspector Jeremiah Lynch of the Flying Squad in Catford. Lynch then lost sight of him but later saw him again, this time in London's Shaftesbury Avenue, and followed him, observing him loitering in shop doorways in the Strand. On being arrested, apart from being found in possession of two jemmies, a torch, gloves, a magazine containing six cartridges and a bunch of skeleton keys, Devereux also attempted to produce a fully-loaded automatic pistol with the safety catch off from his shoulder holster, but was prevented from doing so. 'You know what it's for and why I have it', he told Lynch, adding, 'It's lucky for you that you took me by surprise and that you found it.'

Devereux had convictions for burglary, house- and office-breaking, had only been released from a prison sentence in March of that year, and when he appeared at the Old Bailey he denied making that rather incriminating statement to Lynch. Asked why he had the pistol in his possession he did rather let himself down with the cocky answer: 'Unfortunately, I've always had a weakness for these things.' The Recorder of London, Sir Ernest Wild KC, described Lynch as 'a very fortunate man to be alive' and Devereux as 'a dangerous criminal and a thorough waster'; and for possessing a firearm with intent to resist arrest, Devereux notched up his seventh conviction, sentenced to eight years' penal servitude, with a concurrent four-year sentence for possessing house-breaking implements by night.

Complimented on his courage, Lynch received a £10 award from the Bow Street Reward Fund and five years later, he retired; but not so Devereux.

Somewhere along the line, Devereux collected a further conviction, before police paid him a visit at his Upper Montagu Street flat in Marylebone on 22 January 1948. There he was found to be in possession of a green handkerchief with eye slits cut in it, a steel cosh, a bunch of skeleton keys and jewellery, part-proceeds of four house-breakings, plus a fully-loaded automatic pistol, which he produced, telling the officers, 'Stand back or I'll blow your fucking brains out! Keep away or I'll shoot.'

It was the last time Devereux would threaten anybody with a firearm, and it was not the officers' 'fucking brains' that would be 'blown out'. There was a struggle, the pistol went off, and Devereux crashed to the floor hit, with real bad luck, straight between the eyes. Recording a verdict of accidental death, the coroner and the jury commended Detective Sergeant Butler and Detective Constable Barlow for their courage.

★ ★ ★

Seven months after Devereux's unfortunate demise, post-prandial events began innocently enough in East London; Detective Sergeant Harold Bland and Detective Constable John Baxter were called to Whitehorse Lane, Stepney during the afternoon of 27 August 1948 following a report of a stolen car at the Eastern Auction Mart.

There they spoke to George Edward Dendrickson, a 23-year-old decorator; but while they were doing so, a man suddenly drove off in the car in question. DC Baxter leapt on to the running board in an effort to stop it, but after being carried for some distance he was thrown off.

Dendrickson was arrested and put into the back of a police car between the two officers. They were about 20 yards from Arbour Square police station when he suddenly produced a pistol, shoved it into Bland's side and shouted, 'Stop now, and you've had it if you don't!'

Bland pushed down on the gun barrel, whereupon the gunman said, 'You can have the lot then!' and fired. The bullet passed through Bland's trousers, grazing his leg, and was later found embedded in the car seat. Dendrickson was disarmed and quite possibly appropriately spoken to, because when he appeared at Thames Magistrates' Court the following day, despite appearing to be suffering only from a bandaged finger, he was permitted to remain seated in the dock.

Charged with shooting at Bland with intent to murder him (to which he replied, 'Yes, it's what I expected'), he was also charged with stealing the car, valued at £830, or alternatively, receiving it.

'He doesn't say much about himself', Detective Inspector Barnes told the Magistrate, and indeed, he hadn't; the newspapers referred to him as 'a mystery man'. When Dendrickson appeared at the Old Bailey, Mr Justice Stable provided a better description, telling him that he was 'a menace to society' and sentencing him to seven years' penal servitude, after which both officers were awarded the King's Police Medal.

That was a pretty clear-cut case; the next one played out in rather muddied waters.

★ ★ ★

It appeared that the mother of Aircraftman Leslie George Kaill was in severe financial difficulties, because a torn letter from her was later found in his possession, which in part read:

> . . . and think differently. I could not stop crying today. I never did a thing. It worried me so. How can I find the money? I could not pay the rent this week. I have got to find two weeks on Monday.

It was sufficient to prompt her son – who, by the way, possessed an excellent character – to visit Barclay's Bank in the Euston Road on 28 December 1939 where he sought, and obtained, an interview with the manager, Mr Arthur Edward Pearn.

Kaill requested a loan of £200; when Pearn asked if he was a customer or possessed any collateral, and Kaill replied, 'No' to both questions, the manager replied, 'I'm afraid the bank can't help you' and rose to see him out. It was then that the aircraftman produced a pistol, whereupon Pearn hurriedly left his office and the police were called.

Detective Constable Wood shouted for Kaill to give up the gun, but he replied, 'If you come a step nearer, I'll shoot. I came for £200 and I'm going to get it.'

At that point, Police Constable 526 'C' Peter Slater opened the door, to see Kaill in a corner of the office pointing a revolver at him. Telling the others, 'I'm going to get him', Slater stepped into the room.

'I will bloody shoot you', Kaill shouted. 'Don't come a step nearer.' He repeated this several times.

It was a tense moment; everyone believed Kaill would carry out his threat, police officers, bank staff and especially Slater, who told him, 'I'm going to arrest you whether you shoot or not.'

'I don't care', replied Kaill. 'I've nothing to lose.'

'Don't be a fool', said Slater, who was slowly advancing towards him. "You'll only make it worse for yourself.'

But the gunman kept repeating, 'I'll shoot!'

It was only when the two men were close to each other that Kaill lowered the pistol and Slater grabbed hold of it. 'I wouldn't shoot you if I could', said Kaill then, and Slater realized that what he had been threatened with was a toy pistol.

At Clerkenwell Police Court, Kaill told Mr W. J. H. Brodrick, the Magistrate, 'I've been ill. I don't think I was responsible for my actions', and it appeared that Mr Brodrick agreed, because he ordered medical reports.

But although out of his eight weeks' service with the RAF Kaill had spent six in hospital, he was adjudged to be completely sane and able to stand trial.

Three weeks after the incident at the bank, Kaill appeared at the Old Bailey, where he pleaded guilty to assaulting the bank manager and possessing an imitation firearm with intent to resist arrest. The Recorder of London, Gerard Dodson, usually the most benevolent of judges, told him, 'It is quite obvious that every effort must be made to prevent methods which might be common elsewhere from creeping into the life of this country', and sentenced him to twelve months' imprisonment.

Slater, with seven years' service, was commended by the Judge, highly commended by the commissioner for displaying 'courage, determination and tact' and awarded £7 from the Bow Street Reward Fund; rightly so, since although some people – who have never faced an angry man in their lives – might find it amusing that the pistol with which he had been threatened was no more than a toy, Slater didn't think it was imitation, and neither did anybody else.

But given all the circumstances, I do think that Kaill could have justifiably been dealt with more sympathetically. The character in the last of these accounts certainly was; and that was a big mistake.

★ ★ ★

There was a mysterious personage lurking in Mayfair on the evening of Sunday, 4 June 1939; two passers-by heard the report of a firearm and saw him push something into his pocket and cycle away. The following morning, a housemaid in the employ of the Earl of Harewood at 32 Green Street discovered a hole in the window at that address.

Someone almost as ominous was Laurence Olivier playing Heathcliff in William Wyler's film *Wuthering Heights*, but that was the film that the Duchess of Kent wished to see at the Gaumont cinema on the evening of 5 June. She and the Duke had dined at their address at 3 Belgrave Square, and he left for a private engagement a few minutes before the Duchess, who together with Lady Portarlington got into a car and departed at 8.40pm.

As the car drove off towards Grosvenor Crescent, a man standing by the junction of Halkin Street and Belgrave Square fired at it; the shot missed and hit the roadway. The gunman – the same one as the previous night – then mounted a racing cycle and rode off along Halkin Street.

He was an Australian, his name was Ledwedge Vincent Lawlor and he was as mad as a hatter.

The shooting was witnessed by Police Constable 422 'B' Robert Tice, who stopped a passing car and gave chase. At the junction with Halkin Street and Grosvenor Place, the car swerved in front of Lawlor and he was stopped by PC Tice.

'I didn't hit anyone, did I?' protested Lawlor. 'It's quite in order; I have a certificate for it', which he then produced.

PC Tice was not so much interested in the certificate as in what it referred to. 'Where's the gun?' he asked, and Lawlor produced from his hip pocket a sawn-off rifle 12 inches long, which was promptly seized.

'There's no need for all this fuss', exclaimed Lawlor and, referring to the gun, added, 'I'm entitled to this.'

But on arrival at Gerald Road police station, two matters became immediately apparent. When the gun was opened, its breech was found to contain an empty cartridge case, and when the firearms certificate was examined, two addresses were seen to have been scrawled on the back: '32 Green Street' and '3 Belgrave Square'.

Interviewed by Divisional Detective Inspector Henry Haywood, Lawlor told him:

> I am not making any statement in writing. The gun was sent to me by my brother in Australia. I sawed it down myself because I wanted to have it about with me for fear it was stolen. It jammed a few days ago and I was trying to free it in Belgrave Square when it went off. I carried it about for several days when I went to Buckingham Palace and Windsor. I want to see the dukes and kings. I wrote those addresses down on the back of the certificate because somebody told me that was where they lived. I was in Belgrave Square last night and I wanted to see the duke. I had a solicitor in Australia who told me that if

ever I was in trouble, I need never make a statement and I am not doing so.

At Westminster Police Court, Lawlor's solicitor wished to state at the earliest opportunity that his client had no desire to cause injury to either the Duchess of Kent or the Earl of Harewood.

In fact, the Duchess was blissfully unaware of what had happened that evening and went on to enjoy the sight of Merle Oberon's life slipping away in front of Messrs Olivier and Niven.

However, just in case Lawlor had associates, while his immediate future was being decided by Clyde Wilson, the Westminster Magistrate, police were on hand to scrutinize the tickets for the annual garden party of the Chelsea Babies Club that the Duchess was attending that day; and when she later went to a charity meeting at West Ham Speedway Stadium she was provided with a police motorcycle escort.

Back, now, to court, where the firearms expert Robert Churchill, who had examined the weapon, stated that although the shortening of the barrel made it impossible to fire with any accuracy, it was dangerous at a range of up to 1,000 yards. Lawlor was duly committed for trial at the Old Bailey.

But later that month, when Lawlor pleaded guilty to two charges of possessing a firearm with intent to cause serious injury, an extraordinary decision was reached that the best course of action was to bind him over to keep the peace, on condition that within a month he returned home to Australia.

PC Tice was highly commended by the commissioner for 'courage and promptitude in bringing about the arrest of a dangerous armed lunatic'. 'Lunatic?' The commissioner didn't know the half of it.

* * *

On 7 December 1939, Lawlor met his cousin, George Anderson Kelly, at St Kilda Junction, Melbourne. They had a few drinks before going to a hamburger shop, where Lawlor consumed hamburgers and tea. They separated in some nearby gardens, Lawlor walked off and then Kelly heard an explosion. He had been shot in the back, the bullet passing through a lung and lodging under his chest.

Lawlor returned to the shop, ordered another hamburger and tea and told a waiter, Alan Maloney, 'Kelly will be going to a funeral, tomorrow' – and it was only due to the skill of the surgeons at a nearby hospital that he was not.

Leaving the shop, Lawlor returned to the gardens, where he saw another man, Leslie Glen Giles, who was a complete stranger to him; Lawlor shot him in the back, too, and he fell to the ground, blood spurting from his mouth.

Once more Lawlor returned to the shop, only ordering tea this time and muttering to himself, although the waiter was unable to make out what he was saying.

He was arrested the following day by Senior Detective Porter, who found a loaded pea rifle in his pocket which had been sawn down to resemble a pistol, about eight inches in length.

'I won't discuss the shooting', Lawlor told him. 'If you want to talk to me, talk about cricket or football, but not the shooting.'

It was proved scientifically that the bullets extracted from the two victims had identical marks to those from a test firing of the gun in Lawlor's possession, and he was committed for trial to the Supreme Court on 15 February 1940 to face two charges of shooting with intent to murder.

He was found not guilty on the grounds of insanity and was incarcerated in a psychiatric hospital – a secure one – for the rest of his life, which ended at Arar, Australia in 1971.

The Duchess of Kent, the Earl of Harewood and quite possibly King George VI didn't know how lucky they'd been.

Chapter 11

A Wheeler-Dealer

The possessor of nine previous convictions, 22-year-old John Thomas Galvin was what was known as a 'wheeler-dealer'; or in more prosaic terms, cunning, manipulative and slimy. Mind you, I had no objection to dealing with someone like that as a snout, as long as they didn't break any of the rules I imposed; and especially if they didn't attack a fellow police officer and put his life at risk. But that's just what happened in the case of young Mr Galvin.

The story starts in 1938 when, between 14 and 15 May, Galvin with two other men broke into the Premier Filling Station, Portsmouth Road, Cobham and stole a typewriter, the contents of a cash box and other property, to the value of £36 3s 3d.

Taking care to erase the typewriter's serial number, Galvin sold the item for £3 10s 0d with a receipt saying it was his property to a dealer, but was nabbed a few weeks later in February 1939. Appearing before the Kingston County Justices on 3 March, he pleaded guilty but refused to reveal the names of his accomplices, virtuously telling the Justices, 'They're now in the Army and I don't want to bring them into it.'

In a statement to police, he promised that 'he would go straight in future', and committing him to the Surrey Quarter Sessions on bail, the Assistant Chairman told Galvin that 'the probation officer will do all he can to help you' – and it appears he did; six weeks later, he was bound over to keep the peace for two years. It was a forlorn hope.

Three months went by, and between 17 and 18 August 1939, the White House, Denham was broken into and items including a camel hair coat were stolen. The garage of the house was also broken into during the same period and items were stolen from there, too. Police made enquiries, and as a result, on 18 August, they arrested Edward Hooper at his address at Comeragh Road, West Kensington, where all the stolen property was recovered. A car was seen outside the address; its registered owner, who was also Mr Hooper's roommate and who answered to the name of John Thomas Galvin, was nowhere to be found, and a warrant for his arrest was issued.

But three days later, a garage at 42 Peterborough Road, Fulham was broken into during the early hours and tools were stolen, as was an Austin saloon from the same address. The persons responsible were Galvin and a similar ne'er-do-well, Thomas Latham, who like Galvin possessed a healthy number of previous convictions. They drove the car to Rickmansworth, where they abandoned it, broke into another house, 'Lady Walk' in Long Lane, and stole a cinema projector and other property valued at £110. They drove the owner's car, a Rolls-Royce, back towards London, leaving it in Kingston, and then stole a Humber saloon from Tournay Road, Fulham.

On 29 August, Edward Hooper was at court to be committed for trial at Buckinghamshire Quarter Sessions, when he asked to see his arresting officer, Detective Sergeant King, because he wished to make a statement. He did so, and what it contained must have been especially pertinent, because on the following day, the area of Munster Road, Fulham was staked out from 10.00am onwards by a couple of aids to CID, one of whom was Police Constable 440 'B' William Bridge. They were keeping observation on an SS Jaguar which, they were informed, was going to be used by two local and well-known criminals.

At 1.35pm their patience was rewarded when the stolen Humber arrived, driven by an unknown man; Galvin and Latham were passengers. Galvin went to the boot of the car, whereupon Bridge grabbed hold of him. There was a fierce, brief struggle, and the driver started the car and began to drive off. Galvin tore himself free from Bridge's grasp, chased after the car, jumped on to the nearside running board and scrambled inside. Bridge, too, raced after the rapidly accelerating vehicle and jumped on to the running board, whereupon both Galvin and Latham (who was in the rear of the car) punched him, and the driver swerved from side to side in an effort to throw him off.

After 300–400 yards of very fast and dangerous driving the car came to a halt, and the driver and Latham ran off into Welford Terrace. Bridge, still on the running board, was hanging on to the wildly struggling Galvin, who dragged the officer through the nearside window of the car while he escaped through the driver's door. Bridge got out and chased after Galvin; he, too, had run off down Welford Terrace, and now the first two suspects scaled a fence into a back garden. Galvin tried to follow, but Bridge pulled him back and there was a further fierce struggle, until Galvin broke away once more and ran back towards the car. Another officer then arrived and pinned Galvin down on the ground long enough for Bridge to run up and arrest him.

Meanwhile, at the rear of 260 Munster Road, Police Constable 199 'B' Williams (who was off duty) found Latham hiding in an outhouse.

'What are you doing there?' asked the officer, to be told, 'I live here.'

Just to be on the safe side, the officer confronted Latham with the householder, whereupon Latham lamely replied, 'All right. I'll come. I'm caught.'

After the two were taken to Waltham Green police station, all of the stolen items were recovered from the Humber. Neither replied when they were charged with the Peterborough Road burglary, although when charged with assaulting PC Bridge, Galvin had the cheek to reply, 'I'm pleading not guilty to that.'

He then went on to say, 'With regard to the Humber, we take responsibility for that, as the driver had nothing to do with it', and Latham, nodding, concurred: 'Yes, that's right.'

You may have come to the conclusion that Galvin was one to take control of the situation, decreeing who was who and what was what. At Westminster Police Court, he told the Magistrate, Mr Marshall, 'I didn't steal the cars. I took them without the owner's consent.' He knew there was a world of difference in sentencing between a bit of TDA and larceny of a motor vehicle.

They were committed to the London Sessions, where on 13 September they pleaded guilty to everything – with the exception of the attack on PC Bishop – and each asked for three other offences to be taken into consideration.

Detective Sergeant Fairbrother was keen to tell the court that Galvin had assisted in recovering stolen property, and PC Bridge's part was referred to simply as 'after a chase and a struggle, both prisoners were arrested'. No mention of the fact that Bridge had suffered bruises and abrasions and was put on the sick list for two weeks.

With pleas of guilty and the evidence watered down, unsurprisingly Latham was sentenced to just twelve months' imprisonment and Galvin to fifteen.

But matters did not end there. On the evening the two men were arrested, Detective Sergeant King interviewed Galvin at Waltham Green police station regarding the burglary at Denham, for which Hooper had been charged and for which a warrant had been issued for Galvin's arrest. Galvin denied being involved in any way. While he was serving his fifteen months' sentence at Oxford Prison he was served with a copy of Hooper's incriminating statement and said, 'That's all right.'

Both Hooper and Galvin appeared at Buckinghamshire Quarter Sessions on 6 October charged with the Denham burglary, to which Hooper pleaded guilty and Galvin not guilty. Galvin then cross-examined Hooper so well that he was acquitted. It was probably just as well. Despite his plea of guilty and asking for seven other offences to be taken into consideration, plus what was described as 'his tragic history' – an industrial school when young, progressing to being in and out of Borstal and prison, as well as deserting from the Army – His Honour Judge Digby Coles-Preedy KC was in no mood to be lenient. Telling Hooper that 'you are a public danger and a man with a shocking record', he sentenced him to three years' penal servitude before congratulating the seven-man jury (the reduced number due to wartime restrictions on jury members) upon the fact that their labours had been light and that they could get home in daylight.

Fortunately, someone was sufficiently aware of PC Bridge's pluck and determination to submit a report describing what had actually happened; he was highly commended by the commissioner, received a £7 cheque from Mr McKenna, the Magistrate at Bow Street, and was quite properly awarded the King's Police Medal for gallantry.

Latham? After his release he was found in a house by the owner and the police were sent for. Latham wailed that he was only sheltering from an air-raid but was obviously disbelieved when his pockets were found to be bulging with the householder's jewellery.

I sincerely hoped that John Thomas Galvin Esq would fare less well during his criminal career, and lo and behold, he did.

He was released from prison on 20 November 1940 and a year later, he was arrested for being found on enclosed premises for an unlawful purpose. Once again, Galvin was chased by the police, was caught, broke away and after a longer chase was arrested as he was trying to board a moving omnibus. Listening to his whining excuse for being at the house, the magistrate was less than impressed after hearing of his previous convictions, plus the fact that he had claimed to be in a reserved occupation as a bricklayer but had in fact been working as a chauffeur.

'I would like to accept the prisoner's story', he said with every suggestion of regret, 'but I'm afraid I cannot.'

The Army claimed Galvin – but only for a while. He absented himself, obtaining a false identity card, and all this came to light when he was arrested for breaking into a house in 1944 and stealing a refrigerator.

His comeuppance arrived on 1 December 1951, when he encountered a villainous family named Connell; Galvin was stabbed five times in the back, one of which punctured a lung. Released on bail, Peter Connell just had time, in February 1952, to be sentenced to fourteen days' imprisonment for stealing lead, before appearing at the Old Bailey for the stabbing incident. He was sentenced to two years' imprisonment, as was his brother Patrick; their brother John received five years and an uncle, eighteen months.

It seemed that the genus Connell found Galvin just as tiresome as PC Bridge and quite a few other coppers did, and there's a moral to this story.

Dealing with slime such as Galvin, as soon as it became obvious that someone was going to start saying what he would or wouldn't do, I always found it efficacious to lay a firm hand on the nape of the person's neck, and with a brisk shake, utter the words, 'Right, now you listen up, son . . .'

What would happen thereafter you may guess at, but need not enquire into.

Chapter 12

The Blackmailed Baronet

John Ronald Leon was the son of Kay Hammond, a very popular stage and film actress, and her then husband, Sir Ronald Leon, 3rd Baronet, and they lived in Mayfair. When John Leon had just passed his fourth birthday he was at the centre of a very odd blackmail/kidnapping plot.

Early in June 1938, Sir Ronald and his wife received a letter which read as follows:

> Dear Sir,
> We regret having to inform you that we have planned to kidnap your son; but knowing that you are a wise gentleman and your wife has just given birth to another son we have realised that it would not be playing the game.
> Therefore we decided to forget for the small sum of £250 cash in notes. We don't think we need to remind you of the dangers in a case of this kind when we get double-X.
> Naturally, you will think of notifying the police. You can if you wish. We are well organised and will carry out our intentions at the slightest suspicion of any tricks.
> There's nothing to worry about, old boy, if you do as we say, so cheer up and smile and all with be well.
>
> (Signed) Chick

The Leons were both horrified and terrified. It is not often that a blackmailer suggests to his victims that they should go to the police, and although Sir Ronald was more than willing to pay the money he decided to take the blackmailer at his word and did just that.

The matter was dealt with by Divisional Detective Inspector Peter Beveridge at Vine Street police station, and he was assisted by Detective Inspector Bob Fabian. Sir Ronald was persuaded that paying the blackmailer would be a foolhardy course of action, and Fabian stayed overnight in the Mayfair flat, waiting for the blackmailer to contact the couple; when he did so he told Sir Ronald, 'If you don't pay up, something will happen to your wife and child.' The call was overheard by Fabian on an extension; during a further phone call at 4.00pm on 6 June, Sir Ronald was told to take the money to Whitehorse Street, to wait there until he could take a taxi to the corner of High Street, Bloomsbury and Charing Cross Road, then to go into the men's toilets and wait.

Fabian rushed down the flat's fire escape, hailed a taxi and drove to Whitehorse Street; meanwhile, as Sir Ronald left the flat on foot, he was surreptitiously tailed in a car by Beveridge, who was accompanied by Woman Police Constable (later Detective Superintendent) Amy Ettridge. She was dropped off in Bloomsbury, Sir Ronald was collected in the taxi and dropped off at the meeting point and Fabian entered the men's toilets, where for the next three hours he was ensconced in one of the cubicles with just a periscope for company, in order to spot the blackmailer. But nobody kept the rendezvous.

At 8.00pm there was a further telephone call, this time demanding £50. Sir Ronald was told to take the money in an envelope and to walk to Curzon Street, turn into Shepherd Market and, at the junction with Trebeck Street, to place the money in a telephone kiosk between the directories. This time it was a Flying Squad taxi that was used, with Beveridge and Fabian lying on the floor and using the periscope once more. Sir Ronald arrived and placed an envelope as instructed, containing just one genuine £1 note, which had been marked, and forty-nine pieces of paper cut to resemble the balance, before leaving the scene.

Minutes passed before a thin, gaunt figure arrived, looked cautiously around him, entered the telephone kiosk and retrieved the envelope, which he slipped into his pocket. He then ran off along Shepherd Market, closely followed by the detectives. As he rounded a bend, he flung the envelope into the gutter but then ran into a cul-de-sac in Whitehorse Street and, as Fabian approached him, lashed out with his fist. That was a mistake. Fabian was a good amateur boxer, Beveridge had served a tough apprenticeship with the 1930s Flying Squad, and although the man fought fiercely he was overpowered. 'I have nothing on me', he protested. 'You don't realize, I'm desperate.'

He was right; the man, whose name was Albert Bencivenga, was desperate and had just one penny in his possession when he was searched at Vine Street police station. Upon being charged he said, 'I don't know what made me do it. I went mad. I got the idea from American magazines.'

Again, this was correct. When his lodgings at Victoria Dwellings, Clerkenwell were searched, as well as blotting paper used to dry the actual kidnap letter, there was a lurid American magazine open at a page which read, 'Ten thousand dollars for your wife'.

Some of the stories contained therein bore a marked similarity to the ruse that Bencivenga had used.

The following day, the 21-year-old plaster figure maker appeared at Bow Street Police Court, and when Beveridge asked for a remand in custody, he also asked the Magistrate, Sir Rollo Graham-Campbell, that the complainant's name be kept secret.

'Is it a blackmailing case?' asked the Magistrate, to be told, yes, it was.

It was an open and shut case; found in Bencivenga's possession was writing paper identical to that used in the ransom demand, and Sir Ronald and the detectives recognized his voice from the telephone calls; there was, of course, no gang.

But rather foolishly, when Bencivenga's lawyer applied for bail on 27 June at Bow Street, not only did his client plead not guilty but he stated that the person who had made the demands on the telephone was someone known only as 'Tony'. The lawyer demanded that 'Tony' be arrested and stated that since his client was the only person who could identify this associate, he should be granted bail in order that he might trace him.

It was an imaginative ploy but one doomed to failure, especially after Beveridge told the court that young John was taken to certain public places during the day and that his father was extremely concerned about the little boy's safety.

Bencivenga was committed to the Old Bailey in custody and three weeks later, he pleaded guilty; he was of previous good character and was sentenced to a remarkably lenient nine months' imprisonment.

After his release, nothing more was heard of him; or of 'Tony', for that matter.

Even though the Baronet's name was never mentioned in the press, Bencivenga's lawyer should have taken heed of the Leon family motto: 'Seek the Truth'.

Although Bencivenga vanished into oblivion, rather more was heard of the target of his attentions. John Ronald Leon's parents divorced, and his mother later married a fellow actor, Sir John Clements. Young John was educated at Eton College and Millfield School and later served as a second lieutenant with the King's Royal Rifle Corps. He began his acting career in 1955 and nine years later, succeeded his father as the 4th baronet but did not use the title. He adopted his mother's maiden name, appeared in a great many plays, films and television productions, most recently in *Game of Thrones* and *The Crown*, and is widely known as that fine character actor, John Standing.

Chapter 13

The Battle of Heathrow – the Aftermath

I want to deal with what became known as the 1948 'The Battle of Heathrow' just in passing, because it has already been well documented.[1] Just briefly, about a dozen determined criminals decided to rob the occupants of the warehouse at the newly-opened Heathrow Airport because they erroneously believed that a consignment of gold bullion had been delivered. Nevertheless, in the warehouse were goods valued at £224,000 and in the safe, jewellery worth £13,900 – at today's value a staggering total of £11,895,000 – and to acquire them, the gang was willing to add phenobarbitone to the three security guards' coffee in quantities which were sufficient to kill several very healthy horses.

Fortuitously, the Flying Squad was tipped off about the raid and three Squad officers swapped places with the guards; the coffee was not consumed and the gang entered the warehouse, took the safe keys off one of the 'unconscious guards' and tried to open the safe. It was then that other Squad officers, secreted behind packing cases, sprang the ambush and there was a battle royal which culminated in severe injuries sustained on both sides. Eight of the gang were sentenced to a total of 71 years' penal servitude, and the officers were commended by the commissioner.

But I think it's interesting to consider what happened to some of the officers afterwards.

* * *

Detective Sergeant John Matthews was one of the 'sleeping' guards; his snoring failed to convince gang member Sidney Cook, who cracked him over the head with a car's starting handle, so that was him out of the running. So, temporarily, was Detective Sergeant Fred Allen; a carafe, to be used by the gang to wash

---

[1] For a full account, see *The Sweeney: The First Sixty Years of Scotland Yard's Crimebusting Flying Squad 1919–1978*, Pen & Sword Books, 2011

out the phenobarbitone from the coffee cups, was smashed and jammed into his thigh; but before collapsing, Allen managed to smack his assailant over the head with his truncheon.

Another of those 'guards' was Detective Constable George Draper; he was later posted to Ealing. In October 1954, he received an unexpected commendation from an Army deserter whom he had arrested hiding in a cinema's attic. The man told the Bench at Ealing Magistrates' Court, 'I should like to thank the officer for saving me when he arrested me.'

The mystified Magistrates demanded an explanation. 'He did in fact fall through the ceiling but I managed to pull him back', explained Draper, who had modestly neglected to inform the Bench. Since the drop was 45 feet, the prisoner had every reason to be grateful, and this was probably instrumental when he asked for five other offences to be considered on appearance at Middlesex Sessions and was placed on probation.

The third guard was Detective Sergeant Charlie Hewett, a newcomer to the Squad who quickly established his bona fides with the other members. He had had the safe keys taken from his pocket and now he waded enthusiastically into the fray. His Squad partner, Detective Constable Donald MacMillan (they were known as 'Chas and Mac'), had his nose broken as he defended Hewett from attack; in turn, Hewett beat gang member 'Big Alfie' Roome so badly that later the same morning, he was unable to attend Uxbridge Court, having a more pressing engagement in the local hospital.

Nevertheless, both Hewett and MacMillan went on to better things when they became two of a select number of officers to carry out arrests on behalf of the ultra-secret Ghost Squad.[2] This was a unit set up to combat the black marketeers and hi-jackers who abounded following the end of the Second World War. Acting on a Ghost Squad snout's tip-off, Macmillan arrested a lorry driver for stealing two bales of cloth valued at £100, closely followed by an arrest for possessing two clothing coupon books. There were arrests for store-breaking and stealing wireless sets valued at £100; two men in the tailoring profession were caught receiving stolen cloth valued at £300; and stolen cloth featured once more in January 1949, when MacMillan made another arrest for receiving that commodity to the value of £500.

---

2 For further details of this unit, see *Scotland Yard's Ghost Squad: The Secret Weapon against Post-War Crime*, Pen & Sword Books, 2011

The Battle of Heathrow – the Aftermath

Yet oddly enough, although MacMillan and Hewett were partners they never operated together on Ghost Squad work. Probably that was because when information came into the Flying Squad office from a Ghost Squad snout it needed to be acted upon so quickly that the person taking the call had to grab hold of anyone in the office at the time to make the arrest.

Hewett was busy from the start, arresting a coal porter for receiving cloth, gloves and a camera, valued at £400, followed by two arrests for receiving eleven cases of stolen whisky. More arrests followed as Hewett tore through the underworld, for receiving nylons, more nylons, quantities of cloth and a lorry. Two men were arrested for being in possession of three fur coats and a quantity of jewellery, the results of a burglary in Hertfordshire. More nylons – 445 pairs – were seized. Stolen oak timber valued at £800 was found in possession of a cabinetmaker, who told Hewett, with unintentional humour but unerring accuracy, 'I suppose I'm lumbered?' His next four arrests were for persons receiving timber, but his last case for the Ghost Squad was participating in the arrest of two men who had received a lorry containing silk valued at £18,000. 'That's done it', said one of them, and he wasn't far wrong, since he was jailed for five years and his partner for four.

After six years with the Flying Squad, Hewett was promoted to first-class sergeant and as a member of the Murder Squad he participated in the investigation into the murderous activities of Dr John Bodkin Adams. He retired with the rank of detective superintendent in 1968.

* * *

Other officers who had been involved in 'The Battle of Heathrow' undertook Ghost Squad work. Detective Sergeant Micky Dowse had sustained serious injuries, having been hit over the head with a pair of giant wire-cutters. When another gang member lashed out with a cosh, Dowse raised his arm to deflect the blow and his hand was badly shattered. Nevertheless, just six weeks later, Dowse was involved in the arrest of two men in possession of Sir Joshua Reynolds' unfinished portrait of Georgiana Cavendish, Duchess of Devonshire. Valued at £5,000 (or £183,000 at today's value), it had been stolen from the Kensington flat of the 11th Earl of Carlisle in July 1948; two months later, it was restored to its rightful owner after Dowse retrieved the painting, wrapped up in an old car rug, and felt the collars of two unpleasant characters: one was Peter Martin Jenkins, who had received three years' penal servitude for his part in 'The Mayfair Playboys' jewel robbery in 1937; the other was an old lag named Harry Mann.

Following his release, in 1942 Jenkins was sentenced to eighteen months' hard labour for breaking into a flat and stealing jewellery; then in 1945, he received another three years' penal servitude for receiving a stolen fur coat.

Mann, unlike Jenkins, had not enjoyed the benefit of an education at Harrow. Since May 1939 he had acquired seventeen convictions, which included reformatory school and Borstal, and in August 1947, he was released from a two-year sentence for conspiracy to receive stolen jewellery – that had been a Ghost Squad arrest.

In fact, on 15 July 1948, both men were arrested by Ghost Squad officers for being suspected persons, loitering with intent to commit house-breaking; given their antecedents, both were surprisingly bound over to keep the peace for twelve months. It was shortly afterwards that the portrait had vanished.

Now justice caught up with them; found guilty of receiving the painting, each was sentenced to four years' penal servitude at the Old Bailey, the judge urging them to 'reform themselves'.

It can't be said that they tried, although others attempted to reform them; when Jenkins was convicted of receiving a stolen trunk in 1952 he was told he was also receiving 'one last chance' and was conditionally discharged. All to no avail; in 1955, for obtaining a car and £500 by false pretences, he was jailed for seven years. Whilst on day release in 1959 he was fingered for a robbery in Leeds; instead, he accepted another conditional discharge for receiving two watches from the robbery. He was later found dead from alcoholic poisoning in a Bayswater lodging house.

As for Harry Mann, he was later sentenced to fourteen years for robbery with violence.

★ ★ ★

Allan 'Jock' Brodie had just commenced what promised to be a fruitful career with the Flying Squad – three commissioner's commendations within twelve months – when he was called up for war service with the RAF. The former gamekeeper was now a flight lieutenant and after a four-year interval, having been awarded the Distinguished Flying Cross, he returned to the Met. He was soon promoted to detective sergeant, and was back on the Flying Squad when he was co-opted for duties with the Ghost Squad. In a little over two years he carried out twenty arrests for that unit: retrieving stolen carpets, cases of whisky, timber, a safe and a car, uncustomed nylons and fur coats; and

The Battle of Heathrow – the Aftermath

arresting various people for unlawful possession of US dollars, a series of shop-breakings and possessing a printing press for the unlawful manufacture of clothing coupons. Then came the fracas at Heathrow – after which, in the final year of the Ghost Squad's existence, often in company with Detective Sergeant Johnny Franklyn (a useful boxer who at Heathrow dished out rather more than he received), he notched up seven more arrests, for receiving ladies' watches, stealing a van and house-breakings.

* * *

Detective Constable Acott – his baptismal names of Basil Montague were swept under the carpet and he was known to all as 'Bob' – was already an established CID officer when, like Brodie, he was called up for service with the RAF. Again like Brodie, he was promoted flight lieutenant and was awarded the DFC, and upon his return to the Met he was promoted and posted to the Flying Squad. After twelve months of Squad duties he was put to work on the Ghost Squad, where he made himself busy – the punch-up at Heathrow intruding – carrying out fourteen arrests for receiving bales of cloth, forged clothing coupons, stolen nylons and a mink coat, for house-breaking and, to my shame, arresting a relative of mine for stealing a lorry and electrical equipment valued at £2,200.

Acott rose through the ranks and had a distinguished career; in 1961, he investigated a murder and a rape which resulted in the conviction and hanging of a certain James Hanratty. For years controversy raged over the conviction, the cause being taken up by a host of left-wing academics, writers and lawyers; there were three Home Office enquiries, the last of which was referred to the Criminal Cases Review Commission. Justice was finally served when Hanratty's family demanded an exhumation of his body, to prove once and for all that he was innocent. But he wasn't; his DNA matched exactly the semen found on the rape victim's panties. Not that that made any difference; the family of a murdering rapist who had just been released from three years' corrective training continued to hysterically proclaim his innocence, as did the left-wing intelligentsia who will *never* admit they're wrong.

Acott retired with the rank of CID Commander; sadly, he died before it was decided by the Court of Appeal (Criminal Division) that Hanratty was well and truly guilty – something that Acott and his investigating team had known all along.

* * *

The leader of the Heathrow raid was Detective Chief Inspector Bob Lee, second-in-command of the Flying Squad. He was hit over the head with an iron bar wielded by Alfred Roome which split his scalp; a witness was of the opinion that 'his ears looked as though they had sagged down to his neck.'

Following the unexpected death of Bob Chapman, Lee became head of the Flying Squad in July 1953, but prior to that he was involved in a case with Peter Sinclair, who had similarly been injured during the Heathrow fracas. Sinclair had assisted the Ghost Squad as a detective sergeant in 1947, making an arrest for store-breaking; within sixteen months he would be promoted to detective inspector and during 'The Battle of Heathrow' he sustained a badly broken arm.

Sinclair was an enormously energetic Flying Squad officer, and the following chapter is devoted to some of his caseload; it commences with the case in which he was involved with Bob Lee, a case which started several years before the Heathrow punch-up.

Chapter 14

The Caseload of Peter Sinclair

On 11 December 1944, a ladder was used to break into the home of Mrs Frederika Newton-Deakin at Westerlands, Petworth, West Sussex. Jewellery and a fur coat, valued at £1,303, were stolen. It would be another eight years before Mrs Newton-Deakin, and a number of other wealthy ladies, were reunited with at least some of their possessions.

Three weeks later, on 2 January 1945, it was the turn of Mrs Dorothy Sarah Learman to be screwed – her house, that is, at Oaklands, Gerrards Cross – when jewellery to the value of £1,109 was stolen. Again, a ladder was used to gain access.

There was then a break of over nine months before what was referred to as 'the ladder gang' struck again. This time, on 21 October 1945, the property of Mrs Josephine de Laszlo was broken into and an assortment of jewellery – including an emerald snap and diamond bar brooch, a diamond and emerald brooch, a platinum and ruby ring and a platinum and diamond ring – was stolen.

Now, hang on a minute. All these burglaries, targeting wealthy women, stealing large quantities of jewellery (its final value would be in excess of £12,000) and using a ladder to ease the burglar's entry. Am I being totally prejudiced in suspecting the culprit to have been George 'Taters' Chatham? The same Taters Chatham who was released from penal servitude in 1943?

Well, you never know. But when White Ladies, Oxshott, Surrey, the address of Mrs Gertrude Mary Avicen Ault, was broken into – again by means of a ladder – and jewellery valued at £450 was stolen on 22 January 1949, Taters had a cast-iron alibi; the previous day, he had been sentenced to three years' penal servitude. And therefore, two months later, when a ladder was used to burgle the home of Lady Rachel Neale Brickwood of Liphook and jewellery worth £2,782 went missing, Taters was, once more, as innocent of that crime as a newborn babe. At some stage, the jewellery of Lady Teviot of Adbury, Newbury had also gone adrift – perhaps we should give Taters the benefit of the doubt with that one, too, and turn our attention towards the direction of 'Ray the Cat', of whom more later – but bits and pieces of items stolen from all those victims were discovered in November 1952, when Lee and Sinclair arrived with a search warrant to examine the contents of the safe in the Hatton Garden offices of Charles George Masters, a 45-year-old diamond merchant. His records revealed his secondary trade as a 'fence'; he paid £35 for a ring that was sold on for £1,383, and rings for which he paid £40 were sold for £200.

Masters stood trial at the Old Bailey on seventeen charges of receiving and denied everything; he was found guilty on eight of the charges, of receiving jewellery valued at £7,000. Masters, who had no previous convictions, was told by Judge Bass, 'If there were no people willing to receive the stolen goods, the whole purpose of all thieving would go', and was then sentenced to three years' imprisonment.

* * *

But several years prior to that arrest, Sinclair's arm had healed sufficiently for him to wield a mop, along with five other Flying Squad officers, and convince shopkeepers in The Mall, Ealing that they required their porches to be cleaned – when in fact they were surreptitiously keeping watch on the National Provincial Bank. When a messenger carrying a large amount of cash to pay the workers in a local firm left the bank, mops and buckets of water were flung to one side as the officers chased down the thoroughfare after three ne'er-do-wells who had targeted him. Two of them leapt on to buses, followed by the detectives, and pedestrians looked on in amazement as Flying Squad cars suddenly pulled out of side-turnings to halt the buses before their next stops. The three men's next appearance was at Ealing Magistrates' Court.

Leonard Rutherford, Douglas Stratford and Dennis Petty – the oldest of the trio was twenty-three – were lucky not to be charged with conspiracy. Instead, they pleaded guilty at the Magistrates' Court to being suspected persons, loitering with intent to commit a felony, and although Sinclair spoke up for them ('They had no instruments on them at the time; I don't believe they would have used violence'), the Bench took a dim view of matters and weighed them off with three months' imprisonment each.

* * *

The day after Messrs Pressings and Stampings Ltd, Ecclestone Road, Ealing was broken into, the inner doors forced, the safes interfered with and National Insurance cards fully stamped and worth £1,400, plus other property, were stolen, Leslie Alfred Green and Leslie William Sweetman were stopped in the street by Sinclair in the Uxbridge Road, West Ealing. He was accompanied by Detective Sergeant Alfie Durell, whose career in the police had been interrupted by service in the Royal Navy. 'Darky Durell' as he was known when he boxed as a middleweight, due to his swarthy complexion, was employed by the Flying Squad as a detective constable and sergeant for eleven years and was hugely successful, as he was on this occasion.

'We have reason to believe that you're in possession of stolen property', said Sinclair, to which Sweetman replied, 'No, not us. You're wrong there', and Green said, 'We've got nothing.'

They were not being entirely frank; a search revealed that Green was in possession of 308 used stamps, 26 insurance cards, a watch and some cheques valued at £343, and Sweetman had seven cards, 70 stamps and, at his home, another 75 stamps valued at £296.

'We got them from a pub', said Green, while Sweetman told the officers, 'We were going to try to flog them', but when it was discovered that Green had previously worked at the company, the pair were charged with office-breaking. Convicted of receiving at the Middlesex Sessions, both being possessors of four previous convictions, they probably considered themselves fortunate just to receive nine months' imprisonment each.

* * *

Without information – and I mean rock-solid information, not just the odd rumour – the Flying Squad could not have existed. So when Camberley Post Office in London Road was broken into, between 3 and 4 January 1953, and stamps and cash valued at £23,409 10s 4d were stolen, it was not too long before pertinent information sent Sinclair and a Flying Squad team to a caravan at Mixnams Lane, Chertsey, Surrey.

The occupants of the caravan were Eric Charles Davis and Sylvia Mary Taylor; they were in the company of Eric Davis' brother, Victor Edmund. Also in the caravan were part-proceeds of the loot from the Post Office, which amounted to £10,180, as well as a quantity of explosives.

'I'm keeping them for somebody', said Eric, and of Mrs Taylor he added, 'She is not in it.'

Her response was a little contradictory, however, since she told Sinclair, 'I live here. You found the stamps. I had best say nothing. Life means nothing without Eric.'

Victor was rather ebullient when he said, 'Who shopped us? I told Eric we were being watched.'

Four more people were arrested for receiving more of the loot from the Post Office raid, and when the trio appeared at Feltham Magistrates' Court and Victor Davis applied for bail, Sinclair told the court, 'This man was found in possession of a quantity of stamps which are the proceeds of robberies at Post Offices.'

Eager to show brotherly solidarity, Eric Davis shouted, 'You're a lying fucker!' and Mr Frank Bevan, the Clerk of the Court, told him, 'Don't be offensive; it will not improve your case.'

He was right; it didn't. Mrs Taylor had the case against her thrown out, as did three of the others charged with receiving. However, the two brothers were found guilty of the shopbreaking, and at the Old Bailey Eric was sentenced to seven years' imprisonment and brother Victor, to four. William Henry Sellars was convicted of receiving stamps worth £1,158 9s 7d and was sentenced to eighteen months' imprisonment, with the Judge, Mr Commissioner Stewart, telling him in most un-judicial language, 'You knew the stamps were "hot".'

★ ★ ★

Mixnams Lane caravan site appeared to be a hotbed of crime in the 1950s, because that's where three highly dangerous criminals, Geoffrey Joseph, William Henry Purdy and Ernest Walker Robinson, were staying, in between committing a number of offences, including armed robberies. One Flying Squad officer was injured during the men's arrests, although it was not Peter Sinclair who, it appeared, was on reasonably friendly terms with Robinson. On being told that he would be charged with officebreaking and possessing oxy-acetylene cylinders, goggles, pipes and cutters, Robinson replied, 'I'm admitting that one, Peter, but that's all.'

In fact, he didn't. Joseph (a prison escapee) and Purdy appeared before Lord Chief Justice Goddard, who told them, 'I must treat you as two dangerous criminals' and sentenced each of them to fourteen years' imprisonment, but Robinson never made it to the Old Bailey. Suspected of a murder, he was interviewed in prison and suddenly dropped dead. Squad detractors insinuated that he had been frightened to death but not, surely, by the affable Peter Sinclair?

★ ★ ★

Reginald Langton Swann had first transgressed when he was eleven years of age; in the twenty-three years that followed he collected eleven convictions, and when he was released from prison in 1951 he decided to go straight – alas, not for very long. On 31 March 1954 he was seen by the occupants of a Flying Squad car to drive a lorry into an alleyway by the Gem cinema, Southall. Since this happened at 4.30am, the suspicions of the officers were understandably aroused, especially since the lorry had just been pinched from a yard behind the Railway Hotel, Southall. Detective Sergeant William Lewis contacted Sinclair, who then went to cover the entrance of the alleyway; meanwhile, Lewis approached on foot and saw Swann and 17-year-old David Victor Rooke, plus a third man, load the cinema's safe on to the lorry. Lewis and another officer arrested Swann and Rooke; the third man ran off down the alleyway, but although he was pursued by Sinclair he made a clean getaway.

'All right, Guv'nor', said Swann, 'but where did you come from?'

Rooke said, 'I shan't give you any trouble.'

Both were in possession of house-breaking instruments, including a cold chisel which, in Sergeant Lewis' opinion, matched the marks found on the forced office door of the cinema.

When they were told at Norwood Green police station that the safe contained £30 in cash and £20 in stamps, Swann replied, 'All that work for nothing; I thought there would have been five hundred quid in there', and Rooke agreed, saying, 'So did I.'

It appeared to be an open and shut case, but both men denied the charge at Ealing Magistrates' Court. Swann told the magistrates that he wanted bail in order to find certain persons who would clear him of the charge. 'I only know these people by sight', he said, 'and they are my only hope.'

Sergeant Lewis stated that the police were quite prepared to give Swann every assistance in that respect but objected to bail. The magistrates agreed, and Swann was led away, lamenting, 'This is giving me no chance to prove my case!'

But both had a change of heart at the Middlesex Sessions, where they pleaded guilty to breaking into the cinema. Rooke, who had no previous convictions, was remanded for reports, but Swann was sentenced to three years' imprisonment, the witnesses who would prove his innocence unfound, as was the third man, who had managed to outrun Peter Sinclair.

* * *

Information can often tell the police who is going to commit an offence, where and on what day – but not necessarily at what time. That was the case when George Henry Phillips and John O'Connor were kept under observation at the Grapes and the Wagon and Horses public houses in the Uxbridge Road. Information had been received that they were planning to rob employees of Weston Chibnal Ltd's bakery of thousands of pounds in takings.

Detective Sergeant William Lewis saw a jemmy passed to Phillips, who dropped it, then picked it up and put it in his jacket. When the pair were caught, as well as the jemmy, they were found to be in possession of two fire extinguisher pistols, adapted to shoot white powder into the eyes of the victims, together with stocking masks, false number plates, overalls similar to those worn by staff at the bakery, holdalls, gloves and crepe-soled shoes. Unfortunately, two other men escaped.

But this had been the result of observations carried out on a number of successive Saturdays, and when Sinclair was questioned about this at Uxbridge Magistrates' Court on 20 October 1953, he was able to reply, 'Hope springs eternal in the human breast. That's what I felt. I thought I would be there when it happened – and I was!'

CHAPTER 15

'The Velvet Kid'

Detective Sergeant William Lewis has been mentioned on a couple of occasions with Peter Sinclair, and he proved himself adroit at managing Flying Squad ambushes; but prior to that, he distinguished himself during a rather thrilling encounter with a deeply unpleasant character whose younger brother became rather better known than his older sibling.

Niven Scott Craig (known to the popular press as 'The Velvet Kid') was born in 1926 to a respectable family; he was the first member to go off the rails. He was fourteen when he was convicted of store-breaking, and for that, and two other offences, he was sent to an approved school. He and another boy absconded from there, broke into a Home Guard store and stole a rifle, ammunition and a tommy gun and were subsequently picked up in a rowing boat, stating that 'they intended to have a crack at the Germans.' The popular press picked this up and, it being the early stages of the war, the pair were hysterically given hero-like status.

Unfortunately, Niven's youthful impetuosity had dissipated by the time he was old enough to become a member of the Gordon Highlanders, because in 1947 he was court-martialled in Austria for armed robbery and sentenced to five years' imprisonment. He escaped from his escort and carried out four more robberies, holding up Army lorries with a Sten gun and escaping with the vehicles and their contents. By the time he was discharged from the Army in 1950 he had been convicted of military offences on twelve occasions.

In 1952, five masked, armed men broke into a house at Waltham Forest, Essex, terrorized the occupants and escaped with £4 and some ball-point pens. George Albert King was one of the gang; he was arrested shortly afterwards and after receiving a twelve-year sentence, died in prison.

It was quickly discovered that two more of the gang were Niven Craig and Cyril Burney, and they went on the run for six months before a tip-off brought the Flying Squad – in the form of Detective Sergeant Lewis – to an address in Kensington Garden Square. Burney was quickly arrested, then Lewis bashed in a door to find Niven (who had dyed his hair) and a young woman in the room. Niven attempted to pull out a fully loaded and cocked automatic pistol from under his pillow, but Lewis leapt on him and after a violent struggle, Niven was arrested. 'You've got nothing on us', jeered the heroic duo, but it seems the police had.

Appearing at the Old Bailey before Mr Justice Hilbery, Niven acted in an unbelievably cocky way, giving flippant answers to questions; his alibi was that on the night of the robbery he had been with his younger brother, Christopher, and a friend, staying at Wells-next-the-Sea in Norfolk. It was later claimed that when Lewis burst into Niven's room, it was Lewis who had withdrawn the pistol from under the pillow, saying, 'Now, what would a nice boy like you want with a thing like this?' But the young woman who might have authenticated that statement was not called by the defence, because she had convictions for prostitution and that might have muddied the waters for 'a nice boy like that'.

Found guilty of the robbery and possessing a firearm with intent to endanger life, Niven was told by the Judge:

> You are not only cold-blooded, but from my observation of you I have not the least hesitation in saying I believe that you would shoot down any police officer who was attempting to arrest you.

Both men were sentenced to twelve years' imprisonment, and Niven's sang-froid deserted him. 'I am definitely not guilty of this charge, and I shall appeal!' he cried, whereupon Mr Justice Hilbery quietly replied, 'You will find the necessary forms in your cell.'

It begs the question, if both Craig brothers said they were elsewhere on the night of the robbery – and quite obviously, they were not – had Christopher Craig been one of the rest of the gang terrorizing the occupants of 55 Honey Lane, Waltham Forest? That, of course, is speculation, but the fact remains that even before his brother's trial had started, Christopher Craig and another 16-year-old boy had held up an elderly couple in their home at gunpoint; and matching the paucity of the booty stolen from Waltham Forest, the two juvenile gunmen got away with just £4 0s 0d. Eighteen months prior to that, Christopher and another boy had run away from home; they were found in Hove, Sussex and were fined at the local juvenile court, Christopher for being in possession of a .45 Webley revolver, his companion for possessing a Luger automatic.

It's often said that following Niven's conviction at the Old Bailey, a detective was heard to say, 'At least we've put that bastard away for a few years', and that this was the catalyst that sent Christopher and his friend, Derek Bentley, older but with learning difficulties, on a burglary expedition three days later with Christopher in possession of a sawn-off .455 Eley service revolver. It would culminate in Christopher shooting one police officer dead, wounding a second and firing at a number of others; Bentley was hanged, Christopher, the younger of the two, was not.[1]

But it was unlikely that the injudicious remark had sparked off Christopher's rampage; he was bad before his brother's sentence, bad afterwards and had already possessed somewhere between forty and fifty firearms. After his arrest, 138 rounds of ammunition and the sawn-off end of the murder weapon were found at his home address.

Well, so much for the younger Craig, a poisonous, gun-toting, police-hating murderer, although later to become an engineer and a reformed character. What of his brother?

★ ★ ★

'I cannot be interrupted; there is not time . . . I am sorry. I cannot give way. I must not be interrupted or I might not say what I wish to say.'

What was it that Miss Alice Martha Bacon CBE, PC, MP (later Baroness Bacon), the Labour Government's Minister of State at the Home Office, wished to express to Parliament on 29 March 1965 and, at the same time, shut down the protestations of Brigadier Terence Clarke?

It was the matter of Niven Scott Craig, that's what, who was lamenting the amount of time he had spent inside. Having been sentenced to twelve years' imprisonment in 1952, surely by 1965 he should have been released? Let's see why not.

In 1960, Niven was put on a hostel scheme; under Home Office policy, prisoners might be released during the day to go to work unsupervised before returning to prison in the evening, in order that they might become rehabilitated into society. In fact, Niven went nowhere near the Islington Garage which had been assigned to him as a place of work, nor was the garage owner under any obligation to inform Niven's parole officer that he had failed to turn up.

On Sunday, 30 October 1960, there was a tremendous explosion at the premises of West's the butcher in Islington and

---

1 For further details of this case, see *Death on the Beat: Police Officers Killed in the Line of Duty*, Pen & Sword Books, 2012

four men dashed out of the shop with the contents of the blown safe – £26 16s 11d – leaving their woman accomplice frantically but unsuccessfully trying to catch up with her fellow bandits' car. She was arrested, and a trail of clues led the detectives to Niven Craig, who had been granted weekend leave. He had, he said, been staying with his parents, but at the Inner London Sessions he was disbelieved, with the Chairman, Reggie Seaton, warning him, 'You will find yourself qualifying for preventative detention'; he was sentenced to five years' imprisonment.

So was Niven adhering to his story that he was elsewhere at the time of the safe-blowing, in the same way that he was supposed to have been at Wells-next-the-Sea instead of Waltham Abbey at the time of the robbery? It appeared not. He took the blame for the safe-blowing in a letter to the Inner London Sessions, when his 20-year-old housewife look-out (who coincidentally lived in Kensington Garden Square, where Niven had been arrested in 1952) appeared there the following month and was placed on probation for two years.

In June 1961, Niven was one of ten prisoners who escaped from Wandsworth Prison; he was caught two months later in Ipswich, Suffolk and was one of three men to be charged with assault with intent to rob a night-watchman, as well as possession of two sticks of gelignite and detonators. On 20 October 1961, at Ipswich Assizes, Mr Justice Havers described him as 'a menace to society' and jailed him for seven years, consecutive to his present sentence. So by the age of thirty-five Niven had been sentenced to a total of twenty-nine years' imprisonment – excluding approved school, of course.

So what was it that had got up Brigadier Clarke's hooter in Parliament on 29 March 1965? Simply this. Originally, Craig had spent nine months on the hostel scheme, although it was meant for prisoners serving the last six months of their sentence. Now, however, having breached the conditions of the scheme and having been sentenced to a further twelve years' imprisonment, with almost four and a half years left to serve, he had, once more, been placed on the hostel scheme.

Niven had petitioned the Home Office about his case, had solicited the aid of the Lords Stonham (who contributed to a number of penal reforms) and Longford (who was a consummate drip), and now the cudgels had been taken up by Miss Bacon, who told the house that Niven was 'determined to go straight'.

What was not mentioned regarding Craig's prison escape – either because Miss Bacon was unaware of it, or if she was, because she wanted no further details to be provided, hence her braying,

'No interruptions' – was that it had been a highly sophisticated affair. A mock fight had been staged between prisoners in the mailbag shop. When warders moved in to break it up they were overpowered, gagged and tied up. Other prisoners handed the ten escapees ropes for them to lower themselves down from the workshop and into the yard. Posing as a working party, they marched past the prison's married quarters and reached the prison wall, where other ropes to aid their escape had been secreted for them. They scaled the wall and dropped into Magdalen Road, where a car provided by an ex-prisoner was waiting.

Not that that really mattered. Despite his earliest release date being 1969, Niven was released on parole in January 1966.

In 1971, Niven was one of four people arrested for conspiracy to break into a flat, theft, dishonest handling and malicious damage, but the case fizzled out.

And then, in the 1980s, I feel sure I remember walking past Upminster police station and seeing on the notice board outside a copy of *Police Gazette* which stated that Niven Craig was wanted for attempted murder at Waltham Abbey. This struck me as strange, knowing that he had been convicted for the robbery at Waltham Abbey in 1952 and now finding out that he was now wanted for a rather more serious offence in the same area all those years later.

So, forty years later, I spoke to a local crime historian who lives in Waltham Abbey, searched newspapers and requested assistance from detectives who policed the area at that time: nothing.

Was this sighting of a Niven Craig wanted poster a figment of my imagination? Resourcefulness was something I was often hurtfully accused of while I was in the witness box at the Old Bailey. As I make the transition from old fart into dotage, I do wonder . . .

Chapter 16

The Safe-blowing at Martin's Bank

During the weekend of 5/6 February 1955, a rather spectacular raid was carried out at Martin's Bank, 23 St James' Street, Mayfair. Decorators had been at work next door at No. 23a so that the premises might be leased to a firm of solicitors, but they finished work at noon on the Saturday; when the tradesmen left, and unknown to them, one of the persons responsible for the office-breaking was left behind, locked in.

Glass in a lavatory window had been smashed and iron bars bent aside to permit the gang access to the bank's basement. An attempt to gain entry to the bank itself via the ventilator system was unsuccessful, and therefore a more daring and certainly more direct access was achieved; using gelignite, the gang blasted a hole through the 22-inch wall. Next, the 12-inch thick door of the bank's safe was blown off its hinges at 4 o'clock on the Sunday morning. That was heard by the night-watchman tasked with guarding the next premises but one, but having satisfied himself that his building was intact, he went back to bed.

It was left to the bank's cleaner, on the morning of Monday, 7 February, to discover what was described as 'considerable chaos'.

A total of £20,438 0s 1d had been stolen, which included foreign currency valued at £166. The money included £4,000 in new £5 notes, £4,000 in new £1 notes and £1,000 in new ten shilling notes; but however it was compiled, it still represented the equivalent of £540,000 at today's value.

The matter was reported to West End Central police station and that was unfortunate – to the crooks, that is – for two reasons.

First, West End Central was part of the Metropolitan Police's 'C' Division and therefore came under the umbrella of No. 1 District Headquarters. The man in charge was Detective Chief Superintendent Ted Greeno MBE – one of 'The Big Five', a title he would hold for fourteen years – and he had only moved into his office one month previously. Greeno was now fifty-four years of age but he was no deskbound warrior and he had an encyclopaedic knowledge of criminals, accrued after thirty-four years of concentrated police work. What's more, Greeno was itching for a little action.

The second reason was that the senior CID officer at West End Central was Detective Superintendent Bert 'Iron Man' Sparks. At half an inch under six feet two, Sparks, as his nickname suggested, was as hard as nails and completely fearless; six years previously, as a 42-year-old detective inspector, he had been commended by Tottenham Magistrates' Court, the Middlesex Sessions and the commissioner for assisting in the arrest, while off duty, of three persons, one of whom was in possession of a loaded firearm.

This was Sparks' fourth posting to 'C' Division; he knew the area and the criminals – several of whom acted as informants – like the back of his hand.

The Bank was visited by Greeno and Sparks, and a team of officers was deputed to obtain statements from the staff – and to try to determine if any of them could have been inside agents to the breaking. A car used to transport the loot, stolen 3–4 days prior to the raid and fitted with false plates, was found abandoned. The basement – £1 notes were still scattered on the steps down to that area – was given over to Detective Superintendent George Salter and members of the Forensic Science laboratory. That left the two senior officers free to determine who was responsible?.

In fact, it did not take long. There were very few criminals capable of such a sophisticated safe-blowing with gelignite. They could be traced through the 'Method Index' at the Yard's Criminal Records' Office and their informants; Alfie Hinds could have been a contender, had not Sparks arrested him some eighteen months earlier for a safe-blowing at Maple & Co., a furniture shop in Tottenham Court Road – he was now serving a sentence of twelve years' preventative detention. Then, of course, there were George 'Taters' Chatham and Bob Melrose, both very serious candidates, but as we will shortly discover, that dastardly duo had both been weighed off with ten years' preventative detention two months previously. (a) Were they both locked up? (b) Had either escaped? (a) Yes they were and (b) No they hadn't – so that was them out of the frame.

Leonard Minchingdon, otherwise known as 'Johnny the Boche' and also 'The King of the Twirls' certainly fitted the profile, but he was still serving a five-year sentence for office-breaking with the use of explosives.

But wait a minute; what about Eddie Chapman, the same safe-blowing Eddie Chapman who had slipped through Greeno's fingers after he turned double-agent during the war? What a coup that would be for Greeno! But no. Chapman was impressively alibied by Billy Hill, the self-proclaimed 'Boss of Britain's Underworld', another of Greeno's arch-enemies.

Who else? Well, only one really, and that was 43-year-old Alfie Fraser, not helped by the fact that his nickname was 'King of the Jelly Boys' and whose criminal career had commenced in 1927. He had seventeen previous convictions, since 1939 had been convicted on four occasions of house-breaking – these were interspersed with four occasions of deserting from military service – and in May 1948 had been sentenced to three years' penal servitude for house-breaking. In October 1952, for attempting to force open an office safe at the Hounslow Labour Exchange by the means of explosives, he was sentenced to three years' imprisonment at Middlesex Sessions and had been released from prison in October 1954.

Sparks and Greeno put their informants to work and discovered that just prior to the raid, Fraser had been penniless; now he was simply splashing money about, purchasing a £1,140 Daimler and a greengrocery business in Paddington. What was more, he was associating with another well known underworld character.

This was Howard Henry Lewis, who at twenty-nine years of age had cobbled together an impressive criminal record: he had been convicted on eleven previous occasions since the age of seventeen. In January 1943, Lewis had enlisted in the Royal Navy, and his criminal career got underway six months later when he deserted. He had been convicted on four occasions for house- or office-breaking and had been to Borstal, prison and corrective training; coincidentally, like Fraser, he had been released from prison the previous October.

Lewis, too, had been in debt prior to the raid. He had been lodging with his sister and borrowing money from her on a weekly basis, but now he had been enjoying a spending spree in very smart hotels from Leicester to Torquay, as well as putting down a deposit on a new Riley Pathfinder.

It was this vehicle that he was affixing an AA badge to, parked outside his flat at Heslop Court, Balham, when Greeno and Sparks arrived two weeks after the offence. Lewis was told that he was being detained in connection with the raid and that there was a warrant to search his property.

'All right', he replied. 'You'll find nothing there, and furthermore, I don't know what you're talking about.'

But there was something there. In the horn of an old-style gramophone they found fifty-five £5 notes, eighteen £1 notes and seventy-seven ten shilling notes. These notes were traced back to the bank. A pair of trousers was found under Lewis' bed in a suitcase. They were still damp from having been washed, and the turn-ups had been unpicked to rid them of any fragments that might have been blown into them from the blast. Not, however, very successfully.

Fraser was next paid a visit at his home at Fordwych Road, Cricklewood. On being informed of the nature of their business, he told the officers, 'Some bastard's been chatting. Have the others been tumbled?'

Upon being searched, one hundred £5 notes, three bundles of £1 notes totalling £291 and one ten shilling note was found on his person. Asked for an explanation regarding this windfall, he stated, 'An old friend of mine, Percy Horne, gave it to me. I'm setting up in business as a greengrocer.'

A piece of wire exactly similar to some found at the scene was discovered at Fraser's address, as was a briefcase containing a steel cosh; in his diary were Lewis' and Horne's telephone numbers and a newspaper clipping about the raid. It was headed, '£20,000 Gang Picnic in Bank', to which Fraser, who obviously objected to the term 'Picnic', had added 'bollocks'.

The officers also took possession of a holdall, and when Fraser saw the briefcase into which the detectives had put the money seized from Lewis, it prompted him to say, 'That bastard Lewis has been talking' – an utterance he later loudly denied in court.

Next stop was 40-year-old Percy Horne's address in the rather prestigious area of Highlever Road, Kensington, where the timber merchant initially denied knowing either Lewis or Fraser. He told Detective Inspector John Pattison, 'I don't know anything about any crime or any money.'

That changed when there was a telephone call from a woman who asked, 'What shall I do with the money?'

Pattison snatched the receiver and said, 'Is that Mrs Fraser?'

'Yes', replied the caller. 'Who's that?'

High time for Horne to change his mind.

'That was his wife. She's worried; she's told me her husband has been arrested. I felt sorry for him. I've changed a lot of money for him. I can guess it was the Martin's Bank job, but I give you my word I have had nothing to do with it. I'm a rich man. What do I want to blow up banks for?'

He took the officers down to the basement where, after shifting a considerable amount of coal, he unearthed a biscuit tin which contained a block of 500 £1 notes, two bundles of £1

The Great Ones

Above left: DCS Ted Greeno MBE

Above right: DCS Jack Capstick

Below left: D/Supt Bob Fabian KPM

Below right: DCS Peter Beveridge MBE

Above: 'Peter the Plotter's' country retreat (after being searched!)

And the men who caught him

Below left: DCS Bob Lee

Below right: D/Supt Bob Higgins

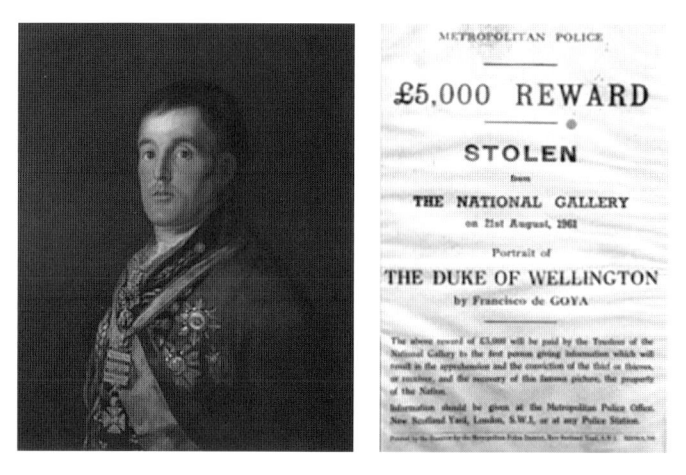

Above left: The stolen Duke of Wellington painting

Above right: . . . and the reward for its recovery

Above: Kempton Cannon Bunton

Right: . . . and the barrister who defended him, Jeremy Hutchinson QC

DCS Greeno and D/Supt Sparks leaving Martin's Bank

Above: Commissioner Sir Joseph Simpson KBE

Left: DAC Ernie Millen CBE

'The Terrible Twins'

Above: D/Supt Peter Vibart QPM and DCS Tommy Butler MBE

Below left: Patsy Fleming

Below right: Butler escorting escaped prisoner Alfie Hinds

Climbers and safe-blowers

Above left: George 'Taters' Chatham

Above right: Eddie Chapman

Below: Raymond 'The Cat' Jones

Above left: D/Supt George Cornish

Above right: Dennis 'Australian Denny' Harris

Right: DCI Fred Sharpe

Left: An old-fashioned way of safe-breaking

Below: . . . and a safe opened with explosives

notes containing respectively £314 and £163, and sixty-one £5 notes: altogether, £1,282.

By the time the trio stood in the dock at the Old Bailey, an impressive amount of evidence had accrued. The deposit that Lewis had put down on the Riley was paid with 521 £1 notes which were traced to the bank, as were some of the ten shilling notes found in his gramophone. The money found in Horne's biscuit tin was similarly traced. None of the money in Fraser's possession had come from the bank, not surprisingly, because it had been changed by Horne. But there was other evidence against Fraser. Ballast, dust, potassium alum and paint were discovered inside the holdall found at his house, and on some of Lewis' clothing. The fragments matched the debris found at the scene, and the minute amount of paint was identical to the six layers and laminations used on the safe door. The crystals of potassium alum came from the fireproof packing inserted between the steel plates of the blown safe door. Found in one of Lewis' gloves were tiny slivers of glass which linked him with the scene; they were found to be of exactly the same density and refraction as glass in the window that had been smashed. The same slivers of glass were found in one of Fraser's shoes.

John Ernest Wilson, an employee of the bank, was in the habit of writing '100' in red ink when twenty £5 notes were bundled up – just like the figure jotted down on some of the defendants' £5 notes.

On the directions of the Common Serjeant, Sir Anthony Hawke, Horne was acquitted of participating in the safe-blowing, and the jury were unable to agree on the receiving charge. He was held over to the next sessions, and after a second jury was unable to agree on their verdict, a third jury was sworn in, whereupon the prosecution threw in the towel on 24 June 1955 and Horne walked free.

But back on 13 May, both Lewis and Fraser were found guilty of the safe-blowing. Having heard details of their lamentable pasts, with Sparks referring to Fraser as 'a persistent criminal and a very dangerous man', his barrister implored the Judge not to 'smash him' by imposing a sentence of preventative detention 'which would be socially, if not actually, a sentence of death for him.'

But the Judge thought otherwise, telling Fraser:

> No court has the slightest wish ever to pass a sentence which will smash a man – to use an expression employed by your counsel – but I cannot lose sight of the fact that this is your

eighteenth appearance before a court charged with crimes of various sorts.

Adding that his last conviction was attempting to force open a safe by means of explosives and that within months of his release he had been found guilty of a crime that was 'well planned and carefully organized', the Judge sentenced Fraser to ten years' preventative detention.

To Lewis the Judge said:

> You are fourteen years younger than Fraser but this is your twelfth appearance in a court and three times you have been convicted of various offences of breaking. Your last offence is about as serious an example of that form of crime as can well be contemplated. But as you are only twenty-nine, there may be some hope for you and sentence will be mitigated.

He then sentenced Lewis to seven years' imprisonment, to be followed by twelve months' police supervision.

It was a clever police investigation, but the fact remained that there was still about £18,000 missing and it was never recovered, although Martin's Bank had a good try. In 1957, they sued Fraser for the missing money. He defended himself, claiming that the money found on him was a loan from the acquitted Percy Horne and that the police had framed him because of his criminal past. But the jury found in favour of Martin's Bank, saying that Fraser owed them £19,602. He had no assets to pay, but the costs of the trial were awarded against him.

Alfie Fraser not only survived his ten-year sentence, he was fit enough to participate with Charlie Richardson in witness intimidation during the famed 'Torture Trial' in 1966; for conspiracy to pervert the course of justice, Fraser was jailed for two years.

It was a forlorn hope that the Judge had expressed in respect of Lewis; practically as soon as he was released, and before the promised police supervision could take effect, in November 1960 he was arrested for two cases of house-breaking at Ramsgate and Faversham, where property valued at £560 was stolen. In January 1961, at East Kent Quarter Sessions, he was sentenced to seven years' preventative detention. Two months later, he escaped from Wandsworth Prison; recaptured, he escaped once more, this time from Chelmsford Prison, two years later.

Drink became a problem in his life; in 1970 he was convicted of drink-driving, and six years later, he was acquitted of the same offence at Warwick Crown Court.

When he appeared at the same court, one year later, again charged with drink-driving, he tried to be clever once too often. He sent a blood sample to an analyst which revealed 34 milligrams of alcohol in 100 millilitres of blood. Unfortunately, the sample the police had obtained from him had registered 152 mgs; and since the legal limit was 80mg, he not only faced the drink-drive charge, but was also prosecuted for attempting to pervert the course of justice. Fortunately for him, the latter charge was allowed to remain on the file, and fining him £500 and disqualifying him from driving for three years, the judge remarked that he was fortunate not to have been standing before the court on a charge of perjury.

What, Howard Henry Lewis accused of telling lies? On oath? The very idea!

CHAPTER 17

'Peter the Plotter'

When the newspapers used to report that in relation to a particular crime wave an Assistant Commissioner at Scotland Yard had barked to his subordinates, 'This will stop – make this your No. 1 assignment!', and scores of grim-faced 'tecs had rushed out to do his bidding, it was normally only *after* arrests had been made that the public were made aware of his orders. He would then be credited with an immense number of brownie points, and readers would marvel at the top cop's acumen, acquired after years of thief-taking; or that would be the general impression.

Between 1952 and 1954, London and the Home Counties were hit by a series of burglaries. Warehouses, jewellers' safes and the homes of the wealthy were targeted; security measures and burglar alarms were sidestepped; and the whereabouts of master keys were made known to the perpetrators.

So in respect of this crime wave, did the newly appointed Assistant Commissioner (Crime), Sir Richard Leofric Jackson CBE, utter those words – or something like them?

Well – no, probably not. Sir Richard had entered the Metropolitan Police in 1953 with the rank of Assistant Commissioner. No gimlet-eyed thief-taker, he – his previous service had been on the staff of the Director of Public Prosecutions and he possibly didn't know what time of day it was. Certainly, he made no mention of such an announcement in his memoirs; in fact, he didn't mention the case at all.

But it must now be described, because it involved both some of London's top criminals and Scotland Yard's top detectives. This is what happened.

* * *

Gordon Simpson was a thoroughly decent insurance broker, earning £15 per week and living with his Viennese wife at Holmedale Road, West Hampstead; additionally, he had a pretty good war record. He had made two bids to escape whilst a prisoner of war in Germany and had helped many others to do the same. In fact, one of his fellow inmates was a former CID officer who would later say that Simpson had put up 'a very gallant performance'.

Perhaps by chance, Simpson's wife fell into conversation with a woman she had met in Hyde Park, and the two became friends. Simpson was then introduced to the woman's boyfriend, and when he discovered Simpson's profession he made him an offer which the insurance broker found impossible to refuse, and the latter started to reveal details of confidential insurance documents to which he had access.

The woman's boyfriend was known to the police and the underworld as 'Peter the Plotter', although the police were unaware that his real name was Harold Lough White.

Tall, balding, 46-year-old White, who habitually wore horn-rimmed glasses, was a former public school boy and the son of a doctor, and he had a chequered past.

He had first come to notice in 1936 in a quite unremarkable manner, having allegedly released a rabbit which had been caught in a trap, which he then deliberately smashed. The gamekeeper, seeing what White had done and also observing that he was in possession of a firearm, gave him a clump. Both appeared in court; White had the charge of trespassing in search of game chucked out but was fined 20s 0d for malicious damage to the trap; and the gamekeeper was fined 5s 0d for whacking White.

White's second court appearance was rather more serious: in July 1939, for conspiracy to defraud, he was imprisoned for nine months.

The next matter would have been even more serious, had it been proved. In December 1945, the bonded warehouse of Messrs Boord & Son Ltd. in Lillie Road, Hammersmith was broken into and 864 bottles of gin were stolen. Five days later, a lorry driver saw White's car outside Bates' Club, in Mayfair's Tilney Street. Men were taking cases of the gin into the premises, and White, of Adams House, South Audley Street was arrested. But not only was the warehouse-breaking charge dropped, the officer in charge of the case also informed the magistrate at West London Court that he was quite satisfied that White did not even know the gin had been stolen.

Well, well, Detective Inspector Norman was a really sympathetic and understanding officer!

White had told him – or perhaps Norman had advised White to say – that he believed it was a matter of a licensee disposing of his stock without a permit. Therefore, instead of incurring the penalties of warehouse-breaking or receiving stolen goods – both of which carried maximum penalties of fourteen years' imprisonment – what White had apparently done amounted to no more than a misdemeanour. The magistrate remarked that had it not been for White's previous conviction, he would have imposed a fine. But because that custodial sentence was on the record, he sentenced him to six weeks' imprisonment.

White, now living at Drayton Court, Kensington, next appeared at West London Court on 8 October 1949, when he pleaded guilty to being concerned in the illegal export of two aircraft. The Magistrate, Mr E. R. Guest, informed him that it involved merchandise 'which it was not desirable to export at a moment of political temperature' and sentenced him to twelve months' imprisonment, also fining him £250 with 100 guineas costs.

By the time police were investigating the series of high-value burglaries, White had acquired the reputation of being a Mayfair playboy, a man-about-town. He was living in a luxurious flat at Thorney Court, Chelsea and he owned not only a Cadillac, but also a Bentley and a Jaguar. Women found his company irresistible, especially when it was accompanied with a voyage around the Mediterranean in his yacht. Additionally, there were trips to be had in his private aeroplane, which he kept on an airfield at Abingdon, near Oxford, or visits to his four-bedroom country cottage in Buckinghamshire. Expensively tailored, White mingled with London's high society and abjured the seedy haunts of criminals.

He was one smooth operator. At a time when a detective sergeant (second-class) was earning £11 4s 3d per week, White's nefarious activities were bringing him in a staggering £15,000 per year.

Minstead Lodge, Lyndhurst in Hampshire, the home of Edith, Lady Congleton, was broken into on the night of 22/23 June 1954, and a diamond brooch, a pair of pearl and diamond earrings and other items of jewellery, valued at £3,461, were stolen.

A premises belonging to Nibs (1929) Ltd, a factory at Westmeads Road, Whitstable, Kent, was also broken into and an unsuccessful attempt made to cut open the safe.

Miss Edith Ellen Harris, a postmistress, was woken in her bed on 16 July and robbed of two bunches of keys fitting the Post Office in the City of London's Eldon Street. While two men stood guard over Miss Harris, others entered the Post Office and helped themselves to £1,256 10s 0d cash plus books of postage stamps, postal orders, insurance stamps and savings certificates valued at £32,747 3s 7d.

The head of the Flying Squad, Detective Chief Superintendent Bob Lee, took charge of the operation. He had spent many years at the Yard's Criminal Records Office (CRO) and had great faith in the 'Method Index', which recorded the traits of criminals when committing specific offences. It was a help, no doubt about it, but there was nothing to beat what the Special Air Service Regiment refer to as 'The Mark One Human Eyeball'.

So the Squad officers needed a break, and they got one on the night of 17 July 1954, when Police Constable Ronald Gibbs was patrolling Heddon Street, Mayfair. At about 11.30pm he was stopped by White, who asked, 'Can you give me six pennies for a sixpence? I want to make a telephone call.' PC Gibbs was unable to oblige him, apologized and saw White get into a Jaguar and drive off. He then forgot the incident until the following morning, when he was rudely awakened from his slumbers in the police section house and told to report to West End Central police station – pronto!

★ ★ ★

The lavatory window of Messrs H.A. Byworth's at 19-21 Heddon Street had inadvertently been left open when the premises closed for business on Friday, 16 July, and the following night, one of White's gang climbed up a knotted rope, entered through the insecure window and let in the others, who brought in explosives and safe-cutting equipment through a side door.

But while White was awaiting entry to the premises he saw PC Gibbs strolling towards him, and rather than have the officer speculate about what he might be doing there, since Heddon Street was a deserted and very short thoroughfare, less than 100 yards in length, he made his unnecessary request for change.

After the officer had left the area, the safe door was blown off its hinges at the premises and gold leaf, platinum, a diamond tiara and other items of jewellery, valued at £37,000, were stolen. An unsuccessful attempt had been made to blow another safe, and fuse wires had been left, along with some fragments of gelignite, and a portion of the rope used to gain entry was hanging from the guttering.

As soon as the report of the breaking landed on Bob Lee's desk, he shot round to 'C' Division's headquarters at West End Central police station. Detective Superintendent Bert 'Iron Man' Sparks was there; he had already been to Byworth's to view what he described as 'the complete disorder' and had called in the night duty patrols – hence PC Gibbs being in attendance.

Lee wanted to know everything – no matter how slight or inconsequential – that had happened while they were on duty the previous night. PC Gibbs gave a good description of the man who had approached him; he even remembered he was wearing a green-coloured overcoat with a small tear in it. He also recalled that the Jaguar that White had got into had a registration number that ended with a '7'. Another constable recalled seeing an impressive-looking Jaguar that night near the location of the safe-blowing – that one had a '7' in the registration number, as well as a 'D'. Then there was the commissionaire at the nearby Albany Club who that evening at about 9.30pm had noticed what he referred to as 'an unusual type of Jaguar' and made a mental note of the registration number. Two men had got out of it and disappeared; two hours later, they returned and drove off.

A search was made of Jaguar registration numbers similar to those recalled by the witnesses and it produced a car belonging to White. Could he be the gang leader? It seemed more than a possibility, and a surveillance operation was carried out on White's Mayfair flat and his country cottage. In the meantime, Lee's men were collating all the crimes of which White and his gang were suspected. It appeared clear that these raids had been the result of inside information, and the backgrounds of servants, night-watchmen and other completely innocent people were scrutinized.

Then, for the second time, White gave himself away, and once more it was a telephone call – a real one, this time – that was the cause. Feeling, possibly with some justification, that the calls at his flat were being intercepted, White entered Piccadilly Circus Underground Station and went to a telephone kiosk; he was followed by a Squad officer, who entered the next booth. White experienced difficulty in dialling the number he required so he spoke to the operator; it was a poor connection and he had to shout out the number he wanted – HAM 7354 – so the detective in the adjoining kiosk was able to jot down the telephone number and the name of the man to whom he was speaking. This was Gordon Simpson, employed as an insurance agent by A.R. Mountain & Sons, Lloyd's underwriters, who covered all of the properties which had been targeted. Now the case was coming together.

There were two prime suspects in the Squad's sights. But neither White nor Simpson had the expertise to have used explosives during the burglaries. A careful trawl through CRO's Method Index, based on the way the safes had been attacked, threw up two possibles. They were presumptions – but pretty certain ones.

As is the case with so many investigations, the problem was whether to strike right away or postpone matters in the hope of gathering more evidence? There's no easy answer to that one, so the Squad officers, using their experience, decided to go in hard straight away, and after obtaining search warrants, the following Sunday, 25 July, the first of four addresses was hit.

This was 1 Lichfield Road, Kew, and an informant had told the Squad that one of the residents there was none other than George 'Taters' Chatham.

* * *

After being released from penal servitude following his bruising encounter with Ted Greeno, Chatham had continued his exploits. On 17 April 1948, after placing a ladder against a first floor window of the Victoria and Albert Museum, he released the catch and, smashing the case containing the Duke of Wellington's ceremonial swords studded with emeralds and diamonds, grabbed the weapons, which today would be valued at £6 million, and disappeared.

He came unstuck after he had broken into 20 Wilton Street in late 1948 and stolen jewellery and a mink coat, valued at £1,819, which he placed in a brown paper parcel and left – just as he had done ten years earlier – in a station cloakroom, this time at Walham Green. He had then returned to Wilton Street, this time visiting No. 17, and with the aid of a jemmy, putty knife, torch and pair of gloves was just about to relieve the occupier, Mr Bradbury-Wilmott, of some of his property when, alerted to sounds coming from his bedroom, the householder surprised Chatham, who was detained after a struggle and on 21 January 1949 at the London Sessions was sentenced to three years' penal servitude.

Following his release, he replicated his success at the Victoria and Albert Museum on 11 June 1951 by propping a ladder against a first floor window at the National Maritime Museum, Greenwich and forcing the window. At 1.57am the alarm signalled that a showcase containing a plume with 300 diamonds on Nelson's hat had been smashed and the contents had vanished – so had Chatham.

The proceeds kept Chatham going until 21 May 1952, when he was one of eight masked man who ambushed a Post Office van in Eastcastle Street and, after savagely coshing the van's occupants, made off with £287,000. The plan had been masterminded by gang boss Billy Hill, and Chatham's share was

£15,000. An inveterate gambler, Chatham lost the lot on the tables at one of Hill's clubs and thinking – probably correctly – that it had been a crooked game, decided to get his own back by breaking open Hill's safe. Hill, being 'the biter bit', took a suitable revenge by giving Chatham a thoroughly good hiding. Since Hill was normally an aficionado of the open razor, there were many who thought Chatham had got off extremely lightly.

It was necessary for Chatham to replenish his funds, but in an effort to do so he overstretched himself when he fell 50ft while attempting to break into the home of the Hon. Mrs Gerald Legge. Making a remarkable recovery after six weeks' recuperation, he was more successful in a second attempt at the same premises and got away with jewellery valued at £50,000.

As in the two museum breakings and the Eastcastle Street robbery, Chatham got away scot-free from the theft of the honourable lady's jewels. However, he was arrested for office-breaking and assault and in August 1953 at the London Sessions, was sentenced to six years' imprisonment. He escaped but was arrested on 2 April 1954; on 29 May, while he was on remand at Brixton Prison, he got into the compound by using a duplicate key. He was in company with a highly dangerous prisoner, Geoffrey Joseph (later to be sentenced to fourteen years' preventative detention for robbery with violence), and together they scaled the scaffolding where building work was in progress to repair a damaged rear wall. A workman seized one of them by the ankle but had to release his grip after his fingers were kicked, and the two men disappeared into the crowds of Saturday afternoon Brixton Hill shoppers.

* * *

Chatham came quietly and when providing his particulars, the 42-year-old burglar gave his occupation as 'retired', but nobody believed him.

'It isn't for me to talk; you'll have to prove everything. I'm in dead trouble now, I know. All right. How did you come to be here? I suppose this is it', he said, as police found a 2ft piece of rope which would later prove to be identical in type to the one used in the breaking at Byworth's, as well as having identically tied knots. He added, 'I'd like to know who told you.' In addition, ballast from the Byworth's safe was found in Chatham's shoes, in the turn-ups of his trousers and even in the hair cream in the teeth of his comb.

But if Chatham's arrest was without incident, not so Harold White's. The police, led by Bob Lee, burst into his bedroom at his Thorney Court flat, and White, who like Chatham was relaxing in bed, decided to make a fight of it. After all, he had a lot to lose and who had he had to contend with before? A gamekeeper, Board of Trade officials and a distinctly dodgy detective inspector. This was his first confrontation with the Flying Squad, and although the Squad's deputy head, Detective Superintendent Bob Higgins, had celebrated his fifty-first birthday three days earlier, he had several years experience as a Squad officer and was a pretty tough cookie. Rising to the occasion, he dived full-length on to White and a battle royal ensued, with the bed-sheets being torn, until White emerged the loser. He had done his best to hide the confidential Insurance Survey Book which he had obtained from Simpson. Apart from the green coat with the torn sleeve which had been noticed by PC Gibbs – who later picked him out on an identification parade – there was White's wallet; it contained three insurance slips which he would later claim were planted.

Told that he was being arrested for the burglary at Byworth's, White replied, 'What are you trying to frame up for me? You'll have a difficult job to prove anything. I was not near Heddon Street last weekend; I don't even know where it is.'

But the evidence began to mount up when police searched his garage at Petersham Place in Kensington. It was fitted with a periscope so that anyone approaching could be observed unseen; a similar item was found at his country retreat. In the garage was his supercharged Cadillac, and in a briefcase were details of safes and burglar alarms which he had acquired from safe-makers on the pretext of wishing to install a safe in his office; in this fashion he had acquired details of all the safes to be attacked. Then there was the old peoples' home at Hindhead run by a relative of White's. In the garage was oxy-acetylene equipment which was able to cut through steel eight inches thick. There was a 2ft transformer, capable of increasing a normal mains voltage from 200–250 up to 750. In this way, an office's power supply could be boosted to run such equipment. That transformer fitted neatly into the boot of the Cadillac; and it was a Cadillac that police patrols had been unable to catch up with following several of the burglaries. There was a half-ton oxygen cylinder, a welder's helmet and a metal shield for protection against the heat, as well as gloves, an apron, fuses, plugs, cables and drills.

Two kitbags were found. One contained half a pearl which matched exactly the other half found in one of White's cars – it was identified as part of the loot from Byworth's – plus dust from that company's safe. The other bag contained sawdust sweepings, plastic fragments and melted metal strands. This was found to have come from Nibs (1929) Ltd, the factory at Whitstable from which the gang were seeking to steal gold, necessary for pen-nib manufacture, worth £100,000. The heat from the safe-breaking cutter had been so intense that the plastic covering the shield had burst into flames, the metal around the strong-room had fused and the gang had left empty-handed. Items taken from the factory exactly matched those found in the kitbag.

Also found was a cystoscope, an instrument used by gynaecologists; White would later say that he used it for inspecting the interiors of gearboxes. In fact, once a hole had been drilled into a safe, White used it for locating the position of the door bolts.

And that instrument was just one of the 125 items found in White's possession.

The other explosives expert was 40-year-old Robert Melrose, who often referred to himself as Robert Melrose Dickson. He had nine previous convictions and had spent nineteen years in prison. In July 1949 at Cardiff Assizes he had been acquitted of safe-blowing but convicted of receiving stolen petrol coupons and sentenced to ten years' preventative detention. The Court of Criminal Appeal had reduced this to seven years' imprisonment, and he was released just in time to join White's gang.

Arrested at a flat in Cadogan Gardens, Sloane Square, Melrose said, 'I don't know where I was last weekend. I suppose you know; anyway, I was not near Heddon Street.' After a little reflection, following the discovery of Simpson's telephone number in his wallet, plus eighty-two £5 notes and forty-one £1 notes – these, he insisted he had won at the races the previous day – he added, 'Have you got much against me? Every fucking blowing job is down to me. How is it the Guv'nor is so long? I must be in trouble, him coming out on a Sunday morning. Has he gone over to Kew for George?'

It appeared police did have much against him; dust from Byworth's was found in his shoes, and in the turn-ups of his trousers tiny particles of fused metal were discovered, identical to that found in the strong-room at Nibs (1929) Ltd.

Simpson was leaving his house as the police arrived. Hidden under a mattress were 140 insurance slips relating to various properties, some of which had been broken into with others marked out for future attention, as were twenty-four more in a coat in the wardrobe. One of the slips described in detail how to get into a cashier's office and bore the phrases, 'always a monkey' (£500), 'big old peter' (safe) and 'light 230 volts'. Hidden away were thirty-nine £5 notes.

Simpson said that he had kept the slips in connection with his work and told the officers, 'I've been mixing with the wrong people. I do know a man named George, but I don't know anything about blowing.' Later, before being put up for identification, he said, 'How can I open up to you? It's too involved, there are too many in it. I'd rather take my chance with the others.'

Different charges were brought against the men: breaking into Byworth's and Nibs (1929) Ltd; White was also charged with receiving the Lloyd's confidential survey book and Simpson with stealing it, as well as counselling or procuring Smith and the others to commit the offences.

Of course, there were many other offences to be considered that could be attributed to the gang, but wisely, charges were only brought on the offences the police believed could be proved.

An exception to this was charging Chatham with robbing Miss Harris of two bunches of keys and the burglary at the Eldon Street Post Office. The evidence against him was pretty thin, but the charge was brought because Mrs Kathleen Muriel Seal, a 35-year-old dress designer, was found to be in possession of eighty 5s 0d books of stamps, thirty 2s 6d books of stamps and National Savings stamps of various denominations, valued together at £6,998 5s 0d. Three weeks after Chatham's arrest, Mrs Seal told Bob Lee, 'I took them from 1 Lichfield Road, Kew, where I was living with George Chatham.'

Identified as being part-proceeds of the theft from the Eldon Street Post Office, Mrs Seal was charged with feloniously receiving them, and Bob Lee probably hoped that she might be compelled to give evidence on her former paramour, but alas, she did not. The case against Chatham was thrown out at the Old Bailey on 21 October, and Mrs Seal, who had pleaded guilty to receiving the items, was sentenced to three years' corrective training.

The case against Chatham and the others got underway at the Old Bailey on 18 November 1954. Various witnesses were called, including Douglas Norman Broad, an insurance broker from the company that employed Simpson, who told the court that Simpson was the general foreign accident broker and that in that capacity he would not normally deal with cases in the United Kingdom. When Simpson gave evidence he stated that he had handled Lady Congleton's jewellery insurance when she had gone to South Africa earlier that year. He had first met White in July and had been to his garage once; the other two defendants he had never met. Simpson firmly denied giving anybody confidential information from the surveyors' reports at Lloyds and also denied stealing the Lloyd's survey book; he had simply borrowed it, he told the jury, in connection with his ordinary work and intended to return it. As for the highly incriminating jottings on the insurance slips found at his house, he had no idea how these had come into his possession; the writing was certainly not his.

White, giving evidence, stated that the arc welding and cutting equipment was used in his capacity as a car repairer; with regard to the three insurance slips, he said that they were not in his wallet when he was arrested and had never seen them before. Additionally, he had never received details of Lady Congleton's house from Simpson, he knew nothing of the burglary at Byworth's, and as for the traces of safe ballast found in his cars, they may have come from the floor of his garage, where a safe had been forced by burglars.

In denying any involvement with the burglary at Byworth's, Chatham agreed that the knotting in the ropes found at his address and at Byworth's was identical but claimed that any similarity between the two pieces of rope was 'coincidental'. He also denied knowing any of the other men in the dock – that was considered a bit rich, since he had known Melrose in prison.

Melrose also denied involvement in any of the offences, saying that the fragments of fused metal found in his trousers must have been picked up in either a garage or a car; and the safe ballast found in his shoes and trousers must have got there in the same way.

Whilst the jury acquitted some of the defendants of some of the charges, the main charges were proved; but when the weekend intervened before sentencing, White produced a card – admittedly, a small one – from his sleeve. He demanded to see Commander Len Burt, the head of Special Branch.

Burt had hit the headlines as an ace investigator and spy-catcher during and after the Second World War, and apart from being commended by the commissioner on thirty-nine occasions, he had been awarded the officer class of the *Légion d'Honneur* by the President of the French Republic, the Order of the Orange Nassau by the Queen of the Netherlands and the Order of the Dannebrog (Chevalier Class) by the King of Denmark. He had been appointed a member of the Royal Victorian Order, and Her Majesty had just advanced Burt to be a Commander of that order; very soon, he would also be appointed a Commander of the British Empire. He had accompanied the royal family on a worldwide tour and more recently supervised the security arrangements for the visit of President Tito of Yugoslavia.

Three IRA terrorists had just broken into the Junior Training Corps Armoury at Felsted School in Essex and stolen a cache of weapons, and Burt was concerned (and rightly so) by information coming in that the IRA was planning another mainland offensive. So whilst he had previously been a first-rate murder investigator, he was now in charge of Special Branch, whose work was as different from that of Flying Squad officers investigating high-value burglaries as the Dogs' Section was from the Mounted Branch.

Of course, thanks to White's pompous self-regard, only someone of Burt's rank could be suitable to hear what the former public schoolboy and Mayfair socialite had to say – certainly not Detective Chief Superintendent Bob Lee, whom he had accused in court of planting the insurance slips in his wallet.

But Burt couldn't have given a rat's arse about what White had to say regarding returning some of the loot from Byworth's – he had enough on his plate supervising the security for the forthcoming visit of the former USSR Premier, Georgi Malenkov, and he passed the matter back to Bob Higgins.

So on Sunday, 5 December 1954, a crestfallen White, his ego in tatters, was taken in handcuffs to the village of Fulmer in Buckinghamshire. In Cherry Tree Lane, about one mile away from White's country retreat, he directed the detectives to walk ten paces south of a lightning-struck oak tree and dig under a clump of ferns. They did so, and unearthed a waterproof bag containing broken-up jewellery from Byworth's worth about £200. It was a gesture, that's all, and a pretty paltry one at that; £36,800-worth of swag was still missing.

The following day, sentencing was carried out at the Old Bailey. Sentencing Simpson to six years' imprisonment, the Common Serjeant told him:

> You were the mainspring of what has been proved to be a most evil conspiracy, the danger of which needs no emphasis at all. Your history is the basis for both respect and admiration – you served your country gallantly and that makes it all the more bewildering to find that a man like you should decide to declare war on the community. How long that might have continued and what damage might have been done, had it not been for the vigilance and thoroughness of the investigation which reflects great credit upon every officer concerned, no one can say.

White was sentenced to seven years' imprisonment, and telling Chatham and Melrose, 'I am afraid the time has come when the law must take its course', the Judge sentenced both of them to ten years' preventative detention.

The case hit the headlines worldwide, being covered in everything from *The Times*, who described it as 'An Evil Conspiracy', to such publications as the *Broken Hill Barrier Miner Newspaper* and the *Sydney Morning Herald* – and then all the fuss died down.

★ ★ ★

So what happened next?

Simpson disappeared from view, and I hope he lived a more lawful and industrious life.

After his release, White was sentenced to four years' imprisonment in 1966, in Dublin, for ringing cars.

Hardly had Melrose been released than he was arrested again, although this time, on 22 November 1961, he was acquitted of receiving part-proceeds from a £11,800 robbery. But the law caught up with him once more, and he was one of five inmates who escaped from Chelmsford Prison on 28 June 1963. He was caught four miles away, 'wet through and tired out', according to an eye-witness.

And Chatham? Nothing was going to stop Chatham. He was released in October 1961 and commenced burgling premises almost immediately. He was aged forty-eight and would continue burgling, sometimes getting caught, sometimes not, often going to prison, until he was almost eighty. It was only old age and general decrepitude, including the result of a fall from a building he was trying to break into – in fact, the only thing he broke was his ankle – that curtailed his activities.

He had spent thirty-five years in prison during his sixty-year career as a criminal, and it's estimated that during that time he had stolen property worth £100 million. So was it all worth it?

When he was eighty-one, using a very selective memory, he told what he wanted to tell of his story to a newspaper reporter, untruthfully whining that he had never used violence. This interview was given in a Fulham tower block with lino on the floor and three cheap pictures on the wall – a far cry from the Matisse and the Renoir he had stolen years before.

Divorced from his wife, their daughter dead, and possessing just a handful of old photos and press cuttings gathering dust, the man who had been dubbed 'The Human Fly' died in that dismal dump, alone, penniless and confused, aged eighty-five, on 5 June 1997.

CHAPTER 18

Diamonds and Accusations

For an astute businessman, Moses Wijnberg was rather lacking when it came to matters of security and common sense. Every week – and this had been the routine for the past six years – he sent his 60-year-old secretary, Mrs Alida Mullen, to the London Diamond Bourse at 57 Hatton Garden to pick up an assortment of cut and uncut diamonds. Having done so, she would return to Wijnberg's chauffeur-driven Rolls Royce, sit on the back seat with the attaché case of diamonds on the floor next to her – just as she always did – and be driven less than a quarter of a mile back to Wijnberg's office at Kimberley House, Holborn Viaduct. There he would trade diamonds twice a week, and the unsold stones would be returned to Hatton Garden.

That was the routine – there and back, every week – over 600 journeys in all, as regular as clockwork, in slow moving City traffic, in an ostentatious, gleaming, chauffeur-driven Rolls Royce. Oh, and Mrs Mullen, who had served her employer faithfully for forty years (and was above suspicion, as was the chauffeur), never bothered to lock the car doors. It was slightly amazing that in all that time nobody had bothered to help themselves to the bag full of sparklers at her feet – until, on 16 July 1956, somebody did.

At 11 o'clock that morning, the Rolls with a consignment of diamonds valued at between £75,000 and £100,000 turned left out of Hatton Garden and into St Cross Street. As it approached the junction with Farringdon Road it was baulked in traffic – and at that moment, a man pulled open the back door, snatched the attaché case and, to the accompaniment of Mrs Mullen's frenzied shrieks, ran off towards a waiting black Ford Zephyr in Clerkenwell Road. He was dressed as a workman, since there were many of these in the area and this had been the best way to avoid attracting suspicion as he hung about waiting for the Rolls. He was chased by the chauffeur, who tripped and fell, and the getaway car roared off, nearly hitting a bus; after 300 yards, the car hit another vehicle, and the thieves – it was believed there were three of them – abandoned it in Vine Hill, got into a second getaway car in Roseberry Avenue and made good their escape.

'It was a dramatic five-second robbery' exclaimed the *Daily Herald*, but that was typical press hyperbole, because it was not technically a robbery at all, since no violence had been used; it was classified as a case of 'larceny simple', although there was nothing simple about the way the theft was executed, or the value of the goods stolen.

So while Mr Wijnberg chain-smoked cigars and spoke volubly to his broker and insurance assessors, the police got to work. But what appeared to be a straightforward snatch turned out to be nothing of the kind. It was a case of smoke (which was dense) and mirrors (that were distorted).

The investigation was headed up by Detective Chief Inspector Tom Shepherd from Gray's Inn Road police station. He had joined the force in 1931 as Police Constable 577 'Z' at Croydon and was a very energetic uniform and CID officer, being commended time and again. On 5 August 1938 he had interrupted a smash and grab gang, leaping on to their getaway car and seizing the driver, the exotically-named Percy Darchambaud, around the throat; this caused the car to crash into the front of a house, trapping Shepherd and a gang member in the wreckage. For this outrage, the smash and grabbers were sent to hard labour, and Shepherd was awarded the King's Police Medal for gallantry.

Gray's Inn Road was part of the Met's No. 3 District, and the officer in charge was the newly promoted Detective Chief Superintendent Bob Lee. When Lee was second in command of the Flying Squad, a mailbag robbery amounting to £287,000 was carried out in Eastcastle Street in May 1952; in September 1954, gold bullion valued at £45,000 was hi-jacked, and at that time, Lee had taken over as head of No. 3 District. He investigated both offences; no one was charged and the property was never recovered. Both jobs had been carried out at the direction of Billy Hill, the self-proclaimed 'Boss of Britain's Underworld'. Hill would later say, 'I can't say I know Lee all that well. But we all know a lot about him. He's not the sort of man anyone can afford to mess about with.' Let's leave Messrs Lee and Hill for now – both will resurface later.

Someone must have provided good intelligence about the diamond snatch, because the following day, police went to an address at Greencroft Gardens, Hampstead; they were looking for Frederick Joseph Harmsworth, a prolific thief and burglar with ten previous convictions. At that time, he was circulated as being wanted; in January 1955 he had been arrested for possessing house-breaking implements by night, but having been committed to the London Sessions he had skipped his bail. In fact, he probably was at that address; but when 22-year-old Phyllis Betty Clark opened the door, she shouted, 'Police officers!'

Of Harmsworth there was no sign; but the premises were searched and a stolen car's registration book was found, also a television set, a suitcase, a clock, a portable radio and electric iron (stolen from a shop a year previously), 6oz of plaster gelatine (an industrial explosive) and four electrical detonators. Then there were a couple of jemmies and a bunch of skeleton keys, unsurprisingly, since Harmsworth was regarded as the best maker of 'twirls' in the business. But to all these compromising items Miss Clark stated, 'I have never seen these things before. I would rather say nothing now', and she was arrested for receiving them.

By now, Harmsworth had stolen a Ford Consul, registration number PXT 63, from nearby Maida Vale Avenue and made good his escape. But two days later, on 19 July, Detective Sergeant Ken Jones was keeping observation on a garage at Princes Avenue, Acton and at 10.15pm he saw Leslie Beavis arrive, open the garage and go to the stolen Ford Consul.

'It must belong to a friend of mine', he told the officer, but when it was pointed out to him that the car had been stolen, he replied, 'I know there's been some nicking going on. I suppose the car is down to me, being in the garage.'

Told he would be taken to Gray's Inn Road police station to be seen by Shepherd 'in respect of other matters', Beavis said, 'Is it in connection with a black Zephyr? I saw about it in the paper and I came home to clear the garage out because I don't want to be mixed up in it. Whatever it's all about, I want you to understand the old man's not in it. It's all down to me.'

The involvement (or not) of 'the old man' had been satisfactorily ironed out, because the following day, Beavis said, 'I will tell you my piece now . . . I want my alibi checked to prove that I was not mixed up in the big job. Believe me, I'm shocked.'

He was charged, together with his brother-in-law William Cyril Manning, with receiving the stolen black Zephyr, which had been taken from outside Park West, Edgware Road in May; a detailed forensic examination revealed their fingerprints on the registration plates. In addition, inside the car were found the fingerprints of Harmsworth and those of a certain John Morley Kelly, a thief with three previous convictions – who had gone missing, the day after the snatch.

In addition, prior to the snatch, police had seen two men drive up in a Standard car at a garage in Chichester Mews, Paddington, owned by Manning. A check on the Standard's registration plate revealed that it belonged to a Mrs Kelly of Lansdowne Lane, Charlton, the wife of the missing John Kelly.

So far, three people were in custody – but not Kelly or, in particular, Harmsworth, who was not arrested until 26 July, when police surrounded a boarding house in Westcliff-on-Sea at 5 o'clock in the morning and pulled him out of that establishment, still in his pyjamas.

He was seen by Shepherd at Southend police station later the same day and arrested for being concerned in the snatch. When charged, Harmsworth replied, 'I know all about the job. I supplied the car. You will find they have put me in the middle. I wasn't there at the time.'

Taken to Gray's Inn Road police station, Harmsworth said, referring to the diamonds, 'I don't suppose you'll get them back. They went abroad soon after they were nicked. The share-out is next Tuesday. My contact will collect my share . . . I might as well tell you the truth about the whole set-up. You can throw the keys away as far as I'm concerned, anyway.'

He then gave a written statement which commenced: 'First of all, you must know I'm on the run . . . you must have found some skeleton keys and jemmies. They are all mine I used to do all my jobs. The girl knows nothing about them.'

Appearing at Bow Street Magistrates' Court, Harmsworth and Manning were remanded in custody until Wednesday, 1 August – the day after Harmsworth's contact was supposed to collect his share of the loot – with Beavis being granted bail.

On 6 August, with a warrant for Kelly's arrest, Shepherd and Detective Inspector Jim Driscoll arrived on board the 13,000 ton *Bloemfontein Castle* which was outside the 3-mile limit off Cape Town, South Africa. Kelly, at the request of the police, had been put under close arrest four days previously by the ship's commander, Captain J.K.R. Wilford.

Kelly, serving as a crew member, was arrested for being concerned in the theft of the diamonds and receiving the stolen Ford Zephyr, two road fund licences and a radio. Initially, he said, 'I know nothing about it', although when he was told that he would be charged with those offences, he replied, 'If that's the case, when I get back to England, I'll tell you all I know and then you'll be able to get the others. I'm not taking the can back for anyone.'

Despite Harmsworth's claim that the diamonds were out of the country, Shepherd, perhaps optimistically, told reporters, ''I'm satisfied the jewels will be recovered.'

Back in England, Kelly told Shepherd, 'All I can say is that I did not steal the diamonds. I know something about the car. I got the plates for it. The wireless set I've had for a long time.'

On 28 August all five appeared in the dock at Bow Street. By then, Harmsworth was a serving prisoner since he had appeared, belatedly, at the London Sessions, where on the house-breaking implements charge he had been sentenced to fifteen months' imprisonment. Phyllis Clark had now been additionally charged with receiving a chamois leather containing a jeweller's ring gauge, a pair of tweezers and twenty-four jewelled platinum weights, and while she was remanded until 6 September on bail, the others were remanded to appear two days earlier; all were committed to the Old Bailey for trial, after the explosives charges were dropped against Harmsworth and Clark.

On 16 November, the charges against Clark had evaporated even further; for receiving a stolen car's registration book she walked free from court, having been conditionally discharged.

Mr Justice Hilbery had postponed sentence after the other male defendants were found guilty on 29 October, when there was an unexpected outburst from Kelly. He told the court that since being on remand in Brixton prison he had seen the police on five occasions and had tried to help them by telling them all he knew. 'This case is not being tried in the dock, but outside', he shouted. 'There is corruption going on. A statement has been made that two police officers have each received £13,000.'

'Which two?' asked the Judge.

'Mr Lee and Mr Shepherd' replied Kelly. 'I have been told by Inspector Shepherd and Inspector Driscoll that they know I had nothing to do with this case, yet they insisted on putting me before the court.' (In fact, during the trial, it was admitted by the police that neither Harmsworth nor Kelly had taken part in planning the theft and that neither had actually snatched the diamonds.)

'You say that two police officers each received £13,000?' asked the judge.

'That is the statement that came to me yesterday.'

'What for?'

'To keep the original people they had in custody and on the identification parade out of this court on this charge.'

Reggie Seaton for the prosecution now intervened. 'You have told us about £13,000', he said. 'Who was going to give the police officers that money?'

'A man in Brixton prison told me; he used to work for these people', replied Kelly. 'He just said the jewellery was sold for

£65,000 and the police – he named Lee and Shepherd – had received £13,000 apiece. The only name the man mentioned was the Dunn brothers.'

'What is the name of your informant?' asked Seaton, to be told, 'A man named Amos. He was in prison but has been released on bail.'

Now, on Monday, 19 November, Beavis, despite having ten convictions, was told that he was being given 'one last chance', since the Judge believed he had been led into this offence by Manning, his brother-in-law, and for being an accessory after the fact in stealing the black Zephyr used in the theft he was bound over for two years.

Manning, with four previous convictions, was sentenced to three years' imprisonment for stealing the Zephyr, but the Judge's disapprobation was reserved for Harmsworth, and he told him:

> I am convinced that at least two of those who stand in the dock with you stand there largely because of your bad influence. You tempted Manning to steal a car for you which was subsequently used in the big diamond robbery. I can find nothing in your favour. You are one of those persons who chooses to be a criminal and lead a criminal life, but you will find that you will spend a large part of your life in gaol.

For the diamond snatch, Harmsworth was sentenced to seven years' imprisonment and for other offences, receiving and breaking and entering, received a concurrent sentence of five years.

The Judge was spot-on regarding his assessment of Harmsworth's character; following his release, he and others used oxy-acetylene equipment to cut open the safe at the Sheerness Co-operative Bank, stealing £13,525 in September 1963; appearing at the Kent Quarter Sessions on 5 December, he was described by the Chairman as being 'the brains behind the planning and the execution of this crime' and received another seven-year sentence.

But back now to the Old Bailey, where it still remained for Kelly to be sentenced; asked if he had anything to say before sentence was passed, he said, 'I am innocent of all the charges against me. My conscience is clear and I only hope that others in this court – but not in this dock – can say the same.'

At this, he looked pointedly at DCS Lee and DCI Shepherd.

He was then sentenced to three years' imprisonment for the diamond theft with a concurrent eighteen-month sentence for receiving the stolen Zephyr.

While this imputation against the officers' characters was temporarily left in abeyance, the press released a story of how the gang was caught and introduced a jilted mystery blonde and a ne'er-do-well known to the underworld as 'Screwie Louie' who tipped-off the police as to the true identity of 'Freddy the Fly' (this was Harmsworth). It was utter bollocks but it thrilled the readers of the *Daily Herald* and the *Daily Mail*. They also speculated about the identity of 'Mr Big' and 'The Phantom', the mastermind behind the snatch, the heavy assertion being that it was none other than Billy Hill; there was no doubt they were right.

The offence had all the marks of Hill's modus operandi – meticulous planning, a high-value theft, several cars used in the getaway and Hill's own pet barrister, Patrick Marrinan (as straight as a corkscrew), who appeared for the defence. Other than claiming, 'If I was involved, those sparklers would have been out of the country within 24 hours' (which was pretty much what Harmsworth had said), Hill had little else to say, since at the time of the snatch he was being busily vilified at the Old Bailey, accused of being the mastermind in a plot to frame his old adversary, Jack Spot, for an offence he hadn't committed.

But the allegations against Lee and Shepherd weren't going to go away.

Kelly had taken part in an identification parade to determine whether or not he had driven the getaway vehicle; seven people (including the chauffeur of the Rolls-Royce) said he hadn't. Furthermore, his mother (plus other members of his family) had alibied him at the time of the theft. It was said that a man named Gosling, who had apparently driven the getaway car, had made a statement exonerating Kelly; it was also said that two brothers named Dunn, who had been named as being active participants in the theft, had been arrested and also immediately released. A very thorough internal investigation was carried out, but Kelly's application for leave to appeal was refused on 11 February 1957 and questions were raised in the House on 2 August 1957; Kelly's MP stated that although the internal investigation had concluded, no one was willing to tell him the result.

Both Lee and Shepherd resigned in early 1957.

As a footnote, in the 1980s a celebration was planned to commemorate the anniversary of the Flying Squad, and a bright-as-a-button university graduate approached the head of the Squad, with whom I was chatting. 'Sir!' he cried. 'I've been in contact with an old Squad officer. He's in his eighties but he's very lucid – just the person to speak at the anniversary celebrations!'

'What's his name?' I asked, to be told, 'Bob Lee'.

'That's interesting', I replied. 'I did hear that following a corruption investigation in the fifties, he had the whole of his back garden dug up.'

'Jesus!' shrieked the graduate. 'We can't have him!' and with that, he scurried off.

He was moving so fast down that 4th floor corridor at the Yard that I didn't have the opportunity to tell him that following the internal investigation, the enquiry completely exonerated both men.

CHAPTER 19

'The Terrible Twins'

What book about the golden age of policing would be complete without a reference to 'The Terrible Twins'?
No two officers looked less like twins: Tommy Butler, born in 1912, 5 feet 9¼ inches tall, dark, hawk-faced, joined the Metropolitan Police in 1934 – and Peter Vibart, born two years later, an inch and a quarter taller and a former lance bombardier with the Royal Artillery who joined the police two years after Butler.

Vibart started his career as a police constable on 'T', then 'H' Division; commended for the arrest of eleven persons for housebreaking and receiving, he was appointed detective constable after five years' service.

Butler served as a police constable on 'K' and 'F' divisions and was appointed detective constable after three and a half years' service, but by 1941 he had been posted to the Flying Squad, having been commended on six occasions. He served with the Squad all through the war and by the time he left, on promotion in 1946, his collection of commendations had risen to eighteen.

On the same day that Butler moved out of the Squad, so Vibart moved in to take his place as a detective constable; it helped that during a twelve-month period at Bethnal Green he had carried out 198 arrests. Butler returned to the Squad nine years later in 1955 as a detective inspector in charge of No 5 squad; Vibart was still there, having risen through the ranks to detective sergeant (first-class), his number of commendations having risen to twenty-eight. It was clear that he was fearless; he had been commended by the Lord Chief Justice in 1949 for the arrest of Frederick Parkyn, who had tried to murder him, three years later for the arrest of a dangerous criminal and in 1955 highly commended by the commissioner for the arrest of a gang of dangerous and troublesome criminals.

He and Butler now teamed up; they would make a formidable duo.

Alfred Hinds, a criminal with eight previous convictions (including safe-blowing), had been sentenced to twelve years' preventative detention in 1953 for a £34,700 safe-blowing at Maples Store, Tottenham Court Road. Hinds, who had been on the run for five months after escaping from Borstal in 1939, now escaped again, from Nottingham Prison in November 1955 with Patrick Fleming, who was serving eight years for warehouse-breaking.

On 16 February 1956, Fleming stole a £600 car from Drayton Gardens, Chelsea and another from the BOAC terminal at Buckingham Palace Road at about the same time. On 1 March, Butler and Vibart were patrolling in a Flying Squad car when they saw Fleming drive one of the cars into Artisan Street, Bishopsgate. Once the car was parked, the officers approached on foot, but Fleming saw them and started to accelerate away. Detective Constable Ken Drury and Detective Sergeant Fred 'Wilf' Pickles ran up to it but discovered all four doors were locked; and although they smashed the car's windscreen with their truncheons, Fleming made good his escape.

That was definitely not to Butler's liking; his informants were pressed into service and an observation was carried out on a garage in Plough Street, Stepney; when Fleming appeared there on 9 March after 104 days of freedom, he was arrested, saying, 'Yes, OK, that's fair enough.' Appearing at the London Sessions two weeks later, he pleaded guilty to receiving the cars and was given a concurrent sentence of eight years' preventative detention. But where was Hinds? Eire, that's where, and after 247 days on the run, Butler brought him back to resume his sentence.

In May 1956, there was a cowardly attack on gang leader Jack Spot and his wife in the street outside their address; Spot was left with seventy-eight stitches in his face. The attack had been orchestrated by Billy Hill and Albert Dimes, who were both impressively alibied. But one by one, the actual attackers were brought in and sentenced. Butler and Vibart flew to Eire, where they arrested Robert 'Battles' Rossi and William 'Billy-Boy' Blythe, a 39-year-old bald, satanic midget with eleven previous convictions who had been released in 1950 after the second of two razor attacks, each of which had earned him sentences of three years' penal servitude.

'You can all go and fuck yourselves', was Blythe's response when Butler told them they were under arrest. 'They came at me with guns tonight', he added. 'I only wish I had one. I'd have blown holes in the lot of them.'

That, and a great deal more impolite discourse occurred, there were court proceedings, threats of habeas corpus writs plus allegations of kidnapping, with Blythe being held down by four large policemen as they crossed the border into Ulster and then travelled on to the mainland. That was followed by the arrest of William 'Ginger' Dennis, and the subsequent trial at the Old

Bailey was loudly filled with disputed testimony which culminated in Dennis and Rossi being sentenced to four years' imprisonment and Blythe, to five. Vibart, in particular, was satisfied with the outcome since the long scar down his face was mute testimony that he had been the recipient of Blythe's first razor slashing in 1945.

Next, the 'Twins' were part of a team of Metropolitan Police officers off to Brighton to investigate allegations of police corruption. Vibart interviewed Sammy Bellson, a bookmaker who, it appeared, liked to run with the hare and hunt with the hounds and said, 'I could tell you a lot. I will help you all I can . . . if I can help you, I will.'

The only person Bellson wanted to help was himself, but he found himself in the dock instead of the witness box and denied the conversations with Vibart. He was found guilty, as were two Brighton detectives in the case who were both sentenced to five years' imprisonment. The Judge was less than impressed with Bellson's scurrilous allegations against Vibart and dealt with him in ten words: 'You, Bellson, the sentence is three years' imprisonment. Get below.'

Within months of those sentences, Butler and Vibart were on their travels again, this time to Cyprus to assist in the fight against the EOKA terrorists. News travelled fast; before they could even leave these shores, a terrorist spokesman stated, 'We will kill them as soon as they land.' The Cypriot police chiefs were not too keen on the idea, either; they had come in for fierce criticism after a Judge at the Nicosia Court declared there were 'lamentable gaps' in the prosecution case against a Greek Cypriot accused of the murder of a British Army sergeant. The Yard issued a press statement saying that the 'Twins' would not be going after all, but it was all a blind. Butler (now a detective chief inspector) and Vibart (now a detective inspector) were infiltrated into the island on 22 October 1958 and within a week they were investigating an explosion at Nicosia Airport. A time bomb inside a bottle of wine had detonated; fortunately, the Comet airliner which should have conveyed it had been delayed and was still on the tarmac.

They stayed for a month, advising on the methods of interrogation used by the security forces; then it was home again, where their report and comments were accepted by the Colonial Office.

Within a year, Butler was back on the Flying Squad, this time as a detective superintendent. Vibart by now was at Chelsea police station and tackled the repellent Ronald Easterbrook, wanted for shooting a police officer in the mouth. Trying to grab a Colt automatic pistol hidden underneath his hotel room pillow, Easterbrook received a punch on the jaw from Vibart so hard that his ability to enunciate was beset with difficulties for some time afterwards. Highly commended by the commissioner, Vibart was awarded £15 from the Bow Street Reward Find and awarded the Queen's Commendation for Brave Conduct. A year later, he was highly commended once more after effecting the arrest of a man wanted for murdering a police officer.

In March 1960, he was one of the officers tasked to set up a Criminal Intelligence unit – initially referred to as C5(2) Department, it became better known as C11.

It came in very handy when Detective Chief Superintendent Tommy Butler investigated the Great Train Robbery in 1963; he immediately demanded the presence of Vibart, whom he plucked from his posting at Kingston to assist. Butler was also helped immeasurably by the fact that C11 also dealt with telephone intercepts, under the control of his old Flying Squad companion, Detective Inspector Fred Pickles.

Working 16- to 20-hour days, Butler sought out his informants, had intercepts placed on the telephones of the most likely suspects and got the fingerprints found at the gang's hideout at Leatherslade Farm matched up with those suspects. The hunt was on, resulting in 30-year sentences for many of the gang, and that wasn't all; when Charlie Wilson escaped from prison, Butler went to Canada to bring him back. Butler pleaded for an extension on his service in order to arrest the gang's leader, Bruce Reynolds – and he did just that.

Vibart retired as a detective superintendent on 4 January 1969, just four days after Butler – he had been awarded the Queen's Police Medal for distinguished conduct – and he died seven years later, aged sixty-two. He was not the easiest man to get on with; David Woodland remembers him as a martinet, and every piece of correspondence was subject to his scrutiny and criticism. 'Don't you argue with me, matey!' he would roar down the phone from his office in Putney to a luckless subordinate. 'Come to Putney!' Others thought him a bully and a glory-hunter.

There was criticism of Butler as well. A single man, he worked tremendously long hours and expected all of his subordinates (married or not) to do the same. As a detective inspector, when he welcomed a newcomer to the Squad, he explained that there were early and late shifts. The early shift was nine till five but, as he made clear, 'You'll be expected to work until ten.' Regarding the late shift, that was two till ten, and then the officer could expect to have a lie-in: 'You don't need to come into the office until nine.'

Thinking that Butler had cracked a joke, the newcomer laughed. Butler was furious. 'If you think that's funny, try coming in five fucking minutes late!' he roared.

He was also fanatically secretive. 'Come on', he'd say. 'We're going to nick someone' – but the name of the arrestee and the address where he was to be found would never be divulged to his contemporaries until they got there.

Butler enjoyed a far shorter retirement than Vibart; appointed MBE, he had just over a year to live, before cancer claimed him in April 1970, aged fifty-seven.

So both had their faults, but they were not without kindness, either. Vibart would back hard-working officers to the hilt; presented with a less than perfect report, Butler's response would be, 'What a load of bollocks', but then he would painstakingly correct the officer's report, line by line.

But one thing was for sure: when the 'Terrible Twins' were on the rampage, the underworld trembled.

Is there such a duo in today's Metropolitan Police?

If there is, do let me know.

Chapter 20

A Pretty Collection of Villains

It's always a help when a barrister can unctuously inform a court that his client has 'an unfortunate background'. In the case of Edward Thomas Rice, it was probably true. He was living at 45 Falkirk Street, Shoreditch, a house containing thirteen other adults, and after his mother died when Rice was seventeen, his father, 'an associate of criminals', ejected him from the premises. How much help such circumstances will provide when facing a serious charge depends on the forbearance of the Judge. In the case of Mr Justice Stable, I suppose the answer would be 'not much', because when Rice appeared before him at Nottinghamshire Assizes on 1 July 1949, the learned Judge told him, 'You are one of those people who are an absolute nuisance to the community.'

Their meeting arose after Rice, who was then aged twenty-eight, and two other men (their identities were never disclosed) broke into Earl Beatty's house at Astrop Park during the night of 21/22 May 1949 and stole a whole variety of items, from bottles of whisky to postage stamps, valued together at £188 3s 8½d.

They were disturbed by the footman at 3.30am and made good their escape, but half an hour later, Police Constable Ostle stopped the three men in an Austin 10 driven by Rice. The other two fled and, his suspicions duly aroused, the officer detained Rice. He was not aware of the burglary but he was pointed in the right direction when Rice produced a packet of cigarettes and said, 'Let's have one on Earl Beatty.' Rice was also found to be in possession of a dog licence in the name of the peer's butler and some postage stamps; and when a new wood chisel and a table knife were found in the car and these corresponded with markings on the furniture and fittings at Astrop House, that, really, was that.

Following his expulsion from 45 Falkirk Street, Rice had deserted from the Royal Navy on several occasions and had already served four prison sentences; now, he received his fifth when Mr Justice Stable packed him off to four years' corrective training.

Rice – whose address at the time was 224 Wick Road, Islington – was a long way from home. It was a habit he would adopt when committing other offences in the future.

* * *

Hardly had Rice been released from his four-year sentence than he was at it again. On 10 November 1953 at 8.45pm, six to eight men wearing stocking masks suddenly burst into the Collingwood Road, Levenshulme, Manchester home of 57-year-old bookmaker Samuel Johnson and his wife Alice and assaulted them with pickaxe handles, demanding the keys to the safe. The family's bull terrier attacked the raiders; it was beaten unconscious, and the gang fled empty-handed.

Police enquiries led them to the home of George Kelly. In the grounds of the Johnsons' house, coat buttons of a particular design were found which matched exactly a coat hanging in the hallway at Kelly's Mytton Street address in Hulme; it was bloodstained, as were a sheet and a blanket in one of the bedrooms. Kelly took no time at all to say, 'These are Eddie Rice's' and, shown two more coats in the house, he told the officers, 'There are Eddie's pals', not mine. I don't know them. He brings them here.' Also in the house was Eddie Rice himself, who stated, 'I slept here last night.' On his legs were scratches and bruises commensurate with being attacked by a bull terrier, and an examination of his car revealed a bloodstained pickaxe handle, torches, a screwdriver and a wood chisel.

Both men appeared at Manchester Magistrates' Court, and the investigating officer told the stipendiary magistrate, 'We have reason to believe several other men are concerned, some of them probably from London.' He wasn't far wrong.

Next to grace the dock was Jeremiah Callaghan from Trinity Square, Stepney, and he had an interesting background.

* * *

Just four months previously, Callaghan and Henry Botton had been acquitted at Leeds Assizes of theft and receiving 1,845,400 cigarettes, a safe and other items from the warehouse of H. Field Ltd, Vicar Lane, Leeds; and what was more, the Judge directed that £300 which had been in Callaghan's possession should be returned to him. The arrests arose after Tommy Smithson, an East End hard man, was savagely attacked by a gang including Billy Hill and Jack Spot. Although he refused to name his attackers, Smithson got revenge by grassing up this gang, which was a Billy Hill enterprise, to former Ghost Squad officer John Gosling, who worked with Leeds officers plus a contingent of the Flying Squad to arrest the villains; seven men and one woman. Hill provided his bent barrister, Patrick Marrinan, to represent Callaghan and Botton, and he got them off.

* * *

Before long, Callaghan was joined in the dock at Manchester by William 'Billy' David Ambrose; he, too, had noteworthy antecedents.

Ambrose had been thought (with considerable justification) to be a contender for the middleweight boxing championship of Great Britain, but his plans went awry in November 1952, when he was one of six masked men armed with truncheons (does this sound familiar?) who broke into the offices of Conway Stewart & Co., attacked the elderly security officer and stole gold pens worth £1,500.

He was sentenced to five years' imprisonment but escaped from the hospital wing of Wormwood Scrubs prison and was on the run for six months. It was believed that Callaghan was one of the other participants in the raid, but that was never proved. It appeared that crime was a family business in the Ambrose household; his mother, Mrs Sarah Jane Ambrose, was acquitted of receiving most of the pens, plus the safe-opening gear, which was discovered at her address. Shortly after Callaghan was acquitted at Leeds, so was Billy Ambrose's wife Elizabeth, who had been charged in the same case with being an accessory after the fact and receiving the cigarettes which were found in her garage on the Eastern Avenue, Ilford. It was thought that Billy Ambrose had also been involved in the Leeds job, but like Callaghan's supposed involvement in the pen robbery, that was never proved.

* * *

Now, back to the attack on Mr and Mrs Johnson. A large Pontiac car which had been driven by Callaghan was recovered and found to contain two jacks and a two-wheeled truck, just right for conveying a safe. And prior to the raid, a detective had seen Ambrose and Callaghan in the Pontiac; he had made a note of the registration number because, as he said, it was unusual to see visitors in the Blackpool area 'out of season'.

At Manchester Assizes, Rice denied any knowledge of the items found in the boot of his car (he did mention it was unlocked), and evidence was given that when Callaghan was arrested in London on 18 November he had said, 'This is a dead liberty. I've got my alibi prepared for this one. It'll need some shaking.'

He provided no details of it, but his mother, Mrs Edith Rose Callaghan, turned up at court to say that on the night of the attack her dutiful son had been dutifully decorating a room at her house.

But neither she nor he was believed; and on 15 March 1954, after Kelly was acquitted and another man was sentenced to eighteen months' imprisonment for being an accessory after the fact, the Judge, Mr Justice Oliver, rounded on the other three defendants, who were all found guilty of the attack, denouncing them as 'scoundrels' and telling them:

> It seems to be becoming the fashion to import men from London to commit desperate crimes . . . One has heard too much about violence, recently. It does not seem to get better. It is worse. The only weapon we have against it – and one which we are going to use – is punishment.

He then sentenced Callaghan to eight years' imprisonment, Ambrose to five years' imprisonment, to run consecutively to his interrupted five-year sentence, and because of his appalling record, Rice to ten years' preventative detention.

★ ★ ★

Released on home leave, Callaghan and Ambrose opened the Pen Club, a louche drinking club in Duvall Street, East London, where on 7 February 1960 a man was shot dead; Billy Ambrose was shot in the stomach as well. But during the trial of the three men arrested for the murder, Ambrose refused to identify either his attacker or the murderer (as did his wife); it was a case which attracted such luminaries as Freddy Foreman, Reggie Kray and the Nash Brothers. There were two trials, after the jury in the first one was well and truly nobbled; witnesses were frightened off, two were slashed with razors and the three defendants were unsurprisingly acquitted of murder.[1]

---

1 For further details of this case, see *London's Gangs at War*, Pen & Sword, 2017

After that, Ambrose could do no wrong; for keeping his trap well and truly shut he was officially 'staunch', and Foreman would later hint that Ambrose and Callaghan were employed in carrying out armed robberies. In any event, both were well heeled enough to buy up a string of betting shops. Ambrose featured on the list of eighteen names that Tommy Butler favoured for the 1963 Great Train Robbery, but he was later eliminated from it.

He next came to notice in 1976; living in a prestigious house by the racetrack in Sandown Road, Esher and driving a Rolls-Royce Corniche, he was arrested for being the head of a gang of international swindlers known as 'The Hungarian Circle', who had the ability, as a jury at the Old Bailey was told, 'to bankrupt a small European country'. The gang were convicted, with sentences of up to fifteen years' imprisonment, but Ambrose was not amongst them. After filling the public gallery with 'heavies' who scowled menacingly at the jury, Ambrose walked free from court.

He died in April 2009, aged seventy-nine, and his wife followed him to the grave four years later.

* * *

Jeremiah Callaghan came to notice in 1969, being named as one of several men who had murdered Frank 'The Mad Axeman' Mitchell, the Dartmoor escapee, after he turned out to be an embarrassment to the Kray brothers. Callaghan – and others – could not be found, but after Freddy Foreman and the three Kray brothers were acquitted of Mitchell's murder, no further arrests were made.

Action was taken in 1975, when Callaghan was one of three men – Freddy Foreman was another – who stood trial for the murder, ten years previously, of Terry 'Ginger' Marks; all of them were acquitted.

'A slippery customer', John Troon (who arrested him) told me, 'and a nasty bit of work', Callaghan died in 2000, taking secrets (and there were a lot of them) to the grave with him.

* * *

This brings us back to Edward Rice, or 'Terrible Ted' as he liked to be known, as well he might have been, after attacking a middle-aged woman with a pickaxe handle.

His sentence at Strangeways Prison, Manchester was interrupted after eight months on 6 November 1954 when he was part of a daring six-man escape. The prisoners, all serving long sentences for possessing explosives, possessing firearms with intent to resist arrest and office-breaking, left the mailbag office just after roll-call to go to a storeroom to collect materials; when they got there, they barricaded the door. A metal bar protecting a window 15ft above floor level had been sawn through from the outside, the window was smashed and a 20ft long rope was found dangling outside. The rope ended in the back garden of a prison officer's quarters; the prisoners scaled the roof of the married quarters, dropped down on to the porch, then into the front garden – and away.

One by one, they were recaptured – but Rice stayed free for three months and during that time he made himself busy.

Some time between 26 January and 5 February 1954, he received five and a half stolen sticks of gelignite, five electric detonators and also 28lb of 2oz tobacco and 200 cigarettes, which had been stolen from British Rail whilst in transit.

On 4 February, Rice was one of the men who had gone to Messrs Skyways Ltd, at Stansted, Essex and forced their way in with a jemmy. Using explosives, Rice blew the safe and helped himself to the money and stamps valued at £1,204 – but his luck had run out. Within 24 hours of that offence, a house at West End Lane, Kilburn (which Rice had rented in the name of Smith) was raided by Detective Superintendent Tom Bradford of the Flying Squad, and Rice, in pyjamas and dressing gown (its pockets contained £123 10s 0d) and just about to go to bed, was well and truly nicked.

The tobacco and cigarettes were recovered, and Rice told Bradford, 'I've been expecting this. You're lucky, because I was going to leave here, tomorrow. Things were getting too hot.' In the garden the police found five sticks of gelignite, detonators and reels of wire, and Rice told them, 'I got the jelly and the dets off some fellows.' Whoever those 'fellows' were, he refused to name them, but when charged he replied, 'I plead guilty.'

He lost no time in selling the story of his story ('The underworld planned my escape') to the Sunday newspaper, the *People*, and on 15 March 1955 he made good his promise when he pleaded guilty at the Old Bailey.

After hearing that Rice had ten previous convictions, Judge Carl Aarvold told him:

> You cannot expect to commit crimes of this character in which explosives are used without calling down on yourself severe and serious consequences. What makes you do it, I don't know – whether it is a sense of excitement or whether it be some misplaced sense of vanity.

> One thing is clear, and you must have realised it after the time you have spent in prison, that that sort of conduct does not pay, and only brings the greatest possible misery on your own head and on your family.

The Judge was right; Rice's wife was carried screaming from court and then collapsed on the bench outside after her husband was sentenced to a thirteen-year concurrent sentence of preventative detention.

★ ★ ★

I forgot to mention Henry Botton, who was acquitted with Jerry Callaghan at Leeds, didn't I?

The possessor of nine previous convictions, Botton had just been released from an eight-year sentence of preventative detention for office-breaking when he was swept up in an affray at Mr Smith's Club, Catford in 1966, where the Krays' cousin Dickie Hart was murdered. The murderer was 'Mad Frankie' Fraser, although he was acquitted of the charge and, like Botton was sentenced to five years' imprisonment for causing an affray. Botton was said to be a police informer; justice (of a kind) caught up with him in July 1983 when he opened the front door of his house in Shooters Hill Road, Blackheath and fatally received the contents of a sawn-off shotgun.

Without wishing to be unduly preachy, I suppose the moral of this particular story is that those who indulge in crime, whether or not they're convicted, seldom reap the rewards of it.

Chapter 21

Convicted by the Skin of his Finger

The Recorder of London, Sir Gerald Dodson, described the crime as being 'An impudent outrage, carried out by reckless criminals', and that was after only two of the gang of four were convicted; Sir Gerald didn't know the half of it.

Over the weekend of 14/15 December 1957, a dedicated gang of criminals broke into Lloyds Bank at Kingston-on-Thames, scaling the wall and using a ladder to climb to a window protected by three half-inch-thick bars, which they opened using bolt-cutters. Using the manager's office carpet to muffle the noise, the gang deployed sufficient gelignite to blow open the strong-room door, which was six feet high and weighed two tons. The sound of the detonation was heard by several neighbours, but nobody bothered to contact the police. Next, they forced open a steel cupboard and acquired the cash contents, £43,087 7s 3d. They then turned their attention to two safes which contained a total of £71,000, the result of the takings from Christmas shoppers and the winnings of bookies from Hurst Park races. Gelignite inside balloons was inserted into the locks of the safes but was not, for whatever reason, detonated – perhaps the gang were disturbed, and they left with the money and split into two groups.

Remember the gelignite-filled balloons; they make a re-appearance later on.

As the smoke cleared, Frederick Clarke, aged forty-six, the possessor of nineteen previous convictions, got behind the wheel of a stolen Jaguar; into the passenger's seat got Sydney James Stanton, a 35-year-old driver with a more modest nine previous convictions. They were circling the area, awaiting a signal from the other gang members, when they were spotted by Police Constable William Gibbons. He challenged them, the Jaguar roared away, and the chase was on, reaching speeds of up to 85 mph. Clarke managed to evade the first police car but not the second, which forced him to stop, whereupon both men made an unsuccessful bid to escape. Stanton was found in possession of seventeen £5 notes and thirty-four £1 notes, as well as a ten shilling note. In the boot of the car were found wire- and bolt-cutters; a later examination would reveal that it was these bolt-cutters that had been used to get through the bank's barred window. Additionally, padding from the scene of the explosion tallied exactly with material found in the car; it was found on both men's clothing together with traces of explosives, and when fingernail scrapings were obtained from both they were found to contain traces of nitrates.

But with the exception of the cutters, all of these discoveries were in the future; now, at the time of their arrest, both men denied any knowledge of the bank raid or the cutters and stated that they had taken the Jaguar from the area of Hampton Court for a joyride.

With those two gang members locked up, a careful forensic examination was made of the scene of the raid. Blood was found on a tree and on the ladder used by the gang, also on top of the bank's 6ft perimeter wall into which broken glass had been cemented – and there was more. A piece of skin was found attached to one of the shards of glass; it was not very big but it was sufficient for the experts to determine that the fingerprint obtained from it belonged to one John Vernon Rees, aged thirty-five.

Rees had an enterprising criminal record which started in June 1945 with a fifteen-month prison sentence for house-breaking. In 1948, for larceny he received a two-year sentence and two years later, he was given a chance to redeem himself when he was placed on probation for attempted house-breaking. It was an act of clemency which failed to work, because in 1954 he was sentenced to twelve months' imprisonment for shop-breaking.

Of Rees there was no sign; and no sign of the stolen money, either – the bank offered a reward of £3,500 for its return.

In the meantime, Stanton and Clarke appeared at the Old Bailey, still adhering to their story of taking the Jaguar and nothing else; but it did them no good. On 25 February 1958 both were convicted of the bank raid, and with the Recorder of London telling them, 'It must be the business of this court to see that it is a long time before you are able to enjoy your share of the money', each was sentenced to ten years' imprisonment.

And still there was no sign of Rees; but enquiries were continuing from the Flying Squad office, not necessarily in respect of Rees, although perhaps tangentially so. Those enquiries led Detective Sergeant John Clifford Austin Hensley – never known as anything other than 'Ginger' – to an office door on the first floor of 60 Chandos Place, a street running parallel with The Strand. It was not luck or speculation that brought 38-year-old Hensley to that address; this was his second of three tours with the Squad, and his sources of information were legendary.

On a shelf in a back room was a plastic bag; it contained two cartridges of Polar Ajax, an industrial blasting explosive, one weighing 2oz, the other 2½oz. There was a cartridge of 2½oz Polar Ammon gelignite and a red rubber balloon containing gelignite; just the right size for inserting into the lock of a safe. Newspaper found inside a plastic bag had been heavily contaminated with Polar Ajax and Polar Ammon gelignite, and a brown-paper carrier bag also had traces of gelignite inside it. Then there was a set of car registration plates, 128 KMM; the car's owner had left it on the forecourt of the Load of Hay public house, Northolt on 12 January and had not seen it since. She had seen the occupant of the office, William Herbert Robertson, whom she knew by sight from the South Harrow area. Not unnaturally, the 58-year-old Robertson, who had four previous convictions, was asked by Detective Constable Cannon about the provenance of these items. 'What can I say?' he replied. 'I've been minding it for you-know-who. I shall have to take the can.'

The officer obviously didn't know who, and said so. 'Joan, of course' was the reply.

The 'Joan' referred to, was present; she was 41-year-old Doris Joan White, who lived with Robertson in Alexandra Road, South Harrow and she had an interesting history.

Born in Leicestershire in 1917, she received a college education and frequently rode to hounds with some of the best packs in the county. She had married in 1937, but her husband was killed in a car crash in 1945. During the war she had driven VIPs and gained a reputation as a fearless driver. This may have stood her in good stead when in 1948 she married (and later divorced) Harold Lough White, also known as 'Peter the Plotter', whose adventures involving the use of gelignite have already been recounted. Was she the woman who befriended insurance agent Simpson's wife to bring Simpson into the conspiracy? Perhaps. At various venues where premises had been broken into and which White had been suspected of (but not charged with) burgling, powerful cars were seen being driven away at speed; police patrols could not keep up with them. Was the driver White, displaying her 'fearless' driving skills? Maybe. She had been part of a team which included three men who lured a householder and his wife away from their premises so that it could be ransacked and property worth £1,223 stolen. She and another gang member had registered in a hotel close to the burgled house, giving the names of Mr and Mrs Jackson. At Chester Assizes in 1951, for house-breaking and larceny, she was bound over to keep the peace, while 'Mr Jackson' was sent to penal servitude for three years.

She had nothing to say at her trial in Chester and not a great deal now, although when Robert Howard Rutter, with five previous convictions to his credit, walked into the office whilst the search was going on, she did manage to slip him a packet of cigarettes on which she had written 'LAW SEARCH'. Most interesting of all, she had been associating with John Vernon Rees, currently wanted for the Lloyds Bank burglary.

Possession of various quantities of explosives, association with two known users of that commodity, dropped right in it by her current paramour, stolen registration plates, possession of a bunch of 'twirls' – oh dear, oh dear. She might have blonde hair right now, but how would it look after seven years in Holloway? It looked as though help was needed, and a little horse-trading – something which desperate criminals and astute Flying Squad officers knew quite a lot about – was implemented. That included the necessity of getting other officers to act on the information obtained, to keep the source of the information and the receiver of it completely apart; Flying Squad officers such as Detective Inspector Bill Baldock and Detective Sergeant Terry O'Connell, for instance.

It was those two officers who were keeping observation in South Acton at 12.30pm on 29 August 1958, when they saw Rees arrive in a stolen Wolseley car bearing false plates. As he was seized, Rees brandished a cosh and a terrific tussle ensued; however, since O'Connell was a 6' 1½" former wartime Royal Marine attached to 45 Commando, he won.

In the car, O'Connell and Baldock found a stick of gelignite, six detonators, a hacksaw, drill, torch battery, length of wire and pair of car registration plates, and Rees told the officers, 'I've had a good run.' An hour and a half later, John Henry Preedy aged twenty-nine, who had had an eventful life, acquiring nine findings of guilt as a juvenile and nine convictions as an adult, was arrested at his home address in Perryn Road, Acton. That address and another, at Monks Drive, Acton, was searched and a total of eight sticks of gelignite and some detonators were found at both addresses.

Asked to show his damaged finger, Rees held it out to the officers, telling them, 'That was a classic, wasn't it?'

'I know about the jelly, but don't put the blowing down to me', said Preedy. 'The other fellow you have in is the one who has been doing them. He's an expert at the stuff.' When he was asked where the cash had come from for his recent purchase of a £3,300 house and a new car, he replied helplessly, 'I suppose I have no explanation.'

When he was charged he replied, 'Yes, the charge is true.'

Rees' response to the charge was 'The jelly, yes, but not the detonators', although later in court, he suggested that the detectives' hearing was defective and his reply had actually been 'The charge is absurd. I'm not guilty.'

He must have had a change of heart, because he and Preedy both pleaded guilty to the Lloyds Bank caper plus other assorted offences at the Old Bailey on 5 November 1958. Rees was sentenced to ten years' imprisonment and Preedy to four.

One week later, White, Robertson and Rutter appeared at the same court and were found guilty of possessing explosives. The Common Serjeant, Sir Anthony Hawke, told Joan White:

> I do not think I would be justified in speculating what you were doing with this dangerous criminal stuff . . . if I thought this was a case where you were dangerous safe-breakers, you would have gone to prison for many years.

He sentenced all of them to seven months' imprisonment; wearing a smart black suit, Joan – who received an allowance of £650 per year from her former husband – waved at friends in the public gallery as she left the dock. She had spent five months in custody awaiting trial, so with that time deducted from her sentence, plus time off for good behaviour, she had just a few weeks to serve.

Understandably, as she made her way down to the cells, she was smiling.

Chapter 22

A Zealous Cop

Now it's a funny thing – and the views that follow will resonate with many serving and retired police officers – how officers who have never done a stroke of police work in their careers, after thirty years' service unencumbered with complaints, commendations or court appearances, can wander off into retirement. Their mortgages have been paid off, and they're clutching pensions which to my mind have been obtained by false pretences. It's something I find irritating.

But take matters one step further, and there are those whom their contemporaries regard as being some of the biggest villains unhung but who nevertheless, once they've reached twenty-two years' service, have been presented with their Long Service and Good Conduct Medal. Officers' shocked incredulity deepens further when a tainted person retires and the commissioner signs a certificate saying that his conduct has been 'exemplary'.

My Flying Squad driver, Tony Freeman, always referred to the award as the 'Long Service and-never-been-caught-Medal', and there are those who might agree with him, especially my grandson Sam, who as a ten-year-old with a precocious talent for slanderous irony, asked me if I'd borrowed mine.

This brings me to the case of Charles Sydney Clifford Careless. Judging by results he was a pretty successful police officer, but given what transpired in both his later career and thereafter, was he a wrong 'un or unlucky – or what?

Careless joined the police in 1937. His service was interrupted during the war years, when he was a sub lieutenant in the Royal Naval Volunteer Reserve, and then it was back to the West End's 'C' Division, where within two months of his discharge from the Navy he was commended by the commissioner for ability and determination in the arrest of two persistent thieves; that was followed, the next month, by another commendation for ability in a case of shop-breaking. He would serve as a detective constable and second-class sergeant on 'C' Division until 1954, and by the end of his career his commendations would total thirty-two.

Peter James Sheppard was a determined villain; he had served Borstal training and imprisonment with convictions for robbery with violence, and his record was so bad that in November 1953, for burglary, shop- and house-breaking, when he asked for ninety-two other offences to be taken into consideration, he was sentenced to ten years' preventative detention. He escaped from prison in April 1955 and was arrested three weeks later. He escaped once more in May 1962, when he had just nine weeks of his sentence left to serve, and was arrested within nineteen days.

Sheppard was nicknamed 'The Thin Man' because at the time of his first escape, prior to his sentence, he had wriggled through an eleven inch square ventilator. He remained on the run until 27 August 1953, when he was spotted in Trafalgar Square by Careless and arrested. It did Careless' reputation as a thief-taker no harm at all, and this was enhanced the following month when he arrested Jack Spot, the self-proclaimed 'King of the Underworld', in a telephone box for being in possession of a knuckleduster. Spot loudly proclaimed his innocence, stating that he had been fitted up by Careless; not at the time, though – much later, because on 23 September, Spot pleaded guilty at Bow Street Magistrates' Court and was fined £30 after he told the bench he had bought the knuckleduster for his protection from a store, a fortnight previously.

Careless was promoted to detective sergeant first-class in 1954 and was posted to the Flying Squad. His career continued to glitter, and he collected commendations for ability and persistence in cases of conspiracy to steal, receiving and arresting a team of house-breakers, as well as mopping up gangs of persistent criminals. He was promoted to detective inspector and then hit the *Daily Mirror* headlines with an idiosyncratic case: 'The Lovelorn Crook and the Clippie'.

There had been a dawn smash and grab raid on a Regent Street jeweller's window, and seven diamond rings valued at £2,580 had been stolen. Bill Smith had helped the thieves dispose of six of the rings to a fence but kept one back for himself, for a very good reason.

He was besotted with Krithia, a clippie on a No. 27 London bus. He pestered her to accept presents like chocolates and jewellery, even though he knew her husband was driving the bus. He offered her the ring – valued at £385 – which she refused, so he left it for her on the front seat of her bus. She and her husband took the ring to the police, and as the lovelorn fence sat once more on the No. 27 bus he was arrested.

Careless had a quiet word with Smith in the cells and made him an offer he found difficult to refuse. The following day, an unshaven and shabbily dressed Inspector Careless arrived in

West Kensington, at the Welbeck Court flat belonging to Stanley Nicol, told him Smith had sent him and suggested that he was a shop-breaker who wished to dispose of stolen goods. Later, Richard Liddle, a fence, arrived at the flat and asked Careless, 'What have you got for me?'

'I've got a shock for you', replied Careless. 'I'm arresting you both.'

After a three-day trial at the London Sessions, during which Smith, currently serving a two-year sentence, gave evidence, Liddle was sentenced to twenty-one months' imprisonment for receiving six of the rings, and Nicol, for being an accessory, was gaoled for fifteen months.

The press had a field day, Careless was commended by the chairman and later by the commissioner, and after the case he told reporters that he was going home to his wife, who 'doesn't like my shabby crook disguises'.

It may or may not have been his wife that he was returning to; but four months later, Careless was on the start of a particularly slippery slope that would end in an almighty tumble.

* * *

George Madsen was a prolific thief who had spent twenty of his forty-two years behind bars. He and Ernest Norris had blown two safes at a laundry in High Road, Enfield and escaped with £400. Since his release from prison in April 1958, the Flying Squad had kept Madsen under sporadic observation; eventually, both men were found in a one-room flat in Bethnal Green, and with them was a quantity of gelignite and some of the stolen money.

Norris had been particularly difficult to trace; but now that the pair were arrested, they were remanded in custody and on 13 October 1958 appeared at Enfield Magistrates' Court. Inspector Careless was there as well, not, as he later told the court, in connection with that case; he had simply arrived there to speak to fellow Flying Squad officers about a completely different matter. But there were eight other people there, five men and three women, and Careless overheard what could be described as pretty incriminating conversations, because it appeared that there was a conspiracy afoot to spring the two defendants. The men were going to be handed a tyre lever and a chisel by a Jean Haddon; these were to be used to break out of the prison van taking them to Brixton prison, and a car would be on hand to spirit them away. Haddon gave Madsen what was described as 'a long lingering kiss' through the bars of the door of the gaoler's office, and it appeared she was doing something with her hands under her coat. Madsen was searched immediately afterwards, and the chisel was found in his right trouser leg suspended by tape from a trouser button; the tyre lever was found down his left trouser leg.

Stopped as she was leaving the court, Mrs Haddon said, 'Oh dear, it was silly of me to do it', adding, 'Someone had to do it – I did.' All of the defendants were committed to the Old Bailey to stand trial on charges of conspiring to effect Madsen's and Norris' escape and conveying a tyre lever, chisel and a car to them; to these charges Jean Haddon pleaded guilty, but the other defendants denied them.

It was an exciting case, with fascinating snatches of the incriminating conversations overheard by two detectives (Careless and Lawless – couldn't make it up, could you?): 'If you're going to use my car for the getaway, then I had better get out of the way' . . . 'Are you sure the girl is going to be all right?' . . . 'Everything is set. George will take the tools when he kisses her' . . . 'I don't know how they hope to get out of the roof of the wagon without anyone seeing them' . . . 'If Ray is close up with his car, they'll only have a few yards to run' . . . and much more of the same.

But when Careless was cross-examined he again said that he had gone to Enfield court in respect of a matter quite unconnected with the case. This sounded (and possibly was) unbelievable. If it wasn't a white lie, it was certainly a grey one. It was clear that information had been received that the escape was going to go ahead, and to protect the source of the information – either an informant or a telephone intercept – Careless had stated that he had overheard the conversations by chance. It is quite possible that he did; after all, the items were found in Madsen's possession and Mrs Haddon had pleaded guilty to supplying them.

The conversations had been recorded in a brand new pocket book – Careless said his old one was full up – and he stated that he had written all the defendants' names in red ink when he returned to the office.

He was just about to be further cross-examined by five other defence counsel when the bombshell dropped. Mr Maxwell Turner for the prosecution asked for an adjournment, and after lunch a conference with all the barristers was held by the judge in his chambers. At 2.35pm on 21 November 1958, Mr Turner stated that he had been instructed to offer no further evidence in the case. This instruction came from the Director of Public Prosecutions, Sir Theobald Mathew, who was sitting in court; he would later submit a report to the police commissioner outlining his reasons for dropping the charges, none of which were mentioned in court.

All of the defendants were acquitted; Jean Haddon was allowed to change her guilty pleas of conspiracy to 'not guilty', although her plea of guilty to actually passing the tools to Madsen remained and she was later placed on probation for twelve months. Four of the male defendants were awarded costs not exceeding 20 guineas, and Veronica Norris, the wife of Ernest Norris, received costs not exceeding 10 guineas. All of the released prisoners vowed to sue the police.

Three weeks later, justice finally caught up with Madsen and Norris who were sentenced to eight and six years' imprisonment respectively for the safe-blowing.

The DPP's report reached the commissioner's office, and it was clear that a rather searching enquiry was heading in Careless' direction, but otherwise it seemed to be business as usual. He was commended by the magistrate at Bow Street and the commissioner for ability and persistence in a difficult case of larceny, and then, three months later, on 28 August 1959, Careless tendered his voluntary resignation – and vanished.

It was later established that eleven days before his departure, Careless had submitted a false declaration for a joint passport with Eileen Bergmann – also known as Eileen Walsh – in which she was identified as his wife, Ethel Careless. It may or may not have had something to do with the fact that Mrs Bergmann's attendance was required at Thames Magistrates' Court for supplying intoxicating liquor outside permitted hours at a club she had formerly run in the East End. The passport had been authenticated by a Dr Beecher, who had known Careless for thirty years; unfortunately, Mrs Beecher stated that her husband, the doctor, had died eight years previously in 1951.

A warrant for Careless' arrest was issued; although it was suggested he might be in South Africa, the Yard had no idea of his whereabouts.

Within days of leaving the police, Careless and Mrs Bergmann left the country, going first to Trinidad, then Toronto, Canada, where initially he was employed in a store, then by Pinkerton's Detective Agency.

The couple returned to England on 30 June 1960, to find Norman Rae, crime reporter of the *News of the World*, and William Hemming, a former police officer and now a barrister, waiting for them at London Heathrow Airport. There was also a strong contingent from the popular press, as well as Detective Superintendent Stanley Shepherd and several other police officers. The dodgy passport was not found.

Careless was whisked away to Bow Street Magistrates' Court, and Mrs Bergmann to Thames Magistrates' Court, where she was fined £50 with £20 costs; their son, born in April 1959, was temporarily placed in the care of a woman police officer.

Bill Hemming did a good job, stressing that the relationship between his client and Mrs Bergmann had come about as a result of Careless' loveless and childless marriage, that he was 'the scourge of the underworld' and that many people of a 'certain mentality' were glad to see the back of him. He added that there was 'something' – he did not elaborate – that had occurred in Mrs Bergmann's past life which meant she was unable to procure a passport in her real name. Superintendent Shepherd was called to provide details of Careless' past career – the proposed escape from custody case was not mentioned – and on 11 July 1960, the Magistrate, Mr Bertram Reece, fined Careless £25 plus five guineas costs.

But if the escape plot was not mentioned at Bow Street Court it was at the Royal Courts of Justice when, four months later, Veronica Norris sued Careless for malicious prosecution and false imprisonment.

She told the court that the prosecution had withdrawn the charges because they believed Careless' story had been fabricated and that other police witnesses would have had to let him down and retract their earlier evidence. The allegation was, said Mrs Norris, fortified by the type of man Careless was: associating with 'a woman of bad character' who had run 'a low-down basement club in Stepney which was the resort of criminals, pimps and murderers'.

Careless' defence was that he was not actuated by malice and that he had reasonable and probable cause to believe that Mrs Norris had been concerned in the commission of a felony.

Summing up, Mr Justice Streatfeild stated that Careless was not the first man to throw up 'the prizes of a great career for the love of a woman', nor did it necessarily mark the defendant as a liar in his job, or brand the other officers as liars, and he entered judgement against Mrs Norris, who was obliged to pay costs.

Careless went on to provide often sensational copy for the *News of the World* before he disappeared for good.

However, there were anomalies regarding his leaving of the police. First, although he did not qualify for a pension by length of service, he was nevertheless handed a gratuity which at today's values was worth £11,710. Next, he left after twenty-two years and forty-one days' service; so he was entitled to a Long Service and Good Conduct Medal, to add to his war medals.

A Zealous Cop

And lastly, although he had committed a criminal offence punishable with a maximum of two years' imprisonment, eleven days before his resignation – and of course was later convicted of it – his conduct was described as 'exemplary'.

It did leave me scratching my head.

Chapter 23

An Old Master

When is a theft not a theft? Well, the answer used to be, when it's of a well-known and extremely valuable painting, because under the 1916 Larceny Act it was usually difficult to prove that the thief meant to permanently deprive the owner of it. A ransom was often demanded which, if successful, meant that the painting would be handed back. It was an anomaly plugged by Section 11 of the Theft Act 1968, which catered for 'removal of articles from places open to the public' and made the offence punishable on indictment with five years' imprisonment. On the one and only time I made such an arrest, for the much-nicked portrait by Rembrandt of *Jacob de Gheyn III*, valued at £2½ million, from the Dulwich Picture Gallery in 1982, the culprit admitted theft and copped three years' imprisonment, so the question didn't arise.

But it did back in 1961 when Francisco de Goya's portrait of *The Duke of Wellington* went missing from the National Gallery in London. It was valued at £140,000 (equal to £3,150,000 at today's values) because that was how much the Texas oil millionaire and art connoisseur Charles Bierer Wrightsman had paid for it at Sotheby's in June 1961. He required an export licence to take it back home, but questions were raised in the House and funds were made available by the Wolfson Foundation and the Treasury to keep the painting in this country, so Mr Wrightsman sportingly sold it to the National Gallery for the same amount he had paid for it.

The portrait was displayed for the public to admire until someone admired it so much that he helped himself to the 24 × 29 inch painting by climbing in through a lavatory window; the loss was discovered when the gallery reopened on 22 August 1961.

If the investigating officers at West End Central police station cast suspicious, accusing eyes in the direction of Mr Wrightsman's apartment, 3,455 miles away in Fifth Avenue, Manhattan, they were barking up the wrong tree. The purloined portrait was much closer to home; 282 miles away, in fact, at Newcastle-upon-Tyne, but they were not to know that. Nobody knew; not even the guilty man's wife.

But there was enormous speculation about the loss: could it be the work of a gang of international European art thieves who had stolen twenty paintings valued at £230,000 from the Colombe d'Or in April 1960 – or twenty-four paintings from Antibes, valued at £200,000, in April 1961? Then there were the fifty-seven paintings, valued at £750,000, stolen from a St Tropez gallery in July 1961 – plus the £7,000 painting stolen in Cannes, the same month – or the eight Cézannes worth £730,000 taken from Aix-en-Provence during the current month. Were these the work of one gang – or several? And was the gang – or the gangs, if they were linked – responsible for this outrage at the National Gallery?

Hundreds of people were questioned; the concept of an art-loving, eccentric millionaire drooling over the prize in a cellar was discounted by the police, and in that they were correct. However, the notion of a bunch of beastly 'foreign Johnnies' coming to our shores to nick a treasure belonging to the nation could not be disregarded. Interpol and the FBI were alerted, together with Special Branch officers, who cast a jaundiced eye over holidaymakers and suspicious-looking foreigners leaving the Channel ports.

It was all in vain; the portrait's £100 frame was three miles away in a cupboard under the stairs of a King's Cross boarding house, where the thief had been lodging; the portrait itself was hidden in a cupboard in the bedroom of a council house at Yewcroft Avenue, Newcastle-upon-Tyne.

It was not a daring English 'Raffles-style' crook that the police were searching for, nor was it a suave, smooth-as-silk, international European gang. In fact, it was a fat, 57-year-old unemployed lorry driver who was arguably as mad as a bag of bollocks; and although he had a prison record, having twice received custodial sentences for obstinately refusing to pay his television licence, the police did not include him in their list of suspects. In fact, it would take almost four years before he came to the attention of the authorities – and that was because he offered himself up on a plate to them.

But in the meantime, speculation continued to run riot; a man contacted the police two days after the theft to report that he had seen the painting on the back seat of a car in Tottenham Court Road; he hadn't. Additionally, a £5,000 reward was offered by the Trustees of the National Gallery for the safe return of the portrait.

On 31 August, a woman telephoned Reuter's News Agency, saying that she represented the persons responsible for stealing the Goya and for its return demanded that £140,000 should be given to charity. She then phoned the *Daily Mirror*, twice, informing them that the painting would be returned 'if we're given a free pardon'. The caller was later identified as 19-year-old Marcia Anne Phillips, a copy typist who was arrested after she stole a £10 portrait tablet from the National Portrait Gallery. She had nothing to do with the theft of the Goya and admitted the hoax. She had a history: in October 1959 there had been a jewel robbery that attracted a great deal of media attention, and Phillips went to a newspaper claiming she had found a book on the Underground containing details of the robbery. Her photograph appeared in the newspaper, but her story was fictitious. In April 1961, she was arrested after stealing two handbags from Lady Loraine's Wilton Crescent house; Phillips was found in possession of a knife, a pair of pliers and a screwdriver. Since she was into four months of the twelve-month probation order imposed for that offence, when she appeared at Bow Street Magistrates' Court a lenient approach was deemed out of the question and she was committed to the London Sessions for sentence. There she was sentenced to Borstal Training, having been told by the chairman, 'You have a chip on your shoulder . . . and you think exhibitionism is the right way to deal with it.'

She was not the only one. The culprit responsible for the theft had also telephoned Reuter's, demanding that a ransom of £140,000 should be paid to the Campaign for Nuclear Disarmament (CND) and adding that if the money was not forthcoming, the painting would be returned 'but not in a good condition'; that was followed up by an offer to reduce the ransom to £50,000 if it was paid in good time. CND haughtily repudiated any involvement with the demand and concentrated on organizing peaceful demonstrations where police officers could be routinely attacked.

Letters flooded in to the national press as well as the National Gallery: 342 of them in all, but just eight letters were from the person responsible, the first arriving eight days after the theft. Three of the letters were typewritten, one of which, sent in May 1963, was addressed to Lord Robbins, the chairman of the National Gallery's trustees, demanding £5,000 for the return of the painting; and on one of the letters was the sender's fingerprint. Another letter sent to Reuter's News Agency stated, 'This act is an attempt to pick the pockets of those who love art more than charity.'

Cinema audiences were delighted when the first James Bond film, *Dr No*, was released on 5 October 1962 and even more so when the doctor's sumptuous subterranean quarters on the Caribbean island of Crab Key were shown to contain the stolen painting. 'Sho there it ish', murmured Sean Connery.

The matter was still prominent in the public eye when on New Year's Eve 1962 a letter was received saying the sender would return the painting if he might wear a hood whilst doing so and was granted anonymity – but he didn't, so he wasn't.

And then, for two years, the trail went cold; until 6 May 1965, when a letter was sent to the editor of the *Daily Mirror* enclosing a ticket to the left luggage office at Birmingham New Street train station. There was the stolen Goya, and it was restored unharmed to the gallery.

But there was still no indication as to the identity of the perpetrator – the fingerprint found on the letter was not on file – until 19 July 1965, when a man walked into Scotland Yard claiming that he was responsible for the theft.

This was 61-year-old Kempton Cannon Bunton – he had been christened thus after the fortunes of his father had been improved by a jockey named Kempton Cannon, who rode the winner of the Derby in 1904 and who had won his first ever race on a horse named Bunting.

If he was not mentally disturbed he certainly gave a good impression of being so. Refusing to pay his television licence, he demanded that the magistrates commit him to prison – and they did. He launched a campaign to back his stance; but in the event he only received three letters, one of which expressed deep scepticism at his motives. But mentally unbalanced or not, there was something about him that was abundantly clear: Bunton was domineering, dictatorial and controlling, wishing to take command of every situation in which he found himself. This was demonstrated when he was confronted by Detective Chief Inspector John James Conrad Weisner and the following conversation took place:

'What is it you want?'

'I'm turning myself in for the Goya.'

'Are you saying you stole it?'

'Of course. That is why I'm here.'

'What is your name and address?'

'That can wait. As soon as you decide to charge me, I will tell you who I am but not before. Are you going to charge me?'

'Numerous people come here and confess to crimes they have not committed. If you can satisfy me that you committed the offence, then you may be charged. Why have you waited all this time before coming forward?'

'Is there still a reward for the person giving information about this?'

'I don't know.'

'I have let something drop and I believe someone may turn me in to get the reward. If the reward still stands, I want to give myself up to stop them getting the reward. If there is no reward, then we can forget it as the job is as dead as a dodo. Now, make up your mind. Are you going to charge me, or not?'

The extraordinary conversation continued, with Bunton describing how he had made up the parcel containing the portrait; he said that he had put an envelope addressed to the editor of the *Daily Mirror* on the outside of the parcel and thought he had printed the envelope, most probably in pencil. He then produced a small piece of pencil, saying, 'Are you convinced now that I took the painting?'

'You have not convinced me that you stole the painting', replied Weisner. 'If what you have told me about the parcel is right, then you may have been present when the parcel was packed, but that doesn't prove that you stole the painting. Can you tell me how you took it?'

'I am not saying anything more', said Bunton. 'You have got enough there. If you tell me I am going to be charged, I will tell you then.'

Detective Sergeant William 'Johnny' Johnson from West End Central was summoned who had more specialist knowledge of the case and who said, 'You've not mentioned one important thing about the wrapping of the parcel', to which Bunton replied, 'Oh, yes – it was wrapped in a pink plastic coat cover.'

Bunton then produced a pre-written statement, signed it and then said, 'Carry on. You'll make a big blunder if you don't charge me.'

Asked how he got into the National Gallery after closing time, Bunton replied, 'They were building at the back and I took a ladder when the guards were having a cup of tea or were asleep . . . I went through the open toilet window and along a passage and took it. I was by myself. I was not after this painting more than any other. I stole it to ransom it. I thought there would be an immediate collection for it.'

After being charged, Bunton told Sergeant Johnson, 'I shall fight this case on the goodness of it.'

Appearing at Bow Street Magistrates' Court, Bunton produced a further statement in which he said that the sole object of the theft was to set up a charity to pay for TV licences for old and impoverished people. He could not have been too happy if he had known that, four days after the theft, the BBC was demonstrating colour television at the National Radio Show when a picture of the missing portrait was flashed up on the screen. It would continue to be shown, every hour for a week, until the Radio Show ended.

Bunton was committed to the Old Bailey for trial, charged with the theft of the painting and its frame, uttering a letter demanding money with menaces to Lord Robbins, uttering a similar letter to the editor of the *Daily Mirror* and causing a public nuisance by removing the portrait from the gallery. To these charges, he pleaded not guilty.

He was defended by Jeremy Hutchinson QC, who asked a number of largely immaterial questions, including asking Lord Robbins if he thought the portrait was a fake, which prompted the Recorder of London, Sir Carl Aarvold, to say, 'I am going to interfere at this stage. It seems to me to be utterly irrelevant to this case. You need not answer that.'

When the charge of committing a public nuisance was raised, Hutchinson said, 'If you are stopping someone going to see an old bit of canvas with paint slapped on it, there might be some difference than if it were a painting worth £140,000.'

'Whether it was a genuine picture or rubbish . . . I think it would still be a picture of interest to the public', said the Recorder. 'If you are going to try to prove that this picture is a fake, I shall be interested but I doubt whether I shall allow it.'

Bunton was the centre of attention and he was loving it, especially when he was asked if he had told his wife that the portrait was hidden in the bedroom cupboard. 'No', he replied. 'The world would have known if I'd done so', and the public gallery in No. 1 Court howled with laughter.

'It was the defendant's desire for power which induced him to remove the portrait from the gallery', said Mr E.J.P. Cussen for the prosecution, and he hit the nail fairly and squarely on the head.

On 16 November 1965, the jury cleared Bunton of the two blackmail charges, plus the public nuisance charge, but found him guilty of stealing the portrait's frame. Sentencing him to three months' imprisonment, the Recorder told Bunton:

> The jury have accepted that at the material time you intended to return this picture and they have accepted that you made no demands for money with menaces for yourself or for charity, as such. I, of course accept the jury's verdict on these matters but motives, even if they are good, cannot justify theft. Creeping into public galleries to extract pictures of value in order to use them for your own purposes has got to be discouraged.

Although Bunton claimed that he had acted alone, in 1969 his son John was arrested for an unrelated, minor offence and stated that he had been responsible for the theft of the portrait. At six feet tall and quite conspicuously overweight, somewhere between seventeen and eighteen stone, the thought of 57-year-old Kempton Bunton scaling the outside wall, climbing a ladder, then squeezing through a lavatory window had raised some serious doubts, but Sir Norman Skelhorn, the Director of Public Prosecutions, decided that there was insufficient evidence to prosecute the son. Furthermore, it would be even more difficult to prosecute the father on a charge of perjury since reliance would have to be placed on the testimony of the son, who was quite clearly an unreliable witness. Therefore no further action was taken.

It's unlikely that Bunton had ever read Dale Carnegie's best-selling 1936 book *How to Win Friends and Influence People*, but in it the author mentions seven things that people aspire to, and top of the list was 'The Desire to be Great'.

That was what Bunton desired, but he was doomed to failure – because *he* was a failure. He had drifted from one job to another, each of them inevitably ending after a row with the management. He wrote articles, plays and a novel; none was ever published. He lived in a £2 per week council house on National Assistance with his wife and five children. When he went to prison for refusing to pay his television licence, having run the unsuccessful defence to the Newcastle Magistrates that he had modified his television so that it could only receive ITV, he was pitied rather than scorned.

But when he appeared in No. 1 Court at the Old Bailey – the same court where luminaries like Oscar Wilde, Crippen and Christie had stood in the dock, just like him – to be tried by the Recorder of London, the most senior judge – well, that was different! What was more, having a senior and junior counsel provided for him was completely free, courtesy of the Poor Prisoners' Defence Act of 1930.

It's true that at that three-ring circus of the judiciary Jeremy Hutchinson QC was the ringmaster, but there was no doubt whatsoever, that between 4 and 16 November 1965 the star-spangled attraction was none other than Kempton Cannon Bunton. In his later admissions to the police, John Bunton stated that both he and his brother Kenneth had been ordered by their father not to come forward, and that certainly had the ring of authenticity about it; no one would be allowed to steal the star attraction's thunder.

The media interest, already high as a result of the theft, intensified with Bunton's arrest – 'Johnny' Johnson described to me separating two reporters at Bow Street who were fighting each other to get a quote from Bunton – and although the expression was not in use at the time, it 'went viral'. His every utterance was repeated worldwide; his photographs graced all the newspapers. Here was a jolly 'man of the people', someone cocking a snook at authority – 'You would never have found it in 800 years,' he told the police – and all to pay for old and impoverished people's television licences. He may have come from 'up north', but as far as London readers of the *Daily Mirror* were concerned he was 'a diamond geezer'.

And then came the very lenient sentence; and that was that. 'I have nothing further to say' he said – and he hadn't. An appeal was discussed after he was moved from Wandsworth to Ford open prison one week after sentence, but by 1 December he decided not to pursue that course of action.

When Kempton Bunton died in Newcastle, eleven years later in 1976, he had already milked Andy Warhol's '15 minutes of fame' to the limit; and the public's memory of this egocentric, conceited man drifted into obscurity.

CHAPTER 24

The Enigmatic German

It was after several of the Great Train Robbers were handed down thirty-year sentences that, rather like sulky teenagers, they started muttering, 'We might as well 'ave used guns; we wouldn't 'ave got no more if we 'ad!'

It was after this that gangs did start using firearms during robberies and firing them as well; mind you, it was almost certainly the abolition of the death penalty, to prevent their necks getting stretched (in case of 'accidents'), that prompted that line of action, rather than the disgruntled wittering of the train gang.

But it was a fact that prior to the GTR, while armed robberies were carried out, they were few and far between. It makes it all the more surprising that six months prior to the Glasgow to London mail train coming to an unscheduled stop in Buckinghamshire, there was a sudden outbreak of armed robberies in Central and North London.

The person responsible lived south of the River Thames, worked alone and used his own car for getaways. He was an oddity; a 24-year-old German national, he had no known criminal associates, was married to an English girl and was employed as a decorator.

However, he had no hesitation in using a gun that fired gas projectiles which injured three of his victims; in the space of a few weeks he had stolen cash and jewellery worth in excess of £20,000 (approximately £423,000 at today's values), and his name was Volker Joseph Hans Von-Machazek.

It would have been a good idea to have coordinated these investigations – with the advent of the Robbery Squads in 1978 they would have been – but because the offences occurred during 1963 within the boundaries of different police stations, they were investigated separately.

Machazek started off modestly; he held up Jack Singer, the manager of a betting shop in Caledonian Road, and robbed him of £107. Next, he was more adventurous; threatening John Cremin, the manager of a jeweller's shop in South Moulton Street and David Woolmark his employee, he relieved them of cash and jewellery worth £15,500; and that was followed at Edwards'

Jewellers, Marble Arch, where he robbed Ronald Thomas Goldsmith of cash and jewellery valued at £4,500.

On 6 March 1963, Leon Weinstein, the 67-year-old manager of a jeweller's shop in Great Portland Street, was in a back room when he heard his assistant say, 'Don't be a fool; put it down,' and realizing, quite correctly, that a robbery was in progress, picked up a cosh and advanced into the front of the shop.

There he saw Machazek pointing a gun at his assistant and, as he later told the Bench at Clerkenwell Magistrates' Court, 'I jumped on him and caught hold of the gun. We had a good fight and he eventually wrenched the gun from my hand. He fired the gun and I was nearly blinded. He fired it in my face. I closed with him again and we eventually finished up in the corner and he fired again . . . I could not see anything.'

Machazek then fired the gun at Mr Weinstein's assistant and ran out of the shop.

His final attack was on 61-year-old Charles Johnson, a garage hand at the Russell Court Garage, Woburn Place, Bloomsbury at 10.30 on the evening of 13 March. Machazek, wearing a grey overcoat and a trilby hat, demanded that Mr Johnson open the safe. When he refused, Machazek fired the gun into his face, and although Mr Johnson was unable to see he raised the alarm and was able to provide a good description of his attacker, adding that he spoke with a Dutch or German accent and that afterwards he had heard the sound of a car driving off.

It was at about this time that two Flying Squad cars that were allocated night-duty cover for the whole of the Metropolitan area and provided assistance for provincial forces were on patrol. They were known as 'Night-Duty Provs', and in charge of one of the cars was Detective Inspector Ian Forbes (later Deputy Assistant Commissioner Forbes QPM).

He once famously said, 'The CID has no place for cowards or look-before-you-leap types. They must be resolute and determined men who are ready to act upon information, no matter where it comes from.' In view of what would happen that evening, it was a dictum well worth heeding.

This was 49-year-old Forbes' second posting to the Squad; he was a well-respected detective, hard as nails and with reliable informants.

But on this occasion it was Detective Constable John George's informant who came up trumps. As Forbes' car patrolled the streets of London's East End, George radioed him to say that an informant had told him that the man responsible for the attacks

The Enigmatic German 173

was a German whose name sounded like 'Makijik' and who lived somewhere near the Elephant and Castle, Southwark.

A check at Criminal Records Office revealed that a man named Volker Machazek had one previous conviction, and further searches provided an address at Queen's Buildings, a block of flats in Collinson Street, Southwark. Both 'Night-Duty Provs' cars met up, and six officers ascended the five flights of stairs to the top floor flat. It was now two o'clock in the morning, and when pyjama-clad Machazek opened the door, from the description of the suspect that had been provided the officers were quite satisfied that this was their man and, with a complete lack of ceremony, they grabbed him

But he appeared quite self-possessed; told the nature of the officers' visit, he replied, 'I don't know what you're talking about. I've been playing chess all night, here with my wife' and permitting the officers to search his flat, he told them, 'I am innocent.'

Nothing was found in the premises, but a search of his car produced the goods: a grey overcoat and a trilby hat, plus a revolver containing five cartridges and a spent one. This had been found behind a section of the dashboard, and under the floor carpet in the back of the car was a paper bag containing a further seventeen bullets, plus a box containing a valuable ring stolen from one of the held-up jewellers. Apart from that one ring, none of the rest of the stolen property was recovered.

Presented with the evidence, Machazek said, 'I'm saying nothing more until I've seen a solicitor,' and he was put into the back of one of the Squad cars. He was accompanied by John George, a very fit officer and one possessing a temper fuelled by a short fuse, plus Forbes, whose last encounter with a member of the German nation had been in the Reichwalde Forest in 1945, when he was a member of the 2nd Battalion of the Seaforth Highlanders and a bullet from one of their snipers had creased his face, entering behind his ear and passing through his shoulder.

By the time they reached Gray's Inn Road police station, Machazek had abandoned his thoughts about legal representation and taken the more sensible route of confessing to all five offences.

Telling Forbes that he had obtained the gun during a visit to Germany, he added, 'I knew that these bullets blinded people,' and said somewhat surprisingly, 'I tried one on myself once.'

But there was a far more worrying aspect to the case. Although the bullets in the gun were gas projectiles, the seventeen cartridges in the paper bag had been modified. The nose of each had been opened and in place of the gas heads, roughly-shaped pieces of metal had been inserted, turning them into lethal dum-dum bullets, capable of causing life-threatening injuries. There were no more gas projectiles left; if Machazek had needed any more bullets, he would have used these.

After Leon Weinstein gave evidence at Clerkenwell Court, the Magistrate, Mr L.E. Barker, told him, 'You acted with quite extraordinary courage; you are a very brave man. I think it is something of which public acknowledgement should be made.'

Machazek, meanwhile, pleaded not guilty, reserved his defence and was committed to the Old Bailey, where before the Common Serjeant on 1 May 1963 he reverted to pleading guilty to everything.

Sentencing him to eight years' imprisonment, the Judge told him:

> You armed yourself with a terrifying weapon . . . you carried out your plans with determination and a vicious disregard for the safety of your victims. Each of these offences would call for a sentence of imprisonment for life and only your youth prevents me from passing such a sentence. The only refreshing aspect of this case is the personal courage shown by your victims.

That, of course, was not the end of the story. On Wednesday, 18 March 1964, Machazek, together with fellow prisoner Leonard Joseph Smith, scaled the wall of Wormwood Scrubs prison. Smith broke his leg but fortunately, Hammersmith hospital was directly opposite, so he received the best medical care along with his loss of remission.

Machazek on the other hand made it all the way to Woolwich but he had no real escape plan. He asked for a glass of water at a house; the occupier didn't like the look of him at all and phoned the police. A passing police constable spotted him, and without a murmur the fugitive surrendered.

Following his release, he changed his name by deed poll to Volker Von-Lauer and went right off the radar for almost twenty years. Divorced, he was now living at Garden Cottage, Elmwood Close, Reading Street, Broadstairs, Kent and was a property developer/builder, running several businesses in the Thanet area as well as a kitchen furniture shop in Ramsgate.

But at the beginning of January 1983 he was being sought by the local police in connection with an assault in Margate. Their investigations led them to Von-Lauer's flat, where on 5 January he was found dead from a gunshot wound to the chest.

A gun was found next to the body, and no other person was sought in connection with his death, but at his address as well as in his warehouse next door were found tubes of explosives and wiring. These, said a police spokesman, 'were sufficient to give cause for concern' and were taken away for examination, while thirty local people were evacuated overnight and a controlled explosion was carried out on a briefcase. Sniffer dogs were used to search for any other devices and 'certain documents' were retrieved from his house but were not thought to be connected to any subversive organization.

Von-Lauer – aka Machazek – died as he lived; a complete mystery.

Chapter 25

'Ray the Cat'

Nantyglo is a village in Monmouthshire and in the mid-nineteenth century it was regarded as the most important iron-producing centre in the world.

One of the outstanding sons of that village was Jack Henry Williams, who for his gallantry during the First World War was awarded the Victoria Cross, the Distinguished Conduct Medal, the Military Medal and Bar – all on the same day. He had been badly wounded by shrapnel; in fact, the wounds opened up during his investiture, so badly that he had to receive medical attention before leaving Buckingham Palace. The French also awarded him the *Médaille Militaire*, of which, more later ...

Unfortunately, it is rather a lesser personage whom many prefer to remember as a champion of the village.

Born three years before Williams' investiture, a burglar named Raymond Jones – who liked to be known as 'Ray the Cat' and 'Ray the Climber' – claimed that he had almost had a shot at the British middleweight boxing crown; except that he hadn't, because he was not a professional boxer. He also claimed that during his criminal career he had stolen anything between £60 and £100 million; but he ended up in a Dalston council flat, on benefits. He was almost supernaturally boastful, alternately whining that he had been 'fitted up' and then demanding to be arrested for serious unsolved crimes. He got women to alibi him in court, to write to the Home Secretary to prove his innocence after he had been 'fitted up' and then to have pamphlets printed to hand out to passers-by, detailing the crimes that he had committed and for which the police had declined to arrest him. When he broke out of prison Jones was championed by his widowed mother, who stated he was never violent. This was the same mother who, according to Jones, had tied him to a bed with a clothesline when he was a boy, having discovered that he had stolen 'thousands of pounds', and whipped him with a leather belt until 'it ripped the whole of the flesh off my body'.

Much of Jones' self-proclaimed CV that was slavishly accepted as the truth by Jones-worshippers consisted of lies; the rest was bullshit.

His formative years from the age of twelve were spent in and out of remand homes and Borstal. In June 1936, he stood trial at Breconshire Assizes on a charge of breaking into the home of the Hon. Miss Mabel Bailey and stealing jewellery to the value of £96. His alibi stood up and he was acquitted. On 29 October 1936, the home of Mrs Nellie Paine was broken into and a gold and a silver wristlet watch were stolen; Jones stood trial at Abingdon Petty Sessions, where the bench was told that other charges would 'probably' be preferred against him.

It appeared that they were, although that was not made clear at Blaina Police Court in November 1937. He had been summoned to appear on charges of punching one woman on the chin, striking another woman in the eye and also knocking out the son of one of them.

His mother, Mrs Julia Jones, and several other women were similarly accused of assault and bound over to keep the peace, but Mrs Jones staunchly defended her son, telling the Bench that Raymond had not attended court 'because he was working in London and could not afford the fare'. Although Raymond Jones was described in court as 'the villain of the piece', the summons against him was dismissed after his mother and three members of the Edwards family stated that he had not touched the women.

His inability to afford the fare was not the reason why he had failed to attend court; the truth of the matter was that since June 1937 Jones had been on the run, having been circulated as being wanted for house-breaking and assault at Abingdon, Berkshire.

Going on the run became a habit. In December 1937, police had spotted Jones and another man attempting to steal from a car at Marble Arch (although his fans maintain he was engaged in nothing more than 'a pre-dinner stroll'); Jones then knocked an officer unconscious. He was circulated as wanted, and the following month, a police officer at Nantyglo recognized him and was similarly assaulted; it was not until February 1940 that he was arrested, in Lambeth. It was probably on this occasion that Jones, who should have kept his big mouth shut, didn't. He told Detective Constable Donald Hope, who was taking his antecedents and wanted to know his employment history for the past two years, that during that time he had assaulted 'numerous police officers' who had had the impudence to try to arrest him and that he had lived on the proceeds of house-breaking, which had brought him so much profit that as well as having £50 in his pocket he had managed to acquire twenty-one suits.

The officer felt impelled to share details of Jones' good fortune with Judge Beazley at the Old Bailey in March 1940, and the Judge, telling Jones that he had been guilty of 'a savage attack', sentenced him to two years' imprisonment.

Now, here come details of that commodity beloved of most criminals – justification. No professional criminal worth his salt will ever say, 'Well, I decided that breaking into people's property and nicking their belongings was far easier than getting a regular job – and what's more, if I couldn't get away after punching a copper, I could always say I was fitted up.' Oh, no, justification is needed – and in Jones' case, it came in the form of his brother Dai. Jones' worshippers could never decide whether their hero was serving his two-year sentence – then again, it might have been six years – at Chelmsford or Pentonville Prison, but details like that hardly matter. Legend has it that having visited his incarcerated brother, Dai was killed in a wartime bombing raid on his way back to the railway station.

The two things that Jones said mattered most to him – his brother and becoming a British – sorry, World – boxing champion – had been taken away from him, and there and then he swore revenge upon the establishment. As he would later say, 'Like Robin Hood, I'd steal from the rich in order to settle a few of the all-too-many scores between the privileged elite and the endlessly abused working class.'

Leaving this confused sociological bullshit to one side, it raises a question, since it was Hitler's Luftwaffe who had killed his brother: why didn't this 23-year-old, supremely fit and possible (if not probable) contender for global honours in the world of pugilism, join the armed forces when he was released from his two-year sentence in 1941? Probably because if he had been captured, escaped and continued to pursue his day job in Germany, he would have discovered that due to a sharp rise of house-breakings in Berlin, Hitler's chief of police, Heinrich Himmler, had decreed that in future those found guilty of that offence would be decapitated. No, far better to stay over here and commit burglaries in comparative safety, as he did between 9 and 10 April 1942, when he and brother Harry Horace Jones and another man broke into a clothier's in Victoria Street, stole clothing valued at £110 8s 0d and clumped a police officer who tried to stop them.

Fast-forward now to 11 November 1943, when Jones and Harry Edmund Bowalls broke into a house at Dulwich Wood Park, West Norwood and stole jewellery and other items valued at £208. Later the same day, a Norwegian sailor named Frede

Kjergaard was picked up by a young woman to whom he handed £1 for the rent of a room. Jones and another man – who may, or may not have been Mr Bowalls – threatened the sailor with a knife and demanded another £4, which was duly handed over.

Jones was caught on 5 January 1944 as he was leaving Wandsworth prison, having visited a chum; possibly Bowalls, who by then had been sentenced for the West Norwood housebreaking. Told that he was being arrested for both offences, Jones replied, 'You've made a mistake. Do me a favour and grant me bail. My father is dead and I want to go to Wales for the funeral. I'm not worried about the job with Bowalls but I've never done a robbery job.'

Told that he would be put up for identification, he said, 'I want the parade at Brixton prison. There are no private witnesses in the Bowalls job, are there? They're all police. I know why you picked me up, because you found my ration books at Bowalls' place.'

His ration books had indeed been found at Bowalls' address at 46 Claverton Street, Pimlico, and on 6 January Jones was put up for identification. Detective Inspector Fluendy of the Flying Squad took him from his cell, whereupon Jones asked to have a wash. Having done so, he combed his hair in a completely different style, tied a white silk scarf round his neck in choker fashion and donned an overcoat. Despite continually changing his position in the line-up, he was picked out by two constables from 'P' Division (where the house-breaking had occurred) and also by the Norwegian sailor.

At the Old Bailey, Jones recalled that 11 November was Poppy Day and called his mother plus two other women witnesses to say they had been in his company for several hours before, during and after the robbery.

It did him no good; the jury disbelieved Jones and his distinctly dodgy witnesses. The court heard that he had fourteen previous convictions, and in what Jones and his followers would describe as another miscarriage of justice, he was weighed off with eighteen months' imprisonment.

* * *

The most fortunate couple at the 1951 New Year's Eve party given by Lieutenant Colonel Martin Charteris at his home in Ingram Avenue, Golders Green, were Lieutenant Commander Michael Parker, equerry to the Duke of Edinburgh, and his wife; because they left the party at 11.30pm.

Meanwhile, Colonel Charteris, private secretary to the (then) Princess Elizabeth, and his twenty guests continued with the celebrations and dancing ('It was rather noisy; reels, you know') and heard nothing untoward such as a ladder being shoved up against a second floor window. Neither did the three Charteris children, Mary, six years old, Andrew, four and Harry, almost two; all were fast asleep on the same floor.

But at 1.30am on 1 January 1952 it was quickly discovered that something was very wrong, when the ladies went to Mrs Charteris' bedroom on the second floor to collect their fur coats – only to find them missing. The dyed ermine coat belonging to the younger daughter of the Earl of Sandwich, Lady Elizabeth Montagu, which was valued at £400, was gone; so was the coat belonging to the niece of the Prime Minister, Miss Clarissa Churchill, worth £600. Then there was the £460 coat belonging to Miss Vella Abul-Huda and the fur coat valued at £10 less than Miss Abul-Huda's which was the property of the Hon. Janet Margesson, daughter of Viscount Margesson, wartime Secretary for War – both missing.

There was Mrs Ann Martelli, not to mention Mrs M. Padev, formerly the Princess Priscilla Bibesco, daughter of the former Romanian Minister to the United States and granddaughter of Lady Oxford – their coats had also vanished, and the haul, with a total value of £4,095, represented a nice little New Year's present for Alan 'Jock' Grant and Raymond Jones.

Time to call in the Flying Squad; fortunately, Detective Inspector William MacDonald was already on the case.

MacDonald had previously served a four-year wartime tour with the Flying Squad; now he was back again and had achieved astonishing successes working with the Ghost Squad. It's fair to conclude that he had retained his various sources of information, because within 24 hours of the burglary MacDonald and his team were inside an observation van keeping watch on a house in Willesden and saw Jones and Grant enter the premises. The following afternoon, they saw Jones back a black car out of a garage – it had been stolen in November 1951 and bore false number plates – and then drive to the Willesden address. Grant handed Jones a suitcase, the police pounced and, while Jones made good his escape, Grant was arrested and ten out of the eleven stolen fur coats were recovered.

★ ★ ★

At the end of January there was a burglary with the use of a ladder at 'Silverwood', West Drive, Wentworth, Surrey, where jewellery and a satinwood gem case, valued at £2,010, were stolen. Although Surrey police threw a cordon around the area, the gang got through – and vanished – and it was quite possible that their number included Raymond Jones. Their getaway car was left behind, but MacDonald knew who he was looking for: George Pyser, a 22-year-old illiterate barrow boy, who over a period of two years had been hiring cars for the gang, sometimes at the rate of two per day. MacDonald kept observation on his Drury Lane address for five days and nights, before Pyser decided to walk into New Scotland Yard and report that the car he had hired had been stolen.

At the Surrey Quarter Sessions nobody believed that a costermonger earning £10–£15 per week could afford to pay for cars simply for 'pleasure trips' into the country. Pyser had five previous convictions, mainly for very minor offences, and although the headmistress of St Clement Dane's School, which he had attended until the age of fourteen and left without being able to read or write, informed the court, 'He had never been known to do anything shady, was most honest and truthful', Sir Tom Eastham, the senior deputy chairman, took a different view.

'The only way to stop these offences is to deal with them in such a way that it will be a deterrent to others', he said, and after he sentenced Pyser to five years' imprisonment, it took four gaolers and police officers to remove him from the dock, as he repeatedly cried, 'Five years? Oh, no!'

By now, Alan Grant (coincidentally, also a costermonger) had appeared at the Old Bailey and been sentenced to seven years' imprisonment for his part in the burglary at the Charteris premises – but where was Jones? Not buying fruit for costermongers (which was how he would describe his profession), that was for sure.

In February he was seen, still driving the stolen car, in Monmouthshire, but on 4 April he was spotted in London's Baker Street and arrested. Questioned by MacDonald, who informed him that Grant had been arrested, Jones replied, 'Don't I know it! Because I was carrying the case with the gear in it doesn't mean I did the job. I've got my defence, all right. I know you and I can beat you. I can still get out of it.'

He had a good go at it and he could afford to be defended by Petre Crowder QC, MP (who would later defend Ronnie Kray in the first of the gangland murder trials); Jones' defence was a complete denial.

The car? He had hired it from Grant, to go to Wales; he had no idea it belonged to anybody else.

The burglary? He was nowhere near the scene of the burglary; from 9.00pm on New Year's Eve until 2 o'clock the following morning he was at a friend's house in Westminster. He had not seen Grant during that period.

The arrest the following day? Ah, that was because he hadn't known the men who had rushed at him were police; he thought that they were members of 'The West End Mob' who had stabbed his brother the previous July. He had had a fight with the gang leader – a man named Billy Hill – and Hill, boasted Jones, had got the worst of it. In fact, he called Detective Inspector Edward McKechnie to court to confirm that his younger brother, Harry Horace Jones, had been stabbed in the chest in Dean Street, Soho on 8 July the previous year.

It was a fairly imaginative ploy, except for this: if there had been a fight with Billy Hill, Hill would have ensured that Jones' knuckles had been pulverised to the consistency of semolina, to see how many ladders he could climb thereafter. So there was no fight with Hill. It was Hill who had approached Jones, since his brother had named Frederick 'Slip' Sullivan as his attacker. Since Sullivan was Hill's able lieutenant, he wanted the charges withdrawn against him, and Raymond Jones obliged Hill by persuading his brother to do just that.

But in the end, Jones' protestations didn't work; and on 23 June 1952 he was found guilty and sentenced to six and a half years' imprisonment. He could not go without making a profound Jones-style statement; leaning over the dock, he picked up his girlfriend, to ostentatiously kiss her goodbye.

Jones was released just in time to be arrested for housebreaking and larceny; according the Jones-worshippers this was a real fit-up, a proper travesty of justice, because in October 1957 he was sentenced to eight years' preventative detention.

Within a year, Jones led a five-man team in an escape from Pentonville prison; with 630 out of the 1,350 inmates on 'free association', Jones and another prisoner scaled a 20ft ladder, but three others were seized before they could follow them. The two men were believed to have been picked up by a car that was waiting for them, but perhaps this was press hyperbole, as was the suggestion that Jones had spearheaded a grand escape of 20–30 inmates, organized by the underworld. Jones' co-escaper was recaptured the same day after he answered a knock on the door by police at his home address in Chingford.

'He may be violent' was a classic understatement by Scotland Yard but hotly denied by Jones' mother, who also stated that his escape had been carried out to draw attention to his 'wrongful conviction'; this was in addition to asking his sister to present a petition to the Home Secretary demanding an enquiry into evidence which would prove that Jones – by now referring to himself as 'The Aristocrat of Crime' – had been framed by an underworld boss.

During his escape from Pentonville it was said that Jones smashed his kneecap, broke his ankle, then broke his uninjured leg when he jumped. He then crawled on to a flat roof and fell through the skylight, knocking himself unconscious. Recovering, he dragged himself out of the building, pulled himself along the railings in Caledonian Road and crawled across the thoroughfare to King's Cross railway station. There, he dragged himself across a criss-cross of railway lines, fortunately devoid of passing trains until, screaming with agony, he climbed over a wall and into a garden. Gamely, he kept going until he met some men gathered around a broken-down car and threw himself on their mercy. Quickly repairing whatever was wrong with the car, these strangers drove him to a relative's flat, where Jones' wife was contacted. She rented a secret flat for him, where he stayed until he had recovered sufficiently on 30 May 1960 to steal Sophia Loren's jewellery, comprised of diamonds, emeralds and rubies valued at £185,000, from the Norwegian barn she had rented whilst filming *The Millionairess* with Peter Sellers.

Let's stop right there, shall we? The story of Jones dragging the shattered remnants of his lower body along brightly-lit Caledonian Road, then across the myriad of railway tracks at King's Cross for over a mile before salvation in the guise of a group of good Samaritans nursing a broken-down car spirited him away can be put in its proper context when one realizes that its source was the late Francis Davidson 'Mad Frankie' Fraser, who was not especially noted for his veracity.

Leaving that utter, specious bollocks to one side, let's concentrate on what actually happened. A Jaguar saloon was stolen from Warminster, the day after Jones' escape, and on Sunday, 26 October, driven by a man who appeared to wish to escape recognition by pulling a cap over his eyes, it stopped at a petrol pump station at Five Lanes, between Newport and Chepstow. In fact, the driver did rather more than stop there; when it was discovered that the garage had been broken into and an attempt made to force the petrol pump lock, the police were alerted and a road block was set up on the Gloucester–Lydney Road. The Jaguar swerved around it, the driver escaped across country and the following morning, the safe was blown with explosives in the nearby Caldecote branch of the Co-operative Society store.

Four days later, there was an excited press report that Jones could be in France with Alfie Hinds, a fellow escapee, who had similarly absconded in order to prove his innocence because he, like Jones, had been framed.

And then the trail went cold, until Jones was recaptured at a house in Staines, Middlesex (again by the Flying Squad) on 23 November 1960 and was once more returned to quod.

Released in the 1960s, he came to the attention of Police Constable Mervyn 'Taff' Gee, who was on night-duty patrol in Hampstead and at 2.30am saw him exiting from a driveway of a house. 'He was very well dressed and well spoken', Gee told me. 'He said that he had been taken short and went into the driveway to relieve himself.' Sure enough, there on the driveway was the evidence glistening in the street lamps, and after Gee had searched him he let Jones go.

He later returned to Hampstead police station, and there in the charge room was Jones. The two men started chatting and it transpired that, coincidentally, Gee had been born in Nantyglo, two streets away from Jones. The reason for Jones' attendance in the charge room was soon revealed; shortly after their encounter, Jones had been stopped by the local 'Q' Car. Their attention to Jones had been rather more thorough, and they had found a substantial number of diamonds secreted inside his socks.

Raymond Jones next came to notice after Peter Craig Gulston (alias Peter Scott, 'The Human Fly') published his memoirs, *Gentleman Thief: the Recollections of a Cat Burglar*, in which he stated that – apart from relieving such luminaries as Zsa-Zsa Gábor, Deborah Kerr and Ginger Rogers of their valuables – he was also responsible for the theft of Sophia Loren's jewellery. He was not alone in his assertion; burglar and robber Sidney Cugullere would later lay claim to the same theft, as I feel sure did a few more enterprising screwsmen.

But Scott had not mentioned Jones' alleged involvement in the theft, and this was more than the egotistical Welshman could bear. Matters were not improved when Jones went into a North London police station and demanded to be arrested for it; not only was he rebuffed, but when a *Daily Mirror* reporter described him as 'an emaciated . . . hobbling old man', he hit the roof.

With his grip on reality disintegrating faster than Ronnie Kray's, Jones now took to having leaflets printed proclaiming his guilt which he handed out to passers-by near his council flat in Dalston. 'People may say I'm just trying to get publicity, but I'm not', he said. 'I did carry out the theft and I want the police to prosecute me. I want my day in court.' He took to talking to anyone who would listen, especially an Ulster-born former petrol pump attendant, who was also a spiritualist and who urged him to publish his memoirs. Jones would say that his other victims included R.A. Butler, the former Home Secretary, the Duke of Rutland, Lord McIntosh, Bette Davis and Elizabeth Taylor ('a spoilt and pampered actress').

He clung on to one reporter's hand to stop him leaving; he simply wanted an audience.

Jones, who had spent three decades in prison, died of cancer at his flat in 2001 aged eighty-four. His alleged associate, Peter Scott, followed him to the grave twelve years later. Like Jones, Scott was living on £60 per week benefits in a council flat. The difference was that Scott received an obituary in several leading newspapers and Jones did not. That must have been the unkindest cut of all.

★ ★ ★

As a matter of interest, this brings us back to the beginning of this chapter. Jack Williams, who was the most decorated non-commissioned Welsh soldier of all time, was not forgotten by the French. They had no doubt that Williams' gallant actions, when he single-handedly bayoneted five of the enemy and captured fifteen more, for which he was awarded the VC, had saved their village of Villers-Outréaux from certain destruction. As well as decorating him at the time, in 2018 the villagers dedicated a specially commissioned memorial to commemorate him.

Perhaps their counterparts in Nantyglo might like to do the same; unless, of course, they consider 'Ray the Cat' to have been of more importance.

CHAPTER 26

The Safe-blowing Cop

Whenever police corruption is mentioned, inevitably (and sometimes accurately) the finger is pointed at the CID in general and the Flying Squad in particular. Nevertheless, during the 1950s, the uniform branch at 'C' Division's West End Central police station came under scrutiny, and a huge internal enquiry was launched following allegations that they were receiving bribes from racketeers, gangsters and ponces to permit the smooth flow of traffic in the prostitution industry.

But what follows is a tale that featured a uniformed constable on the beat not in steamy Soho but in a sleepy suburb of London, and when I researched the case, the enormity and sheer criminality of it knocked me sideways.

★ ★ ★

Chingford is situated to the north-east of London, the last outpost of the Metropolitan Police and abutting Essex Constabulary. It has a population of almost 70,000 and the council estates are governed by Waltham Forest Housing Association, whom the residents almost unanimously describe as being 'rude, unprofessional and uncaring'. During one month in 2020, a total of 444 crimes were recorded there, which included 174 instances of antisocial behaviour and 84 violent crimes.

It was not always so. Over sixty years ago, a posting to Chingford was dreamt of by police officers who were past their sell-by date. It meant doing very little until their retirement when, their mortgages paid off, they could spend their days in the bar at nearby Chigwell Sports Club regaling anyone who cared to listen with details of their days as stalwart crime-busters. Anybody in their vicinity who had actually provided an input into proactive police duties inevitably gave them a wide berth.

So in 1959 Chingford was a bit of a sleepy hollow, although there were thrilling moments, such as when the sound of a shotgun being discharged woke up Police Constable George Dorsett, who had been recovering from night duty. Already the recipient of a George Medal, Dorset disarmed the youth who threatened him with the firearm, and when he was awarded a bar to his George Medal, that event just about coincided with a sudden outbreak of serious crime in torpid Chingford...

Westcott's Sweet Clean Launderette, Chingford Mount Road was broken into on the night of 26 June 1959, and although the safe was found to be packed with explosives, there was no detonation and nothing was taken; the perpetrators had obviously been disturbed and had decamped.

Next, came an attack on the Westminster Bank, Station Road. This was over the weekend of 29/31 August 1959. Gelignite blew a hole two feet square in the wall of the strong-room; the noise was deadened by covering the wall with a water-soaked mattress. A second explosion only succeeded in jamming the safe containing £10,000; nevertheless, jewellery and cash from deed boxes were stolen, amounting to £2,578. Mrs Kathleen Willis, who lived next door to the bank, stated that she had heard three explosions, but due to the proximity of Chingford railway station, a commuter terminal, she thought the noise had emanated from there and went back to sleep. Entry to the bank – a smashed window with the bars sawn through – was discovered by a vigilant passing constable, who telephoned Scotland Yard.

Two months later came the next attack, this time at the National Provincial Bank, Oldchurch Road, again over a weekend, 31 October/2 November 1959. This time the gang had climbed an iron staircase up to a flat roof. They had already helped themselves to a small ladder from a nearby greengrocer's yard and used this to climb to a higher roof, where they removed a pane of glass from a skylight, then dropped the ladder inside and climbed down. Their first attempt to blow the locks on the strong-room failed; the charges only jammed the locks, much as had previously happened at the Westminster Bank. This was because the safe-makers had implemented a 'fail-safe' device, which in the event of an explosion threw bolts behind the door of the safe as well as immobilizing the handle. However, there was a ventilator shaft in the strong-room wall and they used gelignite to blast their way in, once more resulting in a two foot square hole, and now they ransacked the deed boxes, obtaining jewellery, gold sovereigns, half-sovereigns and cash to the value of £18,182. Mr David Spender, the manager of the shoe shop next door, heard an explosion, but since Guy Fawkes' Night was just around the corner he thought it was mischievous youths setting off fireworks. Later on, he recalled a lot more...

The Safe-blowing Cop

It was common during those halcyon days of policing to call in the night-duty patrols following overnight serious crimes, to ask them where they were, what they were doing and what if anything they had heard or seen. And then something became quite clear. The officer patrolling these beats at the time of all of the occurrences had been Police Constable 564 'J' George Albert Askew. That could have been a coincidence, except for the fact that on each of those occasions, Askew had actually volunteered for night duty. And even stranger than that, he had been offered a posting as a wireless operator on the area car – a plum job for any keen young copper, but also a very acceptable one for 39-year-old Askew, who could have comfortably settled down on cold October nights in the snug interior of a Wolseley 6/90 and been effortlessly chauffeured around by a Class I driver. But Askew had turned it down, preferring to walk the beat.

And that didn't seem just odd to Detective Chief Inspector Henry Baker; it seemed insane, and it begged the question: was there a wrong 'un in 'J' Division's uniform branch?

Askew was certainly rather odd; a former Palestine Police officer, he had first joined the Met on 16 August 1948 as Police Constable 472 'N', but after six years of undistinguished service he received a medical discharge and a gratuity following an accident and suffering depression. Two years later, on 23 September 1956, he rejoined the Met and was posted to Chingford. Tony Pepper, then a constable (and later Superintendent) at neighbouring Hackney, recalled him as 'a boring, old-soldier type'.

But on 7 November, five days after the breaking at the bank, when Askew bought a new car and paid £351 of the asking price in cash, then put down a deposit of £1,500, also in cash, on a bungalow – bearing in mind that his weekly police constable's wage was £10 3s 0d – Baker decided it was sufficient to authorize a team of detectives to carry out surveillance on Askew at his house at Lloyd Road, Walthamstow. It commenced on 14 November and continued until 6 December 1959, but although it was carried out clandestinely it soon became common knowledge at Chingford police station, as John Benstead discovered. He was attached to 'G' Division at the time and had spoken to one of his contemporaries based at Chingford. As Benstead said, 'He told me of the suspicions and goings-on and even named the officer!'

However, it appears that Askew was unaware of the sudden interest in him and his movements, and during that time he was seen in the company of John Thomas Young, aged seventy-one, who lived in Eade Road, Harringay. Askew was also seen in a car with Young and Edward John Irving, aged thirty-four, of Compton Crescent, Tottenham; and on another occasion, Askew met up with William Ernest Goodwin, a 30-year-old window cleaner from North House, Harlow, in a pub. In turn, those men were tailed off and their backgrounds investigated.

Irving already had sufficient convictions to qualify him for three years' corrective training in September 1950 for shopbreaking, and Goodwin also had four previous convictions when he appeared at North London Magistrates' Court in November 1947; the magistrate described him as being 'a perfect little spiv' and sentenced him to six months' imprisonment for taking and driving away.

Young was a real old-timer; he had already been referred to as 'a habitual criminal' when he appeared at the Old Bailey for stealing a car in October 1921 and was sent to penal servitude for three years.

So that was a pretty trio for Askew to be mixing with, and matters were not helped when they all denied knowing one another. That happened on the morning of 7 December, when Askew reported at the police station for early turn. His address was searched and cash amounting to £1,559 10s 0d, plus eight sovereigns and six half sovereigns, was seized. He told the officers that the notes had come from horse deals.

When he was charged with the breaking at the National Provincial Bank, Askew replied, 'It's impossible. Mr Harvey, the Conservative MP, and Mr Fellowes, the solicitor, can prove I was not there. I was on the same table with them at a dinner until two o'clock in the morning. I remember it because that's the day I went sick.' (This statement was later furiously denied in court; Jimmy Fellowes, loyal defender of the better class of criminal, could not afford to be put up as an alibi witness by a copper!) When he was charged Askew replied, 'I emphatically deny it and have done so from the outset.'

But as well as all the booty found at Askew's address, a forensic examination of a pair of Askew's uniform trousers revealed explosive material in the hip pocket.

At the same time as Askew's arrest, other searches were carried out. Police went to Irving's address at Compton Crescent, where at 5.30am Police Constable Westcott saw a bedroom light come on and the window being opened; it appeared that two women, Irving's mother Rose and his 24-year-old sister Beryl, were wrapping something in paper and throwing it into a neighbouring garden. When Detective Sergeant (later Chief Inspector) Arthur Maxwell recovered and unwrapped the parcel, it was found to contain seventy-four £1 notes and four £5 notes. Mrs Irving said, 'I threw it out' and Miss Irving truthfully said, 'I didn't.' Mrs Irving went on to say, 'Eddy gave it to me a few days ago to mind for him. When you came, I got frightened and threw it out of the window.'

When Goodwin's house was searched, money in bundles of £100 ('because I am tidy in everything I do') was found in a basket under his kitchen sink covered with newspaper and potatoes; the seven sovereigns found, Goodwin stated, had been purchased from a kerbside dealer in Hatton Garden. He would later mournfully tell a jury that he had hired a private enquiry agent to trace this shady customer, but without success.

Now the evidence started to come together. Mr David Spender, manager of the shoe shop next door to the National Provincial Bank, told police that he saw two men carrying a cardboard box in the entrance to an alley leading to the bank at about 11.30pm on the Saturday of the weekend that the bank was attacked. The next night, at about 8.30pm, he saw one of the men standing at the foot of the iron staircase looking towards the strong-room. He picked out both men – Irving and Goodwin – on an identification parade.

Goodwin agreed that he had spent £1,500 in November and had banked £470. This was money he had saved in order to buy a shop; when he decided against it, he had spent the money 'on necessities'.

On one occasion when Askew had been in his car with Young it was involved in a slight collision; the following day, Askew reported that his car had been stolen. When his deal on the bungalow fell through, Askew retrieved the £1,500 deposit and paid the money into his bank account.

Goodwin, who was practically unemployed, purchased a car, paying £300 for it in three instalments; some of the notes were very cold, as though they had been kept in a refrigerator, and the furniture in his bungalow was almost new.

At Irving's address an electric drill, three masonry bits, three jemmies, skeleton keys and two driving licences with the names and addresses bleached out were found. Irving was charged with receiving £170; he was further charged with receiving one £2 gold piece and £892 1s 4d, Askew with receiving £3,623 2s 7d, eight sovereigns and six half-sovereigns and additionally £570, Young was charged with receiving £171 10s 0d, a metal match case and two sovereigns and Goodwin with receiving £1,840 14s 3d and seven sovereigns.

These were only holding and alternative charges; all four men were charged with breaking into the National Provincial Bank, at which Irving replied, 'I was not on that job.' However, as DCI Baker told Chingford Magistrates, 'I must say there will be further serious charges. The matter is assuming even graver proportions', and although Tony Pepper recalled Baker as 'a large bombastic man who used to do his morning office work in his braces', he was right. Askew and Irving were further charged with breaking into the Westminster Bank and Askew alone with breaking into the launderette, although as the Magistrates were informed, 'that was not to say that he was the only person involved'. Mrs and Miss Irving, both charged with receiving £94, were allowed bail, but after hearing that a witness had been approached, the four men were remanded in custody and committed to Essex Assizes for trial.

During that trial Beryl Irving was discharged on the counts of receiving and being an accessory after the fact. There was a lady who had wined, dined and danced with Askew over the weekend of the National Provincial bank raid who appeared to be rather confused about the time that she and Askew had arrived home. She had originally told detectives when she was interviewed on 8 December that they had arrived home at 12.15am but now, in court, the time differed. It appeared that she had told detectives that she had seen him with 'hundreds of pounds' – now it appeared it was no more than probably £20, nor could she recall how much money Askew had given her. She admitted she had seen him with 'a roll of notes' when he purchased a gold watch and a £14 coat for her, but as to her conversations with the detectives, she told the court, 'I was confused with the whole affair and made a mistake, I can assure you' – and she denied she was trying to help Askew.

But nothing could help Askew, nor cunning old Young, despite his being described as 'a sociable, friendly old man with a lot of time on his hands', or Goodwin, 'that perfect little spiv', who asserted that he had spent the weekend of the bank raid with his wife since she had been 'advised by her doctor that she should not be left alone'.

With the exception of Mrs Irving, who was acquitted of receiving the £94, all the others were found guilty of the breaking offences of which they had been accused.

Having been informed of Askew's medical problems, Mr Justice Byrne told him:

> You were a police officer paid to protect the public. Instead of that, you became a thief. It may be that there is something in

your background as far as your health is concerned that may explain the situation but it is a very serious case so far as you are concerned.

He then sentenced Askew to two concurrent terms of seven years' imprisonment for the bank raids, plus a concurrent five-year sentence for the breaking at the launderette.

Irving, found guilty of the breakings at the banks, similarly received seven years' imprisonment, as did Goodwin for the National Provincial breaking; Young received five years' imprisonment for that offence, the Judge telling him, 'Having regard to your age, the sentence is less than it otherwise would have been.'

The press coverage was tremendous, as a Woman Police Constable based at Wanstead police station (which was also part of 'J' Division) discovered. Deidre Bonner was seconded to 'C' Division to help with shoppers on the three-week run-up to Christmas 1959. But when the tell-tale 'J' was spotted on the shoulder of her tunic, she received, as she told me, 'So much stick from the officers most days I was there, even though I did not know Askew; I was so pleased to return to my lovely colleagues at Wanstead.'

The memories of those West End officers were very short, considering the exhaustive investigations to which they themselves had been subjected such a short time before, when the Commissioner, Sir John Nott-Bower, had been obliged to deny newspaper reports that all of 'C' Division's 450 personnel were likely to be transferred. That announcement must have caused a deep sigh of relief – to at least *some* of the personnel!

CHAPTER 27

Just When You Least Expect it!

When John Gosling was about to retire he was approached by a senior Flying Squad officer who offered him a sum of money if he would hand over the names of his informants. 'I'd give you their names for nothing', replied Gosling, 'But it wouldn't do you any good; they won't talk to you.'

He had a point; once snouts started working for one officer they would seldom defect to another. It occurred when I had retired from the police; Gerry was my top-rated informant, whose information was so precise that, as Gosling would say, 'You could go in with your head down.' Gerry was approached by a large and rather aggressive member of the Regional Crime Squad but loyally told him, 'I only work for Mr Kirby.'

'Well, he ain't here now, is he?' growled the officer. 'So you're working for me, see?'

I don't really know how that panned out, because (a) Gerry was a pretty tough character who had worked for Army intelligence and wouldn't have taken kindly to that sort of intimidation, and (b) that officer got his collar felt, after which he suffered a number of misfortunes. And Gerry? I dunno; I never heard from him again and he just faded away.

Larry was a snout I did hear from again, in rather unfortunate circumstances – for him, not for me. This is what happened.

★ ★ ★

'Caller on the phone, Sargie', said one of the Flying Squad's switchboard operators. 'Says he's got some info to pass on.'

I took the call; I'd only recently come to the Squad and I wanted to make my mark – and if someone was phoning the Squad with information, this could be the breakthrough I was looking for. But having a snout come in, unknown, cold, 'off the street' was not without its dangers, so I spoke to Larry, laid the law down as to how matters would be conducted between the two of us and arranged a meeting.

I was sitting in the back of a Flying Squad taxi a few hours later, drifting down Knightsbridge, when I recognized Larry, from the description he'd given of himself, standing by the junction with Ennismore Gardens, just round the corner from where the famous Iranian Embassy siege had taken place a few years previously. The taxi slowed, Larry got in and we continued our journey down Kensington High Street.

The information which Larry had on offer was about a very highly-placed gang of villains from the Home Counties who had carried out a raid at a West End furrier's the previous night. He named the thieves and he also named the receivers, telling me that the furs were in transit and that he was trying to find where the transaction would take place between thieves and receivers.

I sat back in my seat and scrutinized Larry; he was a fairly unprepossessing, rat-faced individual, but then again, when had looks counted when it came to being an informant? I took his details, provided him with the 'Snouts' Line' telephone number at the Squad (on an entirely different exchange to the '230' one used at the Yard) and told him to get cracking. I checked out the information; there had indeed been a screwing at a West End furrier's and I obtained photos of the stolen furs; I also checked out the thieves and the receivers, who were top-notch.

Within a couple of days I had a call from Larry, who provided me with an address; raids were carried out, the property was recovered intact, the bad guys were nicked and Larry got a nice reward. And then he disappeared – and I don't mean that in a way that suggests foul play – I mean, he just made himself scarce. In one way it was a pity, because he'd obviously got good criminal contacts, and I was hoping for a bit more work from him. Then again, I'd checked his record; he really was a seedy character, with form for indecency.

So Larry faded from view, and I busied myself with other informants who didn't make me feel the need to have a hot, soapy bath after dealing with them.

Until, that is, I received a phone call from Larry, right out of the blue, several years after leaving the Flying Squad, when I was running the 'N' Division Crime Squad.

'Hey, Dick, how you doing?' he said. 'Listen, I might have a bit of work for you but first I need a favour. See, I got pulled by Old Bill in Essex – a right bunch of wallies. It was about a car or something – anyway, this DC Bennett – right cunt, he is – let me out, but since then I heard he was making enquiries about me, see? So what I need you to do is find out if I'm wanted and if I am, to square it up, see? Then we can get out and you can have a team off.'

I found myself getting more and more pissed off with this cocky little bastard, but it was his next sentence that really put the tin hat on it for me. 'Anyway,' he continued, 'I reckon you owe me; that payoff for the furs job wasn't all that much. Course, I can't do nothing 'til you've sorted that other matter out for me.'

It's difficult to say, 'Sure, no problem – just give me a contact phone number' when your teeth are grinding together, as mine were, but I did manage it.

First, I made a check on the police computer; Larry was there all right, circulated as being wanted for failing to appear at Chelmsford Magistrates' Court on a charge of stealing a car. The officer in the case? DC Jack Bennett, with whom I had an interesting conversation on the phone.

'Dunno how well you know him, Dick, but he's been a right little bastard to us. Gave us a load of fanny about snouting for us and then skipped his bail at court; since then we discovered we wanted him for quite a bit more – nasty stuff, too.' He told me about it; he was right. It *was* pretty nasty.

'Any chance of you finding out where he is? Be glad to come and pick him up if you can finger him for us – buy you a beer as well.'

'Dunno where he is at the moment, Jack, but leave it to me. I'm going to nick the little fucker and present him to you tied up with a pink ribbon – my pleasure.'

'Blimey!' exclaimed Jack. 'Got right up your hooter, didn't he?'

Jack didn't know the half of it; as I'd demonstrated in the past, when snouts thought that simply by being my informant they could commit criminal offences and get away with it, not only did they get nicked – they got nicked by me.

I checked the telephone number Larry had given me. It came down to the occupier of a council flat in Kentish Town, which I also checked out – the occupier's surname was different to Larry's. So Larry was using that address to receive and possibly make phone calls, which meant that he probably lived close by.

I assembled the aids – young police constables in plain clothes, eager aspirants to become members of the CID. 'I've got a surveillance job, followed by an arrest for you this afternoon,' I told them. 'Feel up to it?'

'Course!' was their answering chorus, complete with aggrieved looks for even doubting their expertise.

In the Crime Squad office was a portable R/T set with which I would be in contact with the aids; and once I'd received confirmation that they were in position around the flat I dialled the number.

'Never 'eard of 'im,' replied the elderly gent who answered the phone, but I was not so easily dissuaded. 'Don't piss me about, Pop – go and get him. Tell him it's Dick Kirby calling with some good news for him.'

I could hear some conversation in the background before the phone was picked up again and I was told, "Ang on.'

Just then, the radio crackled into life. 'Sarge, a girl's come out of the flat.'

'Right, don't try to follow her; let her come back to you,' I replied.

A few minutes later, there was a further call on the radio. 'Sarge, she's come back with a bloke – they're just entering the flat.'

'All units, stand by.'

A moment later, the phone was picked up, this time by Larry. 'Hello, mate,' I said. 'I've got some really good news for you – I think you'd better sit down. Oh, bugger – there's the other phone; hang on a moment.'

With that, I went over to the R/T set, depressed the button on the transmitter and said, 'All units, go in now.'

I strolled back to the desk and picked up the phone. 'Well, what's this good news then, Dick?' asked Larry eagerly, and I replied, 'You're just about to find out.' With that, there was a tremendous 'CRASH!' which sounded suspiciously like the front door of a council flat being kicked off its hinges by a group of exuberant aids, some confused shouting, the thud of the telephone receiver falling on to a table and the muffled sounds of someone unwisely offering resistance to an arrest, before the phone was picked up again and I was simply told, 'He's nicked, Sarge.'

Back at Highbury Vale police station, the aids told me about the other occupants of the flat: Larry's sister and his maternal grandfather. 'Gave us a right load of aggro they did, trying to pull him away from us.'

That, I thought, was rather handy and I went to see Larry in the cells. 'You've done me right up!' he shouted as I entered his cell.

'Not,' I assured him, 'as much as you're going to get done up. Thought I was soft, didn't you? Thought I was some big Jaffa you could mug off, didn't you?' (My voice, I must admit, had now risen a couple of octaves.) 'Well, you made a big mistake, mister, and I'll tell you something else. I've phoned DC Bennett and he's on his way. By the time he gets here, perhaps you'd like to get sorted out in your mind the full and frank confession you're going to make to him about all of the other seedy crimes you've committed on his manor.'

'You must be joking,' scoffed Larry.

'It'd save an awful lot of problems if you did,' I said. 'Problems for granddad and your skin-and-blister, I mean; assisting an offender carries an awfully long prison term.' I turned to go out of the cell before I paused. 'Oh, and Larry, don't ever think I'm bluffing, either.'

Jack Bennett was delighted with the immensely detailed confession which Larry provided, and having locked him up took all of us out for a beer.

I saw Larry one last time, as Jack Bennett led him out of the charge room in handcuffs. As he went to get in the back of Jack's car, a penitent Larry looked at me. 'You wouldn't really have nicked my granddad and sister, would you, Dick?' he asked mournfully.

'Probably not,' I admitted, and winked at Jack. 'As you know, I'm just a big fucking softy!'

★ ★ ★

Archie wasn't really a snout at all; he was a character who would pop up now and then and provide me with a bit of information – when I say now and then, I mean that a year or more might pass before I heard anything from him – and when he did get in contact, it might be a piece of information which he wanted to impart, or it might just be the offer of a drink. So I didn't regard him as an informant in the same way as I regarded Gerry or Sammy the Snout who provided me with intelligence on a regular basis, especially since they relied on me as their main source of income. Archie, on the other hand, was an upstanding citizen with a full-time, regular and well-paid job; it's just that from time to time he dabbled on the cusp of criminality.

So when he telephoned me for a meet one evening, there was no indication that he wanted to offer up information. Tony Freeman, driving a Flying Squad taxi, dropped me off outside a North London pub near the Arsenal football ground and drove off – I expect that, left to his own devices, he had some private business to attend to.

Archie was already there and he pushed a large scotch in my direction. We chatted about this and that and then he said, 'Ever heard of Gary Read?'

I thought for a moment, then shook my head. 'No. Who's he?'

'Bit of a toe-rag. He must be, because he's over the wall.'

'No, never heard of him,' I said. 'What was he doing time for?'

'Not sure,' replied Archie. 'Violence, I think. But he sounds a right nasty fucker. He reckons he's got a sawn-off and if the Old Bill come round for him, he going to use it on them.'

'Where is he, d'you know?'

Archie shook his head. 'No. But I know his phone number.'

In his excellent book, *The Ghost Squad*, the late John Gosling described how one of his informants was able to determine the numbers dialled from the distance the dial on a telephone travelled – very clever – and it was a trick which Archie had picked up. He had been in the company of Gary Read's brother who had telephoned his sibling to see if he needed anything, and Archie had memorized the clicks. Not something that could be achieved on modern-day touch phones, but of course this is now and that was then.

So Archie passed me a slip of paper with seven digits written on it, I thanked him, bought another round of drinks and then went back to the Yard to find out a little more about the antecedents of G. Read Esq.

Read had been twenty-three when he was sentenced to thirty months' imprisonment for grievous bodily harm, and he already had a fair bit of form behind him: assaults, burglary, car thefts. Dark haired, about five feet ten, stockily built, Read was a slag who came from a slag family, and the prison authorities should have been aware of this; they had cut him rather more slack than he deserved, and after being assigned to an outside working party he had rewarded their trust by promptly having it on his toes.

So he was going to use a sawn-off on any Old Bill sufficiently imprudent to want to arrest him, was he? Maybe, maybe not. Lots of crims, in a flash of bravado, see themselves as modern-day James Cagneys ('Made it, Ma – top of the world!'), but it doesn't mean they've actually got firearms, or if they have, that they're prepared to use them.

I checked Read's file a bit more. He had been cohabiting with one Gina Abrahams, and this was a name I did know. Ms Abrahams came from what is colloquially known as 'a right family', and I knew that just after the war her grandfather had been sentenced to four years' penal servitude and a flogging for robbery with violence and that Gina herself had previously been sentenced to Borstal training for hacking a girl's face open with a knife.

A right charming pair, I thought – they probably passed the evenings discussing the best way to inflict pain on their victims – and the sooner Gary Read was relieved of his sawn-off and was back behind bars, the better. A quick in and out job, and if he was at the telephone subscriber's address, that'd be that. Of course, it wasn't.

* * *

If you want something done right, do it yourself. The first mistake I made was to give the telephone number which Archie had handed me to one of the Flying Squad switchboard operators, the majority of whom were very sound indeed; this one, I discovered, wasn't. There used to be a very simple way of discovering the identity of a telephone subscriber, the details of which don't matter any more because I expect to do so nowadays you'd have to fill in a document the size and thickness of the *Sunday Telegraph* and get it countersigned by the commissioner.

So yes, I should have done it myself, but because it was such a straightforward matter and I had other things to do, I gave it to the dopey switchboard operator and started rounding up some troops. In doing so I remembered Archie's parting cautionary words ('His brother reckons he's got a bleedin' great dog') so I enlisted the assistance of a couple of local dog handlers.

On the morning of the raid I had determined that when we got to the address we would have firearms officers at the rear of the premises, the front door would go in, the dog handlers would be ready, if necessary, to take out Read's bothersome pet and we (including more authorized shots) would go straight to the bedroom and nick Read in bed.

But when I got to the address provided by the switchboard operator, I stopped. Yes, it was in the area which Read had frequented in the past but . . . this house? No. It didn't look right. Nothing I could put my finger on but it looked . . . well, too respectable for a slag like Read. So I didn't kick the front door right off its hinges; instead, I rang the front doorbell. I was glad I did. Mr and Mrs Morris Goldstein were a very nice elderly couple, made somewhat anxious by the presence of half a dozen determined Squad officers outside their house at 6.30 in the morning and more than a little perturbed by the sight of a couple of huge, menacing German shepherds, but quickly mollified when I offered profuse apologies for disturbing them. No, they didn't know anybody named Gary Read, had never heard of him. And their telephone number? It was almost the same as the one I had been given – almost, but not quite. Two of the digits were the wrong way round. I was furious; then I asked if I might use their phone. I got straight on to the switchboard operator and really blew him up – then told him to get the right subscriber and phone me back.

Now I had got the right address: a council flat where the tenant was listed as Ms G. Abrahams – this was more like it! Authorized shots were positioned at the rear, the dog handlers were ready and I checked the front door, putting pressure with my fingers down the lock edge of the door to establish if there were any bolts, top or bottom, but no, there weren't. The door gave slightly, top and bottom, there was no mortise deadlock, just a Yale-type lock; I stepped back, gave one kick, right on the lock, and the door flew open.

There was no sign of the dog, I dashed straight in to the bedroom and there, in bed, were Gary Read and Gina Abrahams. They were grabbed and pulled out of bed, to a volley of abuse from both, and the room was searched. Nothing. 'Right, where's the sawn-off, Gary?' I said sternly.

'Sawn-off?' he echoed scornfully. 'What sawn-off? Somebody's been telling you fairy stories, mate!'

Both of them were arrested – him for being a prison escapee, her for harbouring an escaped prisoner – and they were allowed to dress before they were handcuffed. The flat was really turned over, and although a sawn-off can be secreted in the smallest of places, none was forthcoming. In one of the other rooms was an old man; it appeared he was an elderly relative of one or other of the occupants and was staying with them, but he 'knew nothing abaht nothing, Guv'nor', and I just noted his details. He wasn't going anywhere, so I told him that I'd get somebody round to fit a new front door, he nodded and, for the time being, passed out of the picture.

'Sorry to have wasted your time,' I apologized to the dog handlers, who laughed when I added, 'Looks like the snout was as right about the dog as he was about the sawn-off!'

With the prisoners in the car, I went to pull the front door shut as I left, and as I did so I heard a 'thump!' and the large German Shepherd dog, who had obviously been right behind the door as I kicked it open, slid down the wall from where it had been pinned, shook itself and trotted off to the kitchen. Well, it looked as though Archie had been half-right!

In the charge room at the local police station, I acquainted the station officer with what had happened and then I turned to Gina Abrahams. 'Would you care to take a seat over there?' I asked her. Her face became contorted with fury. 'WOT YEW SAY TER ME, YEW CUNT?' she screamed. I calmly repeated my previous invitation and her face cleared, as if by magic. 'Oh, fank yew!' she simpered.

Jesus, I thought. We've got a right one here!

But that hiccup apart, there were no further problems. When I interviewed Gary, he was nowhere near as aggressive as before. I questioned him minutely about the sawn-off and told him how bad it would look for him if the gun was discovered later with his fingerprints on it and it was found to have been used in crime during the time between his escape and recapture. In addition, it would be far better for him to stick his hands up to any crimes he'd committed whilst he was over the wall, because if he didn't and they were discovered later, he could well get a sentence consecutive to the one he had interrupted. But Gary was too long in the tooth for any tricks like that and he admitted nothing.

Gina, on the other hand, couldn't have been more accommodating. She described in great detail, in a written statement, the extreme lengths she had gone to in harbouring Gary during his unofficial parole.

And I had to contend with the usual paperwork; there were the reports to prepare regarding the damage at the flat and the fact that firearms had been drawn, the entries in the police station's (and the Flying Squad's) Occurrence Book regarding the same, plus a 'Premises Searched' form. Now on all of these items of paperwork the names of the people with whom we'd had dealings – plus their Criminal Record Office (CRO) numbers – had to be mentioned. Well, I knew Gary's and Gina's already, so that left the old boy in the flat. But when I went into the communications office to carry out a check on him, I was told, 'Sorry, Sarge – the computer's down.'

I thought for a moment. By the time we'd finished processing the prisoners it'd be lunchtime, and we had an operation planned for that afternoon. I wanted to get these forms out of the way now, so I thought 'bollocks', inserted the old man's name on the forms and next to it wrote 'No Trace CRO'.

Meanwhile, Gina was charged, went to court and pleaded guilty. Gary, on the other hand, who had admitted no other offences for which he could be charged, was picked up by a prison escort and headed back to stir, where a bit of extra porridge awaited him. It was a simple, straightforward case and I forgot all about it.

★ ★ ★

If anybody ever tries to tell you that internal police investigations are a whitewash, please refer them to me and I'll show them what police brutality is really all about. If I had been afforded the opportunity to delve into every nook and cranny of a criminal investigation, the way police officers carrying out an internal investigation did, I'd have been a happy man. Because when an allegation of misconduct is made by (or, as in this case, on behalf of) a criminal, it's the usual dreary dross – they were roughed up, beaten up, fitted up. They don't say, 'And what's more, the officer neglected to inset an appropriate entry in the Occurrence Book', but it's these minutiae which some of the investigators are looking for.

Four months later, I was informed that Gary Read's mum had complained on behalf of her son and her quasi-daughter-in-law that damage had been caused at the flat, violence had been used in effecting the arrest and firearms had been carried – all of which, she thought, had been completely unnecessary.

The investigating officer was one who, for a number of reasons, was not inclined to be friendly towards the Flying Squad; not that that particularly bothered me. All I hoped for was the sort of fair treatment which I'd received from the majority of senior officers who investigated me; men who'd been given the distasteful task of enquiring into the conduct of one of their colleagues, who did a thorough job and then impartially reported their findings.

I denied the allegations and then answered all of the investigating officer's questions, as his sergeant wrote down the questions and answers. The senior officer was rather antagonistic, and I found myself disliking him more and more, especially when he asked, 'Did you conduct this search as a result of information you'd received?'

I acknowledged that this was so, and then he flabbergasted me with his next question: 'What's the name of your informant?'

This was the type of question which was absolutely forbidden in court, and it was not the sort of question which should have been asked in an internal enquiry interview, either. Once that name was written down it was a matter of public record, and there was no end of trouble which might be caused if the identity of an informant started being bandied about. So I was absolutely unequivocal in my answer: 'I'm not telling you.'

'In that case, I can always get it from the Deputy Assistant Commissioner's register,' he replied.

'Do as you please,' I said shortly, but privately I thought to myself, 'Since Archie's never been registered as an informant, you'll have your fucking work cut out, mate!'

I wasn't worried about the reports and other documentation which I'd submitted in respect of this case, because I knew my paperwork was spot-on; or so I thought. But then the senior officer suddenly asked, 'The elderly man who was in the flat – did you check to see if he was known at CRO?'

I'd completely forgotten about him, so I replied, "Yes, of course I did.'

He raised his eyebrows. 'Really? It's just that I couldn't find any record of you having done so at the police station, and in the reports you put "No Trace CRO". It's not what I discovered when I did a check on him; he *has* got a record at CRO.'

I was shocked by this sort of childish nit-picking. 'Christ,' I blurted out. 'Surely you're not going to make a federal case out of that, are you?'

'Please,' he said, with a smirk on his face, holding up an admonishing hand, and continued with more trivial questions until the interview reached its conclusion.

* * *

It took seven months for the Director of Public Prosecutions to come to the conclusion that I had not committed any criminal offences; it took rather longer for disciplinary matters to be considered. In fact, it was at a Flying Squad Christmas lunch that the late Detective Superintendent Peter Gwynne told me that I was to be given 'words of advice' concerning my laxness in filling in official documentation. Just for the record, the old man's one and only conviction had been acquired just after the Second World War. His offence of illegally obtaining a bag of sugar, which was on ration, 'without approval of the Food Ministry' had resulted in a forty-shilling fine.

When strong drink has been taken it is not a particularly propitious moment for news of that nature to be imparted to someone as headstrong as me, and I duly hit the roof. Peter Gwynne, one of nature's gentlemen and a very fine detective, took it all in humorous good part and later, of course, I fully apologized for my unseemly behaviour.

But I wondered then, as I wonder now: why was the senior officer so insistent on discovering the identity of the informant? Curiosity? Some deeper reason? Or did he just have an orderly, methodical mind and wanted everything tidied up – just like the CRO check which he carried out on the old man, and I hadn't?

It's as I always say; it's the little things that come back to bite you in the bollocks!

CHAPTER 28

Scandal in Mayfair

This book is full of tales of cunning conmen, dangerous gunmen, daring burglars who scaled the heights and degenerate blackmailers who plumbed the depths, but the story that follows is one that was right out of kilter for the Flying Squad; and since I started the book with a story about Ted Greeno, it's only right that I should end with one.

The French rather chicly refer to a disorderly house as a *baisodrome*, whereas the Germans (who seem to have a number of words for everything) sometimes – not always – refer to such an establishment prosaically as a *bordell* or else *puff*, rather appropriately since the latter also means 'bang'.

An English 'disorderly house' is not necessarily a brothel but it is a premises where the conduct of its inhabitants is such as to amount to a public nuisance, outrage public decency or tend to corrupt, deprave or injure the public interest; and to habitually keep such a property is punishable by means of fines or imprisonment, both of which are unlimited.

When Detective Inspector Ted Greeno attended Lingfield Races in 1938 he was looking for a winner; but the tip he received was not in respect of a sure-fire favourite – it was concerning a highly placed disorderly house in Dover Street, Mayfair, visited by 'the top people'. Greeno casually conveyed this in passing to his boss, Detective Chief Inspector Bill Parker, and he in turn mentioned it to Sir Norman Kendall, who had entered the Metropolitan Police as a Chief Constable in 1918. The news affronted the schoolmasterish Assistant Commissioner (Crime), who demanded immediate action but at the same time hoped (with some trepidation) that if any of 'the top people' were around when the raid took place, they would not be amongst those who had supported his knighthood, the previous year.

The thought of cabinet ministers in various states of undress being hoiked squeaking into Cannon Row was enough to cause a serious twinge to the wounds Sir Norman had received during the Battle of the Somme. However, he was assured that if the raid took place at about 8.00pm, any parliamentarians desirous of partaking in the exotic delights offered by the owner of the premises would probably be dining, taking their seat in the House or participating in some other non-salacious pastime. But a great deal of planning would be required first, and to discover who was who and what was what, starting with the owner.

★ ★ ★

Whether 14-year-old Carmen Smith was accompanied by her parents when she arrived in Britain in 1912 from Jamaica is not known. What is known is that by 1919 she had quickly acquired four convictions for soliciting and one for insulting behaviour, and in May 1923 she came to the attention of the authorities for keeping a disorderly house. Four months later, she was arrested on a Home Office order and taken to Holloway Prison, pending deportation. She was released after she claimed British citizenship.

She made sure of her citizenship when in May 1924 she married the seedy Max George Rosenz, who had been convicted in 1920 after swallowing a packet of cocaine which he had offered to sell to a lady; he was sentenced to three months' hard labour, as was his cousin Conrad Regensburg for the same offence. Two years later, Rosenz was stopped in possession of four packets of cocaine and after telling the police, 'I'm working for the biggest man in London. You know him quite well, but I can't spilt on him, can I?' he was sentenced to six months' hard labour. 'The Biggest Man in London' was also known as 'The Worst Man in London' and that was pimp and drug pusher Eddie Manning who, like Carmen Smith, had strayed from his native island. Manning would later die in Parkhurst from syphilis while serving a term of penal servitude, but Carmen would go on to better things – and if Rosenz and Regensburg do not sound particularly like valid British names, neither was the marriage in Liverpool, which was purely one of convenience.

We need bother no more with Mr Rosenz who, handsomely rewarded for his efforts, was nudged out of the picture while his 'wife' moved into Bury Street. Between 1929 and 1936 a number of complaints were made about her house, which was described as being disorderly, and now she moved into Dover Street.

But her time in Bury Street had not been wasted; Post Office savings books held between October 1933 and May 1937 revealed that £2,287 had been withdrawn; in 1934 she had purchased a bungalow in Lancing, West Sussex; and two years later, she had invested £1,100 in shares in a brewery.

The observation was set up, beginning on 15 February 1938, and on 25 February it was overseen by Detective Sergeant (later Detective Superintendent) Henry Stuttard, who would later achieve great success in running the post-war Ghost Squad. That was from the outside of the premises; the inside was covered by Detective Sergeant Kenneth Murray, an officer of outstanding virtue who, like Duncan Webb, the reporter for the Sunday newspaper, the *People*, a decade later could be relied upon, when a situation became inflamed with lust, to 'make his excuses and leave'.

All I can say is that one would have expected no less rectitude from any Flying Squad officer.

Murray's work commenced the day before Stuttard started the observations. He arrived at the flat at 5.30pm on 14 February and was admitted by Ellen Shaw, the 48-year-old maid, who brought in tea after he had met Carmen Rosenz. She told Murray that she gave parties at the flat and if he was unable to come in the afternoon he should come in the evening.

After she told him that she was 'having a little show here', Murray made an appointment for the following day, and Rosenz told him:

> I won't sting you. My fees are very reasonable, really. It's a big risk and I have to work under a cloak. Nobody knows what goes on but I know I can trust my friends. I have to pay a big rent for this flat and I don't give these shows just for love, you know.

She was quite right; the annual rent of the flat was £265. The next afternoon, Murray arrived once more and Rosenz brought in 24-year-old Fay Williams; they drank stout, whisky and gin. Elaine Hardinge joined them, appearing somewhat shy, and when Murray commented that she looked rather young, she demurely but mendaciously replied, 'I am not yet twenty', although in fact she was twenty-eight.

They went into a bedroom – Rosenz referred to it as a 'theatre' – and drinks were brought in. Other men were there; Rosenz asked for a 'contribution' of £5 plus £1 for the drinks, and Murray and the other men handed over money.

Murray's next meeting at Dover Street was in the afternoon of 25 February; Rosenz mentioned that there would be 'a party that night' and that amongst the guests would be an author and 'a director of a big place in the West End'. Veronne Hardinge, the 22-year-old sister of Elaine, was introduced, and also present were 48-year-old Frederick Ashton Redfern and William Feldgate, a 19-year-old tailor. More drinks were provided, as were sandwiches and fruit, and Rosenz told Murray, 'I shall want some money from you.'

'How much?' said Murray, and she asked, 'How much have you got?'

He then handed over five £1 notes; all of them were marked. They then went into the theatre, together with Fay Williams; Veronne Harding joined them later.

Fast-forward now to that evening, when at 8.20pm Greeno, in the guise of a taxi driver, knocked on the door; the maid, Ellen Shaw, answered it and before she could slam it shut, Greeno's size 12 shoe prevented it closing and the 'tecs rushed in. Every one of the occupants – with the exception of the maid – was naked. Two men and four women were on a bed indulging in what DCI Parker referred to as 'obscene acts'.

Rosenz, at six feet tall and encased only in a pair of thigh-high boots, was a formidable sight; she rushed at Greeno, her fist outstretched, but he promptly dumped her on a chair and told her to get dressed. As she did so, she shrieked at the luckless maid, 'Why did you let these people in? You know I've always told you to let me know if anyone comes to the door!'

Carmen Rosenz was not the only occupant to become over-excited. Reaching for her handbag, Elaine Hardinge (who according to DS Murray appeared 'rather shy') started tearing up a piece of paper, and when Greeno tried to stop her, she bit him on the thumb. She then attacked Greeno with a pair of fire tongs and screaming 'Let me go! Let me go!' she collapsed, sobbing, 'What will my mother say?'

A little sanity was brought to the proceedings by 27-year-old Irene Harding (no relation to Elaine and Veronne), who told her, 'Keep quiet. We're all bad girls but I'm the worst of the lot. You're making it bad for everyone, carrying on like that.'

During the search of the premises a box was found which contained women's clothing, a photograph of a man dressed in women's clothing, several women's wigs and high-heeled shoes. Obscene books and photographs were found, as well as handcuffs, whips, racks and spiked girdles. There was also the rather incriminating matter of letters addressed to Carmen from three people who had received payment for sending clients round to her.

When Rosenz was arrested for keeping a disorderly house she replied, 'No, not on the fifteenth. All my parties have been small. That's why I came here.'

The others were arrested for aiding and abetting her, and Irene Harding said, 'When I first came here, I didn't know what it was like . . . Will this get into the press? I know I have been a bad girl but Carmen is such a formidable woman, and having been in contact with her so long I just couldn't help it.'

Fay Williams commented, 'This seems to be very serious. Can we have bail? Can I explain my position? This is awful; I will never be such a naughty girl again.'

Veronne Hardinge said, 'Where is my sister? I should not have been here, but for her. This is the first time I've been here.'

The tailor, William Feldgate, told the officers, 'You find me in an awful state. It was Carmen's suggestion. I wish I hadn't come. Maybe you'll let me explain?'

Detective Sergeant Benson let him do just that when he took a written statement from him, whilst pretending he found no humour in Feldgate's comment, 'I wish I hadn't come.'

Irene Harding also made a statement, and Sergeant Murray's five marked £1 notes were retrieved from the interior of Carmen's left thigh boot; this was comforting for Sir John Moylan CB, CBE, the Receiver of the Metropolitan Police, who liked all his money to be accounted for, no matter what its provenance.

On 5 April 1938, they appeared at the Old Bailey before the Recorder of London, Mr Gerald Dodson. He informed potential female jurors that what was going to be recounted in court was so revolting that if they wished they could remove themselves from the jury box, and in fact, two women did just that. (This was a mirror image of the committal proceedings at Bow Street Police Court, when a notice was initially put up saying that the case would be heard in camera, until the Magistrate, Mr Fry, decided otherwise.)

DCI Parker, in mentioning Carmen's financial position, produced a further Post Office savings book which showed a balance of £1,458 and told the court, 'The premises she ran can only be described as one of the vilest houses with which the police have ever come in contact.'

Carmen – described in court as 'a coloured woman' and 'a half-caste' (perhaps to distance her from their shores, Jamaica's *Daily Gleaner* referred to her as 'a coloured native of New Orleans') – pleaded guilty and was told by the Recorder:

> The charges disclose a terrible state of affairs. This court is not concerned with a mere question of morality but by pandering to the weaknesses of human nature it is terrible to contemplate than in this Metropolis there should exist an

> establishment like yours – a veritable mausoleum of morals –
> a vault of vice. You have broken the law in a most serious
> manner . . . there are degrees of disorderliness. You have
> accomplished the extreme degree of depravity.

He then sentenced her to three years' penal servitude and ordered that she paid £150 towards the costs of the prosecution.

Irene Harding, a civil servant's daughter who described Carmen as being such a formidable woman that 'I couldn't help myself', was sentenced to nine months' imprisonment, and Ellen Shaw, the maid, was bound over to keep the peace. She was said by the Recorder to be 'a poor working woman, who ought to know better than to work for a woman who had the most unsuitable name of Carmen', although if he was comparing her employer with the eponymous cigarette-maker in Bizet's opera, her morals were nothing to write home about.

Veronne Hardinge was found not guilty on the directions of the Recorder and was discharged.

The other defendants were remanded to the next sessions; Fay Williams and Elaine Hardinge were both penitently clothed in black, their heads bowed, when the Recorder told them:

> It would be little short of a tragedy if your lives were wrecked
> by sending you to prison. For two English girls to stand here
> and confess to this kind of conduct is a disgrace which I
> trust will prevent you from repeating actions of this kind for
> the rest of your lives.

Although Feldgate and Redfern had been remunerated by Carmen for their services, the younger of the two managed to dodge any of the Recorder's sermons on morality, even though he had told the police that Carmen paid him £5 per week, whereas his normal weekly wage at his day job was £3 5s 0d. Not so the 48-year-old Redfern, who obviously should have known better. 'Shame on you!' snapped the Recorder. 'The disgrace of it – it is appalling!'

Three weeks later, with the exception of Fay Williams who was placed on probation for three years, the others were bound over to keep the peace.

Fay Williams was not her real name; she was permitted to use it in court to protect the identities of her relatives. Her father – now dead – had been a clergyman, while her mother attended court and wept when she heard her daughter's barrister say, 'She is thoroughly ashamed of herself.'

Greeno admitted that he felt sorry for Fay. She had met Carmen in a tea room, had later been taken to her flat where she was introduced into the intricacies of lesbianism, and from then on it was all downhill.

Irene Harding had been deceived by her husband, considered suicide, took to drink and was gathered up by Carmen when she was at a particularly low ebb; it also went some way to explain her erratic behaviour when she was arrested.

But among all the ozone of morality there was also room for double standards. It came at Bow Street Court, when Carmen wanted bail and put forward as a surety an elderly solicitor who was in the habit of writing incredibly filthy letters to her. Having seen the letters, Greeno objected most strongly to bail, but he was rebuked by Carmen's solicitor in court who protested that Greeno had referred to the proposed surety as 'this man'.

The Magistrate, Mr McKenna, turned to the officer and said, 'Mr Greeno, will you please observe that by virtue of the fact that this man is a solicitor, he is a gentleman?'

'A rose by any other name' observed Shakespeare, 'would smell as sweet . . .'

Epilogue

Well, there you have it; that's how it was.

To the criminals who read this, be honest – difficult for you, I know! – but aren't you glad that these cops don't exist any more? I'll bet you are!

To ordinary decent members of the public, aren't you upset that police officers of this calibre don't patrol London's streets any longer; officers you could chat to and to whom you could report offences, secure in the knowledge that they'd be investigated? I'll bet you are!

And to serving members of police services, anywhere, this was the way things got done. Called to a rowdy gang of youths, as uniformed officers, we grabbed the biggest, mouthiest one of the group and hauled him into a police van; and having witnessed that display of non-nonsense policing, the rest of the crowd invariably melted away, the situation defused. As CID officers we were trusted to work on our own initiative and we cultivated informants, met them in sometimes dark, unfriendly places, evaluated what they told us and went to work. We kicked in doors, went into pubs, took the glasses out of the hands of protesting ne'er-do-wells and dragged them outside. We worked crazy hours, usually a bare minimum of 12-hour days without overtime; that wasn't paid until 1975. It was a vocation; it was for love of the job.

Most mornings were spent attending court, especially if that had been preceded by an early morning arrest; and if that arrest was simple and straightforward (and let's face it, so many of them are) the matter could be disposed of there and then. There was seldom any need for a case to be remanded for reports, or legal representation; we were able to set out the facts of the case and sometimes offer mitigation on behalf of the prisoner for his transgressions. If that resulted in a non-custodial sentence, it might also result in information being forthcoming.

When we were successful, there were commendations – sometimes – and when we weren't, there were condemnations. But there was camaraderie, too – we backed each other up. Some of our senior officers weren't perfect; but they had been brought up in the CID the same way as us. As they rose through the ranks they accrued investigative skills, and there was nothing they did not know about criminal investigation. They were professionals.

Compare this with the experience of a friend of mine – of the same vintage as me – who recently retired, having served in the Met for forty-four years, spending thirty-five of them in the rank of detective sergeant with the Flying Squad and murder squads. 'I reckoned to know just about everything there is to know about criminal investigation', he told me. 'But if something came up where it turned out that I didn't know the answer, there was no one – and I mean *no one* – that I could turn to, to get the answer.'

What a sorry state of affairs. University degrees have replaced common sense, proficiency and sheer hard work. Promotion has often depended upon the candidate's ethnicity, gender or sexual orientation rather than their expertise, propelling people into ranks and specialized departments way beyond their experience or capabilities.

So these were the days prior to the Police and Criminal Evidence Act which, coupled with the iniquitous Crown Prosecution Service, has dragged the criminal justice system down to a snail's pace. These were the days before hurt feelings spilled over into grassing up one's colleagues for making an injudicious remark. The days when sergeants and inspectors provided real leadership.

Do you wish those days were back again and that you could be part of them? If you do, I'm sorry to disappoint you, because they never will be.

Glossary of Custodial and Punishment Terms

Approved School Young offenders (or those beyond parental control) were sent to approved schools, which replaced 'industrial' or 'reformatory' schools in 1933. Caning or 'strapping' was used on recalcitrant boys and girls, and those who absconded could expect a maximum of eight strokes of the cane on their clothed buttocks. These schools ceased to exist in the early 1970s.

Birching The birch consisted of leafless twigs bound together and used to beat a prisoner's bare back, shoulders or buttocks. This form of corporal punishment could be ordered by the judiciary in cases of violence, usually those deemed not serious enough to merit flogging. After a magistrate ordered a young offender to be birched, the sentence was often carried out by a police officer. In approving a new pattern of birch rod in 1888, the humane commissioner ordered: 'Great care is to be taken in whipping juvenile offenders that the birch rod is not used too severely, especially in the case of small or delicate children.'

Borstal Training Instituted in 1900, young men and women aged sixteen to twenty-one (increased to twenty-three in 1936) who committed indictable offences were sentenced to not less than one year and not more than three, in the often forlorn hope that this would be a reformative exercise. Offenders could be recalled to Borstal, and birching could be ordered for inmates who mutinied or assaulted officers. Borstal was abolished by the Criminal Justice Act 1982.

Carpet Three months' imprisonment. So called, because that was the time taken to weave a carpet on the prison loom.

Corrective Training Under the Criminal Justice Act 1948, if a person over the age of twenty-one was convicted of an offence punishable with two years' imprisonment or more, and having been convicted on two occasions since the age of seventeen, they could be sentenced to corrective training (CT) for a period of not less than two years and not more than four. Abolished by the Criminal Justice Act 1967.

Flogging What was known as 'The Cat-o'-nine Tails' was used to flog prisoners; it consisted of nine leather, knotted straps attached to a handle, and like birching, could be ordered by judges for violent offences. While flogging was abolished in 1948 as a judicial punishment, it nevertheless continued inside prisons as punishment for mutiny or offences of gross violence against the staff until 1967.

Habitual Criminal Under the Prevention of Crimes Act 1908, persons over the age of sixteen who had been convicted of crime on three occasions and were leading a dishonest life were classified as habitual criminals and, having been sentenced to penal servitude, could be sentenced to a further period of preventative detention not exceeding ten years and not less than five, for the protection of the public.

Half-a-stretch Six months' imprisonment.

Hard Labour Hard labour was an additional form of punishment for sentences of up to two years' imprisonment. It included industrial work, oakum-picking and using a treadmill. It was abolished in 1948.

Incorrigible Rogue Once a criminal had been convicted at the Police (or Magistrates') Court of being a suspected person under Section 4 Vagrancy Act 1824, he was adjudged to be 'A Rogue and a Vagabond'. If he was convicted of a further or similar offence he could be committed to the Court of Quarter Sessions, to be dealt with as an 'Incorrigible Rogue' and sentenced up to twelve months' imprisonment.

Journeys Colloquial description for a term of penal servitude.

Laggings This was a contraction of 'leg-irons', which shackled recalcitrant prisoners serving penal servitude. It was shortened further to 'lags' or 'old lags' to describe a person who had been sentenced to penal servitude.

No. 1 Punishment Diet Bread and water for a maximum of fifteen days.

No. 2 Punishment Diet Bread, porridge and potatoes, for a maximum of forty-two days.

Penal servitude The Penal Servitude Act 1857 replaced transportation; its sole purpose was not to reform but to punish the prisoner. It covered periods of imprisonment from three years to life; for the first nine months of the sentence prisoners were kept in solitary confinement, and thereafter they were employed on public works or for private contractors, usually in quarries, digging ditches or repairing dry-stone walls.

Preventative Detention   Under the Criminal Justice Act 1948, preventative detention (PD) replaced penal servitude; where a person not less than thirty was convicted of an offence punishable with two years' imprisonment or more, and had been convicted on three occasions since the age of seventeen, having served imprisonment, Borstal training or corrective training, they could be sentenced to a term of PD of not less than five and not exceeding fourteen years. Abolished by the Criminal Justice Act 1967.

Second-division   Imprisonment in the second division meant that these prisoners (usually first offenders) would be segregated as much as possible from the other inmates, would wear uniforms of a different colour and receive more frequent visits and letters.

Stretch   Twelve months' imprisonment. (This also was a reference to capital punishment, as in 'Stretching one's neck'.)

Woodmans   One month's imprisonment. This was a reference to the fact that during the first month of an inmate's imprisonment, they slept on wooden boards.

Bibliography

Beveridge, Peter	*Inside the CID*	Evans Brothers Ltd, 1957
Burt, Leonard	*Commander Burt of Scotland Yard*	Heinemann, 1959
Capstick, John with Thomas, Jack	*Given in Evidence*	John Long, 1960
Cornish, G.W.	*Cornish of the Yard*	The Bodley Head, 1935
Fabian, Robert	*Fabian of the Yard*	Naldrett Press, 1950
Fido, Martin and Skinner, Keith	*The Official Encyclopedia of Scotland Yard*	Virgin Books, 1999
Forbes, Ian	*Squadman*	W.H. Allen, 1973
Foreman, Freddie	*The Godfather of British Crime*	John Blake, 2008
Gosling, John with Tullett, Tom	*The Ghost Squad*	W.H. Allen, 1959
Greeno, Edward	*War on the Underworld*	John Long, 1960
Higgins, Robert	*In the Name of the Law*	John Long, 1958
Hinds, Alfred	*Contempt of Court*	Bodley Head, 1966
Kirby, Dick	*Rough Justice – Memoirs of a Flying Squad Detective*	Merlin Unwin, 2001
Kirby, Dick	*The Real Sweeney*	Robinson, 2005
Kirby, Dick	*You're Nicked!*	Robinson, 2007
Kirby, Dick	*Villains*	Robinson, 2008

Kirby, Dick	*The Guv'nors*	Pen & Sword, 2010
Kirby, Dick	*The Sweeney*	Wharncliffe, 2011
Kirby, Dick	*Scotland Yard's Ghost Squad*	Wharncliffe, 2011
Kirby, Dick	*The Brave Blue Line*	Wharncliffe, 2011
Kirby, Dick	*The Scourge of Soho*	Pen & Sword, 2013
Kirby, Dick	*Whitechapel's Sherlock Holmes*	Pen & Sword, 2014
Kirby, Dick	*London's Gangs at War*	Pen & Sword, 2017
Kirby, Dick	*Operation Countryman*	Pen & Sword, 2018
Kirby, Dick	*Scotland Yard's Gangbuster*	Pen & Sword, 2018
Kirby, Dick	*Scotland Yard's Flying Squad*	Pen & Sword, 2019
Lawrence, Jane R.	*From the Beat to the Palace*	Brewin Books, 2005
Macintyre, Ben	*Agent Zigzag*	Bloomsbury, 2007
Millen, Ernest	*Specialist in Crime*	Harrap & Co., 1972
Morton, James	*Supergrasses and Informers*	Warner Books, 1996
Morton, James	*East End Gangland*	Warner Books, 2001
Morton, James	*Gangland, Volumes 1 & 2*	Time Warner, 2003
Morton, James	*Gangland Soho*	Piatkus, 2008
Morton, James and Parker, Gerry	*Gangland Bosses*	Time Warner, 2005
Murphy, Robert	*Smash and Grab*	Faber & Faber, 1993
Pearson, John	*The Profession of Violence*	Panther Books, 1973

Bibliography

Read, Leonard and Morton, James	*Nipper*	Macdonald & Co, 1999
Sharpe, F.D.	*Sharpe of the Flying Squad*	John Long, 1938
Slipper, Jack	*Slipper of the Yard*	Sidgwick & Jackson, 1981
Sparks, Herbert	*The Iron Man*	John Long, 1964
Swain, John	*Being Informed*	Janus Publishing, 1995
Thomas, Donald	*An Underworld at War*	John Murray, 2003
Thomas, Donald	*Villains' Paradise*	John Murray, 2005
Thorp, Arthur	*Calling Scotland Yard*	Allan Wingate Ltd. 1954
Waldren, Michael, J.	*Armed Police: The Police use of Firearms since 1945*	Sutton Publishing, 2007
Woodland, David I.	*Crime and Corruption at the Yard*	Pen & Sword, 2015

Index

Aarvold, Recorder of London, Sir Carl, OBE, TD 146–7, 168–9
Abrahams, Gina 199–205
Abul-Huda, Miss Vella 181
Acott, Commander Basil Montague 'Bob', DFC 91
Adams, Frederick 26–30
Adams, Dr John Bodkin 89
Alanbrooke, Field Marshal Viscount 28
Aldridge, Insp. 12
Allen, Anthony Richard 64–7
Allen, DS Fred 87
Ambrose, Elizabeth 143, 145
Ambrose, William 'Billy' David, 143–5
Ambrose, Sarah Jane 143
Amos, Mr 132
Anastacio, Agostiono 33
Anson, Hugh 7–10
Archie (informant) 199–205
Askew, PC 564 'J' George Albert 189–93
Ault, Mrs Gertrude Mary Avicen 93
Avory, Mr Justice 12–13
Axford, Vincent–see Raymond, H.

Bacon, Baroness Alice Martha, CBE, PC, MP 101–3
Bailey, Hon. Miss Mabel 178
Baird, David Sellars 52–4
Baker, DCI Henry 'Doughy' 189–93

Baldock, D/Supt William, BEM 152–3
Barker (Magistrate), Mr L. E. 174
Barlow, DC 70
Barnes, DI 71
Barrett, PC Lester 2–3
Barwick, PC 15
Bass, Judge 94
Bathie, Albert Edward, 'Baby Face' 26–30
Baxter, DC John, KPM 70–1
Beatty, Earl 141
Beavis, Leslie 129–34
Beazley, Judge 179
Beecher, Dr 159
Beecher, Mrs 159
Bellson, Sammy 137
Bencivenga, Albert 'Chick' 83–5
Bennett (Magistrate), Eugene Paul, VC, MC 28
Bennett, DC Jack 196–9
Benson, DS 211
Benstead, PS John 189
Bentley, Derek 101
Bergman, Eileen 159–60
Bevan, Frank 96
Beveridge, DCS Peter Henderson, MBE 83–5
Bibesco, Princess Priscilla 181
Bird, Alfred 54–5
Biron (Magistrate), Sir Chartres 37–38
Black, DS, John 19–21

Bland, DS Harold, KPM 70–71
Blythe, William 'Billy-Boy' 136–7
Bonner, WPC Deidre 193
Boswell, Alfred Clyde 39
Botton, Henry 142–7
Bowalls, Harry Edmund 179–80
Bradbury-Wilmott, Mr 118
Bradford, D/Supt Thomas Leslie 146
Brickwood, Lady Rachel Neale of Liphook 93
Bridge, PC 440 'B' William, KPM 78–80
Brinnand, DS Matthew 55–6
Broad, Douglas Norman 122
Broderick (Magistrate), Mr W.J.H. 72
Brodie, DS Allan 'Jock', DFC 90–1
Brooks, DS 15
Bunce, PC 243 'B' William, KPM 22–3
Bunton, John 169
Bunton, Kempton Cannon 164–70
Bunton, Kenneth 169
Burney, Cyril 99–100
Burt, Commander Leonard, CVO, CBE 123–4
Butler, DS 70
Butler, H/Secretary R.A. 186
Butler, DCS Thomas Marius Joseph, MBE 135–9, 145
Byrne, Mr Justice 29, 192–3

Callaghan, Edith Rose 144
Callaghan, Jeremiah 142–4
Cannon, DC 151
Capstick, DCS John Richard 'Jack' xviii, 33–8, 64
Careless, DI Charles Sydney Clifford 151–6

Careless, Ethel 159
Carlisle, 11th Earl of 89
Cartwright, Harry 40
Cerinadas, Abel 33
Chadbourne, DS 57–8
Champion, DS Albert 19–21
Chandler, Joseph 2–3
Chapman, Eddie 7–10, 106–7
Chapman, DCS Robert 'The Cherub' 92
Charteris, Andrew 181
Charteris, Harry 181
Charteris, Lt Col. Martin 180–1
Charteris, Mary 181
Chatham, George Henry 'Taters' 1–10, 93, 106, 118–25
Churchill, Miss Clarissa 181
Churchill, Robert 74
Clark, Phyllis Betty 129–34
Clarke, Frederick 149–50
Clarke, George 33
Clarke, Brigadier, Terrence 101–2
Cockayne, Joseph Henry 40–1
Colbard, Frank 23–4
Coles-Preedy, Judge Digby 80
Collins, PC Arthur 61–7
Collins, Marjorie 61–7
Colman, Gary Cecil 34
Congleton, Lady 122–3
Connell, John 81
Connell, Patrick 81
Connell, Peter 81
Cook, Sidney 87
Corbett, DI 41
Cornish, D/Supt George 44–5, 48
Craig, Christopher 100–1
Craig, Niven Scott 'The Velvet Kid' 99–103
Cremin, John 171

Index

Crowder (Barrister), Petre, QC, MP 182–3
Cugullere, Sidney 185
Cussen (Lawyer), Mr E.J.P. 168

Darry, George 7–10
Davies, Sidney –
  see Morath, S.G.
Davis, Bette 186
Davis, Eric Charles 95–6
Davis, Victor Edmund 95–6
Delaney, David Alfred –
  see Harris, D.
De Laszlo, Mrs Josephine 93
Dendrickson, George Edward 70–1
Dennis, William 'Ginger' 136–7
Devereux, Philip 69–70
Dickson, Robert Melrose –
  see Melrose, R.
Dimes, Albert 136
Dixon, Captain Richard 52
Dodson, Recorder of London Sir Gerald, KC 72, 149–50, 211–13
Dorset, PC George, GM* 187–8
Dowse, DS Micky 89–90
Draper, DC George 88
Driscoll, DI James 130–4
Drury, Commander Kenneth 136
Dummett (Magistrate), Mr 34, 51
Dunn Bros. 132, 135
Dunne (Magistrate), Sir Lawrence 28
Durrant, Edward 47–8
Durrell, DS Alfred 'Darky' 95

Easterbrook, Ronald 137–8
Eastham, D/Chairman Sir Tom 182

Edwards family 178
Eggboro, DI 44–5
Elwell, Major 24
Ettridge, W/Det. Supt Amy 84
Evans (Lawyer), Vincent 51
Evans, William George 64–7

Fabian, D/Supt Robert Honey, KPM xviii, 32, 62–7, 83–5
Fahm, Solomon 56–8
Fairbrother, DS 79
Fairley, John 5–6
Feldgate, William 210–13
Fellowes (Solicitor), James 190
Fleming, Patrick 136
Flood– see Wood, E.
Fluendy, DI 180
Forbes, DAC Ian, QPM 172–4
Ford, James John 26–30
Foreman, Freddy 144–5
Francis, DS 36
Franklyn, DS Johnny 91
Fraser, Alfie, 'The King of the Jelly Boys' 107–11
Fraser, Francis Davidson 'Mad Frankie' 147, 184
'Freddie the Fly' –
  see Harmsworth, F.J.
Freeman, PC 259 'CO' Anthony 155, 199
Fry, Magistrate, Mr 34, 211

Gábor, Zsa-Zsa 185
Galvin, John Thomas 77–81
Gee, DS Mervyn 'Taff' 185
George, DS, John 172–4
'Gerry' (informant) 195, 199
Gibbons, PC William 149
Gibbs, PC Ronald 116–17, 120
Gibney, DS 36
Giles, Leslie Glen 75
Gill, Arthur 46
Goddard, LCJ Rayner 96

Golby. Mr D.J.H. 27–30
Goldsmith, Ronald
  Thomas 171–2
Goldstein, Mr and Mrs 201
Gooch, DCI Daniel 47–8
Goodwin, William Ernest
  190–3
Gosling, Mr 133
Gosling, D/Supt John
  Neville 55–6, 59, 142,
  195, 200
Gould, Arthur – *see* Raymond, H.
Gowan, DS 39
Graham, Charles – *see* Wolfe, C.
Graham, Jimmy – *see* Wolfe, H.
Graham-Campbell
  (Magistrate), Sir Rollo
  6, 20, 33–4, 38, 85
Grant, Alan 'Jock' 181–3
Green, DS, Cyril 5–6
Green, Leslie Alfred 95
Greenacre, DS Albert 32, 36–9
Greeno, DCS Edward 'Ted',
  MBE xviii, 1–10, 105–11,
  118, 207–13
Grant, James 19–21
Groves, Leonard Eric 7–10
Guest (Magistrate),
  Mr E.R. 115
Gulston, Peter Craig 185–6
Gwynne, DCS Peter 205

Haddon, Jean 157–9
Halkett (Magistrate),
  Mr Hay 45
Hambrook, D/Supt Walter 33,
  44–5, 48
Hamilton, John – *see* Gill, A.
Hammond, Kay 83–5
Hanratty, James 91
Harding, Irene 209–13
Hardinge, Elaine 209–13
Hardinge, Veronne 209–23
Harewood, Earl of 72–5

Harmsworth, Frederick
  Joseph 128–34
Harris, David – *see* Harris D.
Harris, Dennis 'Australian
  Denny' 43–46
Harris, Miss Edith Ellen
  115, 122
'Harry the Vain' –
  see Raymond, H.
Hart, Dickie 147
Harvey, MP 190
Havers, Mr Justice 102
Hawke, Common Serjeant
  Sir Anthony 109–10, 153
Hawkes, PC 207 'B' Frederick,
  KPM 23–4
Haywood, DDI Henry 73–4
Heap, William Peter 57–8
Hedley (Magistrate),
  Walter, KC 39–40
Hegarty, Father Joseph 36–7
Hemming (Barrister),
  William 159–60
Hensley, DCS John Clifford
  Austin 'Ginger' 150–3
Hewett, D/Supt Charles 88–9
Higgins, D/Supt Robert Mold
  120–5
Hilbery, Mr Justice 100, 131–3
Hill, Billy 45, 107, 118–19,
  128, 133, 136, 142–3, 183
Hillier, Harold 19–20
Hinds, Alfie 106, 135–6, 185
Hooper, Edward 77–80
Hope, DC Donald 178–9
Horne, Percy 107–11
Humphreys, Mr Christmas 4
Hutchinson (Barrister),
  Jeremy, QC 168–9

Imbert, Commissioner Lord
  Peter, CVO, QPM,
  DL xvi
Insole, Alan Vyvyan 56–8

Index

Insole, Mrs 56–8
Irving, Beryl 190–3
Irving, Edward John 190–3
Irving, Rose 190–3

Jackson, John 15–17
Jackson, AC(C) Sir Richard
   Leofric, CBE 113
'Jackson, Mr and Mrs' 152–3
James, John 44–5
Jenkins, Peter Martin 89–90
Johnson, Alice 142–4
Johnson, Charles 172
Johnson, Thomas 23–4
Johnson, Samuel 142–4
Johnson, DS William 'Johnny'
   167, 170
Joiner, Joe 56–8
Jones, Judge Atherley, KC 45
Jones (Magistrate),
   Mr Chester 13
Jones, Dai 179
Jones, Harry Horace 179, 183
Jones, Mrs Julia 178, 180,
   183–4
Jones, DS Kenneth 129
Jones, Raymond 'Ray the Cat
   93, 177–86
Joseph, Geoffrey 96, 119

Kaill, Aircraftsman Leslie
   George 71–2
Kavanagh, Mrs 11–13
Kelly, George 142–4
Kelly, George Anderson 74–5
Kelly, John Morley 129–34
Kendall, AC(C)
   Sir Norman 207–8
Kent, Duchess of 73–5
Kent, Duke of 73
Kerr, Deborah 185
Kinsella, Joseph 51–4
King, DS 78
King, George Albert 99

Kjergaard, Frede 179–80
Kray Brothers 145, 147
Kray, Reggie 144
Kray, Ronnie 182, 185
Krithia, Mrs 156

Lane, Percy 11–13
'Larry' (informant) 195–9
Latham, Thomas 78–80
Latt, Anthony – *see* Darry, G.
Lawless, DS 158
Lawlor, Ledwedge
   Vincent 72–5
Learman, Mrs Dorothy
   Sarah 93
Lee, DCS, Robert 92–4,
   116–25, 128–34
Legge, Hon. Mrs Gerald 119
Leon, Sir John Ronald, 4th
   Baronet 83–5
Leon, Sir Ronald,
   3rd Baronet 83–5
Lewis, Howard Henry 107–11
Lewis, Raymond Claude 41
Lewis, DS William 97, 99–100
Liddle, Richard 157
Longford, Lord 102
Loraine, Lady 164
Loren, Sophia 184, 185
Lynch, DI Jeremiah 69

MacDonald, DS 51
MacDonald, DI William 181–3
MacMillan, DC Donald 88–9
Madsen, George 157–9
Maloney, Alan 74–5
Mann, Harry 89–90
Manning, Eddie 208
Manning, William Cyril
   129–34
Margesson, Hon. Janet 181
Mark, Commissioner
   Sir Robert, GBE xv–xvi
Marks, Terry 'Ginger' 145

Marrinan (Barrister), Patrick Aloysius 133, 143
Marshall (Magistrate), Mr 36, 79
Martelli, Mrs Ann 181
Martin, Detective Charles, KPM 11–13
'Master 'B'' – see Raymond, H.
'Master 'G'' – see Una, F.
Masters, Charles George 94
Matthew, DPP Sir Theobald 158
Matthews, DS John 87
Maxwell, DCI Arthur 190–1
May, Mr 23–4
McDonald, Mr 38
McDoull, Detective Percy, KPM 11–13
McIntosh, Lord 186
McKechnie, DI Edward 183
McKenna (Magistrate), Mr 80, 213
McWilliams, David Sidney 47
Melrose, Robert 106, 121–5
Millen, DAC Ernest George, CBE, xv–xvi
Minchingdon, Leonard 'Johnny the Boche' 106
Mitchell, Charles 2–3
Mitchell, Frank 'The Mad Axeman' 145
Montagu, Lady Elizabeth 181
Moran, Lord 29
Morath, Sidney George 19–21
Moylan, Receiver Sir John, CB, CBE 211
Mullen, Mrs Alida 127–8
Murray, DS Kenneth 209–13

Nash Brothers 144
Neale, Frank Bernard 49–51
Neale, Leslie – see Raymond H.
Newton-Deakin, Mrs Frederika 93

Nicol, Stanley 157
Norman, DI 114–15
Norris, Ernest 157–9
Norris, Veronica 159–60
Nott-Bower, Commissioner Sir John, KPM 29–30, 193

O'Connell, Commander Terrence, QPM 152–3
O'Connor, John 98
Oliver, Mr Justice 58, 144
Ostle, PC 141

Padev, Mrs M. – see Bibesco P.
Paine, Mrs Nellie 178
Parker, Lt Cmdr Michael 180
Parker, D/Supt William 5–6, 207–13
Parkinson, Thomas Joseph 64–7
Parkyn, Frederick 135
Pattison, DI John 108–9
Pauly, Mr 37–8
Paynter, James Albert 5–6
Pearn, Arthur Edward 71–2
Pepper, Supt Tony 189, 192
Perkins, Edward – see Colbard, F.
'Peter the Plotter' – see White, H.L.
Petty, Dennis 94
Philips, Alan Ivor – see Devereux P.
Phillips, Captain 24
Phillips, George Henry 98
Phillips, Marcia Anne 164–5
Pickles, DCI Frederick 'Wilf' 136, 138
Pointing, James 19–21
Portarlington, Lady 73
Porter, Senior Detective 75
Preedy, John Henry 152–3
Pritchard, Mr Commissioner F.E. 66–7

Index

Purdy, William Henry 96
Purvis, Arthur 34
Pyser, George 182

Rae, Norman 159
Ram, Gurdas 65–7
Rawlings, DC Harry 19–21
Raymond, Harry 'King of the Blackmailers' 49–59
Read, Gary 199–205
Redfern, Frederick Ashton 210–13
Reece (Magistrate), Mr Bertram 160
Rees, John Vernon 150–3
Regensburg, Conrad 208
Reid, DS Charles 15–17
Ressier, George 15
Reynolds, Bruce 138
Rice, Edward Thomas 141–7
Richards, Mrs Phyllis Holman, OBE 27–30
Richardson, Charlie 110
Ricketts (Solicitor), Mr 38, 39–40
Robbins, Lord 165, 168
Robertson, James 5–6
Robertson, AC(A) 29
Robertson, William Herbert 151–3
Robins, John 2–3
Robinson, Ernest Walker 96
Rogers, Ginger 185
Rooke, David Victor 97
Roome, Alfred 'Big Alfie' 88, 92
Rosenz, Carmen 208–13
Rosenz, Max George 208
Rossi, Robert 'Battles' 136–7
Russell, John 44–5
Rutherford, Detective, John, KPM 45
Rutherford, Leonard 94
Rutland, Duke of 186

Rutter, Robert Howard 152–3
Ryan, James 40

Sacks, Simon 39
Salter, D/Supt George 106
'Sammy the Snout' 199
Scott, Peter – *see* Gulston P.C.
Seago, Edward 54
Seal, Mrs Kathleen Muriel 122
Seaton, Chairman Reginald 102, 131–2
Sellars, William Henry 96
Sharpe, DCI Frederick Dew 'Nutty' 46–8
Sharpe, Sir Montague 20
Shaw, Ellen 209–13
Shepherd, D/Supt Stanley 159–60
Shepherd, DCI Thomas, KPM 128–34
Sheppard, Peter James 155–6
Simpson, Gordon 113–25
Simpson, Commissioner Sir Joseph, KBE xv–xvi
Sinclair, DCI Peter 92–8
Singer, Jack 171
Skelhorn, DPP Sir Norman 169
Slater, PC 526 'C' Peter 71–2
Slater – *see* Jackson, J.
Slyfield, DI 53
Smith, DS 2–3
Smith, Bill 156–7
Smith, Mrs Florence 36
Smith, DS Harold 24
Smith, DI John 44–5
Smith, Leonard Joseph 174
Smith, Phillip 34
Smith, William – *see* Chatham, G.H.
Smithson, Tommy 142–3
Smythe, Dr Butler 31
Sparks, DCS Herbert 'The Iron Man' 106–11, 116

Spender, Mr David 188, 191
Spooner, D/Supt 63–7
Spot, Jack 133, 136, 142–3, 156
Stable, Mr Justice 71, 141
Standing, John – see Leon, J.R.
Stanton, Sydney James 149–50
Stevens, Commissioner John, Baron Stevens of Kirkwhelpington, KStJ, QPM, DL, FRSA xvi
Stewart, Mr Commissioner 96
Stone, PC 281 'C' Frederick Mark, GM, BEM, KPM 24–30
Stonham, Lord 102
Stratford, Douglas 94
Streatfeild, Mr Justice 160
Stromberg, Anton – see Anson, H.
Stuttard, D/Supt Henry 209
Sullivan, Frederick 'Slip' 183
Sutcliffe, Patrick Dominic 63–7
Swann, Reginald Langton 97
Sweetman, Leslie William 95

Tarring, Bateman Brown 33
Taylor, Elizabeth 186
Taylor, Sylvia Mary 95–6
'Terrible Ted' – see Rice E. T.
'The Terrible Twins' 135–9
Tester, Percy 2–3
Teviot, Lady 93
'The Thin Man' – see Sheppard P. J.
Thompson, James 47
Thompson, DDI William 51, 55
Thorp, D/Supt Arthur 55
Tice, PC 422 'B' Robert 73–4
Todd, William 2–3
Troon, D/Supt John 145
Turner (Lawyer), Maxwell 158

Una, Francis 57–8

Veasey, DS Arthur Robert 'Squeaker' 62–7
Vevy, Harry – see Raymond, H.
Vibart, D/Supt Jasper Peter, QPM 135–9
Von-Lauer, Volker – see Von-Machazek, V.J.H.
Von-Machazek, Volker Joseph Hans 171–5

Wakeling, DS James 15–17
Wallace, Edgar 49
Wallace, Reginald 31–2
Wallis, PC John 2–3
Walsh, Eileen – see Bergman, E.
Warren, Henry – see Watts, E.H.
Watkins, PC 26
Watts, Ernest Henry 34
Webb, Duncan 209
Webber, John C. – see Colbard, F.
Weinstein, Leon 172, 174
Weisner, DCS John James Conrad 166–7
Welling, Thomas A. 35
Westcott, PC 190
White, Doris Joan 151–3
White, Harold Lough 114–25, 153
Whitely, Common Serjeant Mr Cecil, KC 4
Wijnberg, Moses 127–8
Wilberforce (Magistrate), Mr 47
Wild, PS 61
Wild, Recorder of London Sir Ernest, KC 3, 16–17, 23–4, 51, 69
Wilford, Captain, J.K.R. 130
Williams, PC 199 'B' 79
Williams, Fay 209–13
Williams, Jack Henry, VC, DCM, MM★ 177, 186
Willis, Mrs Kathleen 188

Wilson, Charlie 138
Wilson (Magistrate), Clyde 74
Wilson, John Ernest 109
Wise (Lawyer), Mr 41
Wolfe, Benjamin 35–41
Wolfe, Charles 35–41
Wolfe, Henry 35–41
Wolfe, Jack Kaufman 35–41
Wolfe, Joseph 35–41
Wollington, George 61
Wood, DC 71–72

Wood, Edward 44–5
Wood, Leonard 40–1
Woodland, DI David 138
Woolmark, David 171
Worthington, Dr 67
Wragg, Harry 40
Wrightsman, Charles Bierer 163

Young, DI Charles 15–17
Young, John Thomas 189–93